First Time Pass

First Time Pass

A comprehensive guide to achieving professional level exam success

MICHAEL BELL

FIREWORKS PRESS

Published by Fireworks Press

An imprint of FTP Development Ltd
Registered Office: 2nd Floor, 145-147 St John Street, London EC1V 4PY.

First published in Great Britain in 2010

ISBN 978-0-9567231-0-9

British Library Cataloguing in Publication Data
A CIP catalogue record for this book can be obtained from the British Library.

For Lexie

Overview

Contents

Introduction

When I was a lowly accountancy student, struggling hard to juggle the twin demands of full time employment and study, I would often avidly devour the financial press for the latest job opportunities aimed at newly qualified accountants. Partly, this was to convince myself that all the hard work ahead really would be worth it in the end.

Often, along with the telephone number salaries that I found so interesting, these adverts would include the phrase "first time passes preferred" when listing the attributes of the ideal applicant.

Later, when I had qualified and started looking for a position which would take me the next step up my career ladder, I found that first time passes in a relevant professional qualification were not only *preferred* by the top consultancy and accounting firms, they were an *essential requirement*. It was yet another way of differentiating between applicants, of separating the wheat from the chaff.

In today's ever more cut-throat and competitive job market, an unblemished exam record is a valuable weapon in every successful professional's armoury. Tough though it may seem to those without them, first time passes really can make all the difference in landing that sought after job.

But how to gain those first time passes? This is the sixty million dollar question. And a question which simply isn't answered by all the books currently offering advice on how to study, or how to pass exams. Most of these are aimed fairly and squarely at those in full time education, and as a result, ignore completely the needs of those working towards a professional qualification whilst holding down a demanding job.

This is the reason why this book has been written. To fill that gap, to give you, the career professional studying in your own time, all of the guidance and direction you need.

To ensure you achieve that First Time Pass.

What This Book is About

In a nutshell, this book includes everything necessary to help you pass your professional level exams – the first time you take them. No failures, no resits. The entire study process is covered in detail from start to finish, from the moment you first decide to start studying towards your qualification to the moment you put your pen down at the end of the exam, and beyond.

As such, this book is the ideal self-help guide to give you the greatest chance of examination success.

Why You Should Read this Book

I can already hear the question you're asking. *"Why should I read this book – what's in it for me?"*. This is indeed a fair question. How exactly *is* this book so very different from the hundreds of other books already out there dealing with how to study, or how to pass exams?

It's like this. Traditional books on study have the following characteristics.

- They are written largely for those in full-time education, whether that be school, college or university.
- Because assessment in full-time education tends to be continuous, rather than purely on the basis of examination performance, there is less of a focus on the exam itself.
- There is an almost exclusive concentration on mechanical study skills, rather than any other aspects of the study experience.

This book is different.

- It is aimed fairly and squarely at those of you who are embarking upon on a course of study leading to a professional qualification, for example, in the areas of accountancy, law, finance and so on.
- As a result, this book takes into the account the very different circumstances you are faced with, such as trying to juggle the competing demands of work, home, family and study.
- The unique emphasis on exam performance drives the whole methodology contained within this book. There is a recognition that for many of you, careers really can be made or broken based on the strength of your exam results.
- This book does not just look at those areas traditionally dealt with by the how-to books, for example, giving advice on how to read a textbook, or how to write notes. Instead, it adopts a "*holistic*" approach, looking at the whole study picture. This means it not only deals with the study

skills required, but also at the psychology of learning and the power of the mind.

These are the reasons that set this book apart from all the others already on the shelves of your bookshop and library. If you're serious about success, you need to read this book.

Who Should Read this Book

As already stated, this book is aimed primarily at those attempting professional level qualifications. However, this book can be usefully read by *anyone* attempting a course of study which includes an examination as part of the assessment process. The principles and concepts contained can be applied at all educational levels and by all ages. So whether you're studying for your school certificate, your college qualification or your university degree, there's something here for you too.

How this Book is Structured

This book is split into seven parts.

Part 1 The Success Formula

Looks at the factors that make up examination success, and the relationships between these factors.

Part 2 The Success Factor

Investigates the most often neglected area of study – the individual and their approach to learning.

Part 3 Planning

Shows why producing a study timetable is an essential first stage in the study process, and how to produce one.

Part 4 Study Time and Place

Looks at how environment can have a dramatic impact on the success of your studies.

Part 5 Study Tools and Techniques

Gets down to the nitty gritty, the tools and techniques you'll need to use whilst you're studying.

Part 6 Revision

Takes a long look at the process of revision, and gives essential guidance on how to get the most out of this crucial phase.

Part 7 Exam Technique

Tells you all you need to know about the best way to approach your exam, and the techniques you should be using.

How to Read this Book

Recommended Route

This book has been designed so that the order of the chapters matches the order in which you'll be doing things as part of your studies in the real world. This means that you don't necessarily need to read the whole book from cover to cover before you can make a start. That said, to get the most from this book, I would recommend reading Parts 1 to 5 sequentially before getting down to any serious study. Part 6 and 7 can then be read later when you're approaching the revision and exam stages.

When Time is Short

If you're already nearing your exam date when you first pick this book up, you can still benefit from its contents. I would recommend reading Parts 6 and 7 on Revision and Exam Technique as soon as you can, and also taking a look at Part 2 The Success Factor, which contains some valuable insights into how you can increase your chances of success through the use of simple techniques.

And if you've literally days (or hours!) to go before your exam, at least read Part 7 on Exam Technique.

If You Have Previously Failed Your Exam

You may be reading this book specifically because you have already sat your exam before and failed, either once or a number of times. If so, you might think you already know how to study, and that you just need a few extra pointers to get your through your exam.

I'd suggest otherwise. If you've failed before, there was *something* wrong with your approach. Unfortunately, you're not in a position to identify exactly what that something is at this point. And if you've failed a number of times before, you're clearly stuck in a rut, unable to do anything differently. You have literally learned to fail.

In either case, harsh though it may sound, I'd suggest you need to start from scratch. Follow the recommended route and read this book from the beginning. This way you will get the most benefit from it, and probably identify along the way some of things you were doing wrong before. Then you'll be able to avoid making these mistakes the next time round.

Part One

THE SUCCESS FORMULA

The Success Formula

First Time Pass

You want to be successful in your examinations. After all, that's why you're reading this book. You want to pass first time too. Not only does this minimise the time and effort you have to expend to gain the qualification, but in many industries the very fact you passed those professional level exams first time around adds to your marketability.

So success is the goal – success being those first time passes in the examinations of your choosing.

Defining Examination Success

Let's look a little closer at this idea of examination success. What if I asked you to define the factors necessary to achieve this success? What would you come up with?

You might produce a list of factors which when added together equal exam success. Perhaps something like

ABILITY + DETERMINATION + HARD WORK = SUCCESS

At first sight this seems to make some sense. After all, having the ability but then not bothering to put the hard work in is not likely to lead to that desired pass mark.

But maybe you feel there's something not quite right about this formula, that something is still missing. Maybe you'd define it slightly differently. Perhaps you might say exam success is better defined by

APTITUDE + KNOWLEDGE + HARD WORK = SUCCESS

This seems fair. Many would argue that to pass an exam, not only do you have to work extremely hard and retain a great deal of knowledge, but also that you need a certain aptitude or talent for the subject in question.

In fact, this second formula is wrong too, and here's why. It is based on a number of common misconceptions. Misconceptions which you need to rid yourself of. Let's look at each in turn.

Common Misconceptions

Aptitude

You are taking professional level exams. The vast majority of these have entry requirements, normally educational qualifications of a certain minimum level. This holds true whatever and wherever you are studying. These entry level criteria are there for a reason – they ensure that you have the necessary skills, level of education and aptitude to take on the demands of the examinations.

In other words, that you have the necessary level of aptitude for the exams you embarking upon *is a given.* Remember this whenever you start to question whether you are good enough to be on your particular course of study. You *are* good enough by definition. The difference between a student who passes and one who fails is simply how they *apply* that aptitude during study and exam, not in any fundamental difference in baseline levels of ability.

Knowledge

Another assumption often made is that examinations are all about memorising lots of facts and then regurgitating these in the exam room. In fact, at professional level, this is never enough.

Professional exams are about the ability to *apply* knowledge to different scenarios in a certain way under exam conditions. That necessity to display an application of knowledge means that the mere cramming of as many facts as possible into your head will not lead to success. A completely different emphasis is therefore required when it comes to studying.

Hard Work

Another common misconception, this one goes something like "the more work you do, the better your chances". In fact, this too is untrue. It is not just a question of quantity, but also of quality. It is *what* you do and *how* you do it, not *how much* you do. It is an unfortunate truth that many misguided individuals work late into the night for weeks or months on end before exams, only to find at the end of it that they have still come out with a fail. Poor quality, poorly focussed work is the reason.

So, if the formulae we've seen above fail to correctly define the factors necessary for success, what does?

The Success Formula

Based on my experiences over a number of years as both student and teacher, I have come up with an alternative formula to define what makes up exam success. It is this.

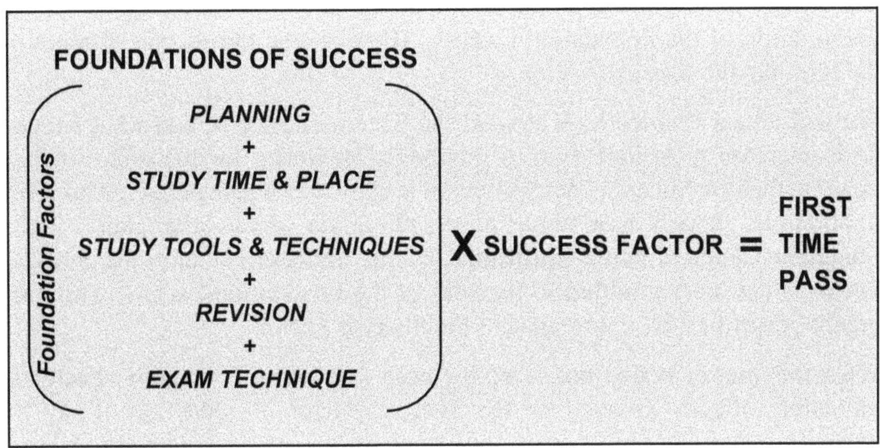

How Does the Formula Work?

The Higher the Better

Put simply, the higher the score given by the calculation contained in the formula, the higher the chances of achieving that elusive first time pass. Conversely, the lower the score, the lower the chances of success.

We can see that the formula is made up of a number of elements. Let's look at each of these in turn.

The Foundations of Success

Each of the elements contained within the curly brackets are what I call the *Foundations of Success*. These are the various processes one needs to engage with during the study process as a whole. These are dealt with in detail in Parts Three to Seven of this book.

Imagine each of these individual elements (which I shall call "Foundation Factors") being marked with a score, say between zero and ten – the higher the score, the better a factor has been dealt with. For example, a score of 2 for planning would indicate poor planning, whereas a 9 would indicate very good planning.

The fact that all of the Foundation Factors are shown within the brackets indicates that they are all interrelated. This is a key point. It is no good having great study technique if one has poor exam technique. A good score in one factor can be cancelled out by a poor score in another. This means that as a student, you need to work on all the Foundation Factors listed in the formula to maximise your chances of success. It is all too easy simply to concentrate on your strong points and ignore your weak.

The Success Factor

But there is more to the Success Formula than this. It is not merely about the interrelation of the Foundation Factors. There is also the second element of the formula, the *Success Factor*.

We will take a detailed look at what the Success Factor is, and what we can do to increase it, in Part Two of this book. However, for the moment, just imagine that the Success Factor element is shown as a percentage. And most importantly, notice how the Success Formula shows the sum of the Foundation Factors being **multiplied** by the Success Factor – the Success Factor is not merely **added** to the sum of the Foundation Factors. This fact greatly magnifies the importance of the Success Factor.

What this means is that the score for each and every Foundation Factor is ultimately directly affected by the Success Factor. A reduction of say 25 percent in the Success Factor will lead to a commensurate 25 percent reduction in *all* the Foundation Factors. Thus one could plan well, study for an adequate time using the correct techniques, revise properly and apply the correct exam technique and yet, due to applying a lack of attention to the Success Factor, still not manage a high score for the Success Formula as a whole.

Remember, the higher the score given by the Success Formula, the higher the chances of passing. And vice versa. So you can see just how important the Success Factor really is in the grand scheme of things. It affects everything you do.

Other Study Books Ignore the Success Factor

This is the premise behind this book, and also what makes it different. There are a number of other books already available out there which set out the basics behind the actual study process, behind the areas which make up the Foundation of Success. Each one of these factors is, as we have seen, important in its own right.

But I believe that there is also another factor of fundamental importance that cannot be ignored by the student who wants to achieve success, and to achieve it in as quick a time as possible. This is the Success Factor. This is a factor ignored by all those traditional books on study and exam technique. This is what makes this book different.

Ignore it at your peril, for it can dramatically affect your chances of success, as we shall now see in Part Two.

Part Two

THE SUCCESS FACTOR

Introducing the Success Factor

The Success Factor

The last chapter made a major claim – that success was based not just on the fundamentals of study, but on something else – the Success Factor. We saw that how well we dealt with the Success Factor affected everything else we did during the entire study process.

Major claims like this need to be substantiated, so let's do that now. Let's visit the idea of the Success Factor.

What is the Success Factor?

You could define it in a number of ways. Positive thinking. Positive mindset. Mental attitude. I prefer to define it in general terms as the *"psychology of success"*.

In other words it's about a way of thinking, a way of thinking which accentuates the positive, the power of the mind, to maximise one's true potential and ultimately, in this case, one's examination performance.

The Big Idea

The idea that mere positive thinking can in any way affect one's exam performance may be difficult for many to believe. In fact, I'm sure that at least some of you reading this book will be wondering whether I am really serious in making such a bold claim.

But I am, deadly serious. The big idea around which this book is based is that what you think really does affect the way you perform. The better the mindset, the more positive the approach, and the higher the chances of examination success.

> ***"Deep within man dwell those slumbering powers;***
> ***powers that would astonish him,***
> ***that he never dreamed of possessing;***
> ***forces that would revolutionise his life if aroused and put into action."***
> **Orison Swett Marden**

To all intents and purposes, the power of the brain and mind is unlimited. For everyone. The potential is there, just waiting to be used. All that we need to do is learn how to tap this potential.

Put another way, the only thing that is holding us back is ourselves.

The Power of the Mind

Prove it, I can hear you say, quite rightly. Where is the evidence to support such a claim? Where is it proven that mere thought can change performance in any measurable concrete sense? Show me the experimental proof.

OK, I can do that. Because I want to convince you that the power over pass or fail really *is* within you. In fact, it's crucial that I convince you, because if you don't believe, then your negative mindset is simply going to have an adverse affect on your ultimate exam result. And I will have failed in my crusade to make the lives of those studying for professional levels exams that little bit easier.

The Proof

Believe it or not, there is in fact a large body of scientific research out there which illustrates the power of the mind, in all sorts of different ways. For the sake of brevity, we'll leave aside the scientific language and detail, focussing instead on a summary of the pieces of research that illustrate the amazing power we all have to improve our lot.

Example 1 – Budding Michael Jordans

The first piece of research I want to tell you about concerns the investigation of the effect of mental practice on sinking basketball free throws (that's getting the ball through the hoop from the free throw line on the basketball court to you and me).

Three groups of individuals were involved. Group 1 was told to practice free throws on court for a total of 20 minutes every day for 20 days. Group 2 was told to spend a total of 20 minutes every day for 20 days simply *imagining* throwing the ball through the hoop. Group 3, the control group, did not practice during the 20 days, either physically or mentally.

Each group was scored on the first and last days of the test so that any improvement in performance over the 20-day period could be measured. The results were astounding.

Group 1, as one might expect, improved performance on average by 24 percent. Group 3 showed no statistically measurable change at all. But Group 2, those individuals who were mentally rehearsing successful hoop throwing, improved their performance on average **by 23 percent** – that's nearly as big an improvement as those who actually practised with a real ball!

> ***"Change your thoughts and you change your world."***
> **Norman Vincent Peale**

Take a moment to consider the significance of that. By no other means than using their imaginations, those in Group 2 managed to improve as near as damn it to the same degree as those who did the actual practice. Concrete, real-world improvements from mere thought. Isn't that truly amazing? Are you still feeling as sceptical about the power of the mind?

How about some more research to back up my claims in case you need further convincing?

Example 2 – Cabbies Grow Bigger Ones

For those who want their proof to be in the form of a measurable physiological change on the individual as an outcome of a particular thought process, how about this. Research has shown conclusively that the hippocampus, an important area of the brain involved in long term memory, is markedly larger in London taxi cab drivers who have been on the job for many years, when compared to their colleagues who have only recent started driving cabs.

The theory put forward to explain this phenomenon is that as part of the job the driver needs to visualise in his own mind the shortest route from A to B for any given fare. In time, this visualisation leads to growth in that part of the brain responsible for carry out such mental calculations.

Again, consider the implications. Our abilities are not set in stone, the brain is not incapable of improvement over time when given the correct stimulus. Just thinking about something (in this case routes through city streets) leads to a physical increase in brain size, and thus to an improvement in performance.

Still not convinced? There's more.

Example 3 – Fingers with Biceps

This research looks at the impact of visualisation on physical strength. Given this focus, for our purposes it is the *principle* of what the evidence suggests in this experiment which is important, rather than the actual effect demonstrated.

The experiment took place over a 4 week period and involved 3 groups. Group 1 was asked to carry out a particular activity, which was tensing and then relaxing a finger on the left hand for 5 sessions a week. Whereas the first group carried out the physical exercise, Group 2 merely imagined, or visualised, the finger exercise. Group 3, as the control group, did nothing.

The strength of the chosen finger was measured at the start and end of the 4 week period. Strength increases measured for the groups 1, 2 and 3 were 30 percent, 22 percent and 3.7 percent respectively. Again, notice how merely *imagining* something had a real-world measurable effect, and a far from insignificant one at that.

Hopefully, by now you are beginning to at least consider the possibility that a particular way of thinking can influence the performance of an individual. As we continue to explore the Success Factor, we will encounter more evidence to back this theory up. But for now, let's look at another example of the power of the mind which, although not rigorously scientific in approach, is nevertheless dramatic. In many ways, the implication to be drawn from the evidence of the following example is even more amazing than the implication that mere thought can affect performance.

> ***"Human beings can alter their lives by altering their attitudes of mind."***
> **Henry James**

Believe It or Not – It Makes No Difference!

I first read about this phenomenon in the best-selling book by Susan Jeffers, Feel the Fear and Do It Anyway. To be honest, on first reading, I was sceptical. What it suggested seemed so unlikely and so counterintuitive. So I put it to the test myself, fully expecting to find that I could not reproduce the results. I was wrong however. Whenever, and on whomever, I carried out the test, I always got the same results – the ones that Susan Jeffers reported. Here's how it goes.

The Experiment

Instructions

Find a volunteer and have them face you. Check that they have no problems of any sort with their arms. Assuming all is well, ask them to clench one of their fists and then raise up the same arm to shoulder height so that their arm is at ninety degrees to their body. Then tell the volunteer to resist with all their strength whilst you stand in front of them and attempt to push their clenched fist and arm back down from the raised position with your outstretched hand.

You will be extremely unusual if you can push down the person's arm with your initial attempt. Even if you manage it, it is unlikely to be easy.

Now ask your volunteer to put their arm down, shut their eyes, and to repeat to themselves ten times out loud the negative statement "I am a weak and unworthy person". They don't need to attempt to believe the statement, only repeat it. After this, get them to open their eyes and raise up the same arm as before with fist clenched. Tell them to resist with all their strength exactly as before, and then try to push their arm down.

Your volunteer will be amazed (as will you the first time you try this!). You will be able to push their arm down to their side with ease and they will offer little in the way of resistance. Assuming that somehow you started pushing before they were ready, some volunteers will ask you to repeat the experiment, thinking that the next time they will be able to resist your downward pressure. But they will be wrong – try it a second time and you'll get the same result.

To continue to experiment, now get the volunteer to close their eyes and repeat the positive statement "I am a strong and worthy person" ten times. Having then opened their eyes and raised their arm, it is now up to you to push the arm down again. What you will find is that you are now unable to budge the arm at all – if anything, the arm seems stronger than the first time you attempted to push it down. Again, you can repeat this with the same results – an inability to push the arm down.

Ah, But You Could be Cheating...

Sceptics might argue that, because you are the one doing the pushing, you are changing the pressure you use to push the arm down, depending on the statements repeated. This is very easily disproved though. Tell the volunteer to select either the positive or negative statement and repeat it to themselves ten times once you have left the room, then leave. When you re-enter the room after a few minutes, you can attempt to push the volunteer's raised arm down as before. If they chose the positive statement, you will not be able to move the arm; if instead it was the negative they chose, the arm will move with little resistance. This is proof that you couldn't have been cheating. You didn't even know which statement they had chosen.

The Implications

I make no apologies for stating that in my opinion, the inferences that can be drawn from these results are staggering. Not only do the things we tell ourselves clearly have an affect on our performance (positive thoughts leading to an increase in strength, negative thoughts having the opposite effect) but, and here's where the staggering part comes in, **it doesn't even matter whether we believe the things we are telling ourselves or not.**

> ***"Self-trust is the first secret of success."***
> **Ralph Waldo Emerson**

What can we drawn from this that is useful for our purposes? Simply this. The power of the mind really is that, a power. We need to ensure we harness it and use it productively. And we need avoid negative self-talk – it seems that somehow the subconscious is unable to filter out fact from fiction and believes all you tell it. Give it those negative thoughts and it will act accordingly. Your performance will suffer as a result.

Brain Power

You may well have been convinced by the evidence I've presented above that positive thinking really can influence results. But I'm aware that many of you will be saying to yourselves right now "That's all very well, but all the positive thinking in the world isn't going to make up for the fact that I just don't have the brain necessary to be successful in my studies".

In other words, you feel that there is some physical and structural limitation within the brain, largely as a result of genetics, which ultimately pre-determines how successful a person will be. Not only this, you believe that your particular brain is limited in this way. You have a lack of brainpower. You can't help it – it's in your genes, predetermined.

I want to challenge this assertion. To show that in fact there is no such limitation in existence. To show that the potential within you is as great as it is in any other person.

To do that though, we first need to look at some basic facts about the brain. Whilst this might appear to be somewhat tangential to the subject of passing exams, stick with me. A basic understanding of the brain will not only begin to make it obvious just how powerful everyone's brain is, but also encourage you to dismiss many commonly-held misconceptions about the brain itself.

Once we've got you this far, we'll be able to look at ways of harnessing all that power to your advantage. But first things first – the background.

Brain Facts

The human brain is the most complex structure, natural or artificial, on earth. And that's a fact!

Brain Structure

Size

The average human brain weighs in at 3 pounds (approximately 1.4 kg). Although only accounting for between 1 percent and 3 percent of overall body weight, the brain receives around 15–20 percent of the body's blood supply, from where it derives its essential requirement – oxygen. Oxygen is needed to act as an energy source for all the cells working within the brain (we'll see just how many cells in a moment). Without oxygen, the brain couldn't function. One can see just how important successful brain function is by the proportion of the body's total blood supply it uses.

Size Isn't Everything

A smaller brain does not mean a lower level of intellectual ability. Einstein's brain was in fact slightly below the average size for the human brain. So don't use the fact you have a small head as an excuse for not having the ability to do well in exams. Size isn't everything it seems!

Two Hemispheres

The brain is a complex structure, but in simplistic terms, it is split into two parts, or cerebral hemispheres, the right brain and the left brain, which look pretty much alike. These two sides of the brain do not operate in isolation – they are connected by a bundle of over 200 million nerve fibres called the *corpus callosum.*

Although the two hemispheres may look exactly alike, they are not. Each hemisphere has functional specialisations – that is, the neural mechanisms for some functions tend to be located in one particular half of the brain. It is research on epileptic patients which has proved this. These patients have had surgery to sever their corpus callosum, thus isolating the left hemisphere from the right. (This is done to stop an epileptic seizure spreading from one side of the brain to the other.)

Right Brain/Left Brain Specialisation

The research carried out shows that each hemisphere of the brain is dominant for certain types of activity. The left side is more dominant for "academic" activities such as

- Language
- Mathematics
- Logic
- Analysis
- Linearity
- Sequence

The right side of the brain on the other hand is more dominant for

- Spatial abilities
- Rhythm
- Imagination
- Colour
- Music
- Dimension

However, don't assume that it's quite as cut and dried as this. Although one hemisphere might be *dominant* for a particular activity, that doesn't mean it acts completely in isolation. In reality, work is *spread* between the two hemispheres. No one single area of the brain is used exclusively during a specific mental task. The difference between the right and left brain is more one of degree (i.e. "this activity is dealt with to a greater degree in one side of the brain compared to the other") rather than an absolute distinction.

Nevertheless, important lessons can be learned from the research. In order to maximise the potential our brains have to offer, we need to use the dominant skills that *both* sides of the brain exhibit during our studies. Learning is often a predominantly left-sided academic activity, but can be much enhanced by including in the learning process some of the abilities the right brain has to offer, by using imagination, colour and so on. We shall see more on this idea later on in Part Two of the book.

Brain Cells

Take a Bow, Mr. Neuron

Sitting centre stage and playing the lead role in the functioning of the brain is a nerve cell known as a *neuron*. There are approximately 100 billion neurons in the average human brain. In addition there are at least ten times as many (i.e. one trillion) other cells in non-computational support roles. That's a lot of cells! And you've got that many too, honest!

Figure 2.1 illustrates a typical neuron.

Figure 2.1

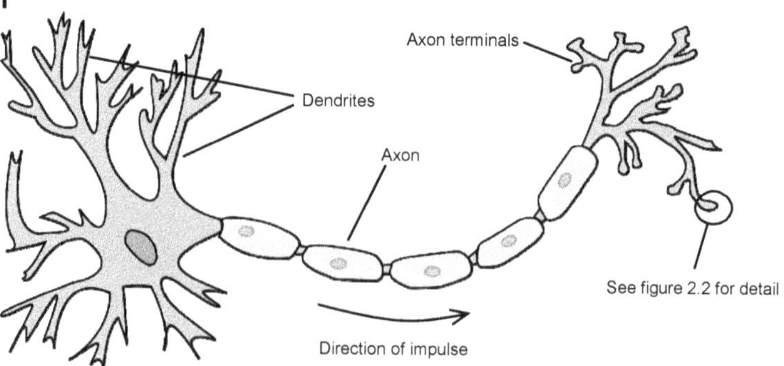

Neuron Connections and Neurotransmitters

Each neuron has branching tree-like projections growing from it called *axons* and *dendrites*. The job of a neuron is to send very rapid messages to other neurons, and it is these projections that allow this communication to take place. The axon from one neuron carries an electrical signal, or impulse, down its length to a connection with the dendrite of another neuron, the connection between the two being known as a *synapse*. However, the axon does not sit in direct contact with the dendrite, there being a small gap (the synaptic gap) between the two. The electrical signal is therefore turned into a chemical one in the form of a *neurotransmitter* by the axon terminal, which is released into the synaptic gap and received by the dendrite. The chemical signal (the neurotransmitter) is then converted back into an electrical one by the dendrite. This signal can now be passed onto to yet another neuron via the neuron's axon. And so on, the process of signal transmission continues.

Figure 2.2

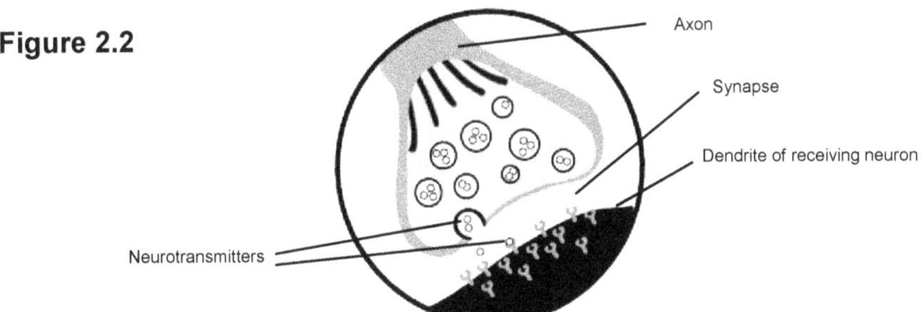

Each neuron will generally have only one axon but can have as many as 100,000 dendrites. Bearing in mind the number of neurons in the brain, it is estimated that there could be as many as 40 quadrillion (40,000,000,000,000,000) different patterns of connections possible in a single brain. This is more than the number of atoms in the entire universe! And it is these pathways of neural connections through which the electrical signals move. The constant strengthening and weakening of these connections and pathways that goes on in the brain form the basis of what we understand as learning and development.

> ***"The number of possible 'on-off' patterns of neuronal firing is immense.....The brain is obviously capable of an imponderably huge variety of activity; the fact that it is often organised and functional is quite an accomplishment."***
> **Daniel J. Siegel**

Your Unique and Powerful Brain

You too have these networks of interconnected neurons. They are what make you who you are, and give you the skills and abilities that you have. No one person will have exactly the same pattern of neural connections – there is almost infinite variety. But note well what was said above – the pathways are constantly changing, as different connections weaken or strengthen. This means, as we shall see in a moment, that what you are and what you can do are not fixed in stone. You can change these pathways, strengthening those that help towards achieving that first time pass, and weakening those that hinder. The power really is within you.

Common Misconceptions Concerning the Human Brain

What They Are

There are two major misconceptions about the human brain which we need to address. In so doing, two major excuses regularly trotted out for an inability to study and pass exams can be shown to be just that, excuses, and no more.

Our Brain's Abilities are Fixed in Stone by Adulthood

The first commonly held misconception is that the brain develops during childhood and by the time we become an adult, the brain and its connections are pretty much cemented into place. Whatever we are at the time that development process is complete, and whatever our abilities and limitations are, these are what we are destined to live with for the remainder of our lives. Thus, if we've never been very good at exams, we never will be, either now or in the future.

Brain Power Declines Rapidly with Age

The second misconception is that the brain's potential declines significantly over time from early adulthood onwards, so that the older we are, the less power we have at our mental fingertips. Nearly everyone believes this to be the case, and it's certainly often used as an explanation by those over the age of 21 (or 30, or 40, or 50, or whatever your age group!) for underachievement.

Why They Are Wrong

Now for the reasons why these are misconceptions and no more.

Plasticity

In reality, the connections in the brain are not hard wired by adulthood, never to change again. It is of course true that a large amount of development does occur in the brain during early childhood, as one might expect. During this time an incredible amount of learning is going on, with connections in the brain being forged to make up networks within the brain's structure. But this is not the end of it. Recent scientific evidence has shown conclusively that in fact the brain continues to change, adapt and develop over our lifetime, certainly way beyond childhood.

> ***"If we did all the things we are capable of doing we would literally astound ourselves."***
> **Thomas Edison**

In fact, if you think about it, our brain, just like the rest of our bodies, is in a constant state of change and renewal. The natural in-built repair process within our body ensures that over a period of weeks or months, no single molecule or cell in our body will remain unchanged. This includes our brain.

The scientific term used to describe the continued flexibility within the brain is *plasticity*. This doesn't of course mean that your brain is made of a synthetic polymer, but rather that throughout its life it remains flexible, malleable – it changes and adapts to overcome obstacles placed in its way.

Real World Examples of Plasticity

Taxi Drivers

In fact, we've already seen some proof of this in-built flexibility. Remember the London taxi drivers' hippocampus? The hippocampus had grown larger due to the greater level of processing it had been undertaking. The hippocampus had, if you like, recruited a greater number of neurons to the task in hand and created new connections between the neurons to deal with the additional load.

This is a wonderful example of plasticity. An adult brain changing, developing, to take account of something new it has been asked to do.

The Blind

There are numerous other examples to back this up. Take those who lose their sight during their adult life. If their brains were not capable of change, of recruiting brain cells to deal with new tasks, then they would not be able to learn the written language of Braille (a system using raised dots arranged in specific patterns to represent letters, and read by the fingertip). But they can, and do, proving that the brain can indeed change and adapt to obstacles placed in its way.

Experimental Proof

Or perhaps some more rigorous scientific research might persuade you? In an experiment, individuals were placed into a number of groups. Those in Group 1 were given a one-handed five finger piano note sequence to practice, 2 hours a day for 5 days. Group 2 was told to play the piano with one hand for the same 2 hours a day, but was given no sequence to practice. Group 3 was told to do nothing.

Images of the individual's brains were taken at the start and end of the task and compared for changes. Group 1 showed a particular area of the brain expanding over the time period as more brain cells were recruited into controlling the necessary movements to perform the sequence. Group 2 showed some expansion in the same area, but no where near as significant as for Group 1. Group 3 showed no change at all. (Interestingly, a fourth group was asked to simply imagine learning the one-handed five finger note sequence. This group showed similar brain changes to those in Group 1 – another example of how mere thought can have concrete, physical results.)

The fact that Group 1 showed changes in the brain as a result of their practice clearly illustrates the concept of plasticity at work in the brain. On the basis of this and the other examples I have highlighted, I would go so far as to say there is incontrovertible proof that *everyone's* brain is capable of development and growth, without exception. And that includes you.

Age Related Decline

No Dramatic Decline

As to the second misconception we mentioned, the idea that the brain starts to decline past a person's early twenties, and that this reduction in brain power is significant, particularly by the time we reach middle and old age – this too can be shown to be a fallacy. There is a very slight decline in mental aptitude from around the age of 25 onwards, but this has been shown to be no more than 5 to 10 percent *over an entire lifetime.* This is neither an overnight change nor a significantly large one.

Active is Good

Even this reduction depends to a large extent on the individual. Because as we have seen, the brain adapts to what's thrown at it. If you like, think of it as a muscle. If you exercise a muscle, it grows in size. The same for the brain. Those people who continue to actively engage their brain cells over their lifetime (i.e. those who exercise their brains by handing it challenges) are far less likely to suffer any significant mental decline when compared to those who don't. The exercise they undertake will ensure that new connections within the brain are constantly being made. But, for those who don't exercise their minds, conversely, existing connections will die through disuse.

> ***"A strong positive mental attitude will create more miracles than any wonder drug."***
> **Patricia Neal**

Plasticity to the Rescue

And remember, the brain displays plasticity. So even if you are 50 years old and feel you haven't really taxed your brain cells since you left school, you're not a lost cause. There's going to be a learning process to get through, yes, because after all those years of inactivity you're going to be rusty, but there's hope. Have faith in your brain – it will adapt, grow, develop, to meet the new demands you place upon it. That's a fact.

No Excuses

In other words, there are no excuses! You are never too stupid or too old to learn. The evidence proves that.

Now all we need to do is find out how to put the theory into practice and make the most of your brain's potential. This we will do in the next couple of chapters.

"One of the greatest discoveries a man makes, one of his great surprises, is to find that he can do what he was afraid he couldn't do."
Henry Ford

Success Factor Theory into Practice – Physical Changes

Putting the Theory into Practice

Right. We've seen that positive thinking equals positive, concrete, measurable results. We've also seen that everyone has a latent power within their brains just waiting to be used. Neither age nor genetics are barriers to accessing this power.

By now then, you should hopefully be convinced that you really *are* capable of exam success if you put your mind to it. But what now? How exactly can you go about making the most of this power, how can you ensure that your Success Factor percentage is indeed the highest possible? You need answers to this crucial question. Let me give them to you.

Methods of Improving Your Success Factor

Improving your Success Factor is all about making changes. To you, to your behaviour, to your state of mind.

You might be surprised to learn though that we are not *just* talking about changes to the way you think, or attitudinal changes, although these might seem the most obvious. We're also talking about physical changes. For example, the introduction of exercise to your lifestyle. Both kinds of changes need to be combined for the maximum benefit.

> ***"Only I can change my life. No one can do it for me."***
> **Carol Burnett**

Introducing both aspects of change, attitudinal and physical, will have a profoundly positive effect on the way you perceive yourself and the confidence you have in your own abilities. This will lead in turn to a raising of your Success Factor percentage, and of course, in tandem with the use of the Foundations of Success factors during your study program, a massively increased chance of success come the day of your exam.

Interestingly, although common sense may suggest otherwise, of the two types of change, it is in fact the physical changes which are easier to implement, and the ones to reap a more immediate noticeable benefit. For this reason, we shall look at the physical aspects of change first in this chapter. In the following chapter we will consider the attitudinal changes you can introduce to improve your Success Factor.

Physical Changes

There are a number of areas of your life where you can introduce physical changes to positively affect your whole mindset. And the good news is that many of the changes you can make are easy to introduce, requiring little or no preparation and no prior experience.

The rest of the chapter looks at these physical changes, in no particular order of importance. Read through the text and see which ideas appeal to you the most, then have a go at incorporating these changes into your life.

Humour

Laughter is the Best Medicine

What, you might ask, has humour got to do with passing exams? After all, most people would find it difficult to even raise a smile when contemplating a forthcoming exam. It's hardly a laughing matter!

It's like this. Once again, there is a multitude of scientific evidence which proves the beneficial effect of humour on an individual. It seems that laughter really is the best medicine.

> ***"Laughter is by definition healthy."***
> **Doris Lessing**

Laughter has been proven to have many beneficial effects. Experiments show that it lowers blood pressure, reduces muscle tension, has a beneficial effect on the immune system, lowers the level of stress-related neurotransmitters, and increases levels of natural painkillers, such as endorphins. All in all a pretty potent get-well-soon medicine, I'm sure you would agree. And best of all, it can be got for free!

Laughter and Study

In the context of study, gaining access to these benefits can be nothing but good. Not only do the immediate physical effects do you good, but the more general "feel-good" factor which comes from the physical state produced by laughter is itself good for improving your overall mood. The better and more relaxed you feel, the more positive your state of mind. The more positive your state of mind, the better you study. And so on.

Where Do I Get My Free Laughter?

There are numerous methods of accessing these benefits, of course, and I'm sure I don't really need to give you instructions here on how to do so. Maybe you like tuning into Sienfield re-runs on cable, or maybe you prefer your Frasier DVDs. Then again, it might be the local nightly comedy club venue or the neighbourhood bar comic.

Do whatever it is that works for you. If classic Monty Python is your thing, great – watch the Dead Parrot sketch yet again and let those guffaws out. But just do it. The important thing is to make the time.

> ***"Laughter is inner jogging."***
> **Norman Cousins**

But what if you can't find the time right now? What if, with study and work commitments, you just haven't got a free time slot? Well, in this case, even a smile helps. Experiments have shown that a smile is enough to produce those same "feel-good" chemicals that laughter does.

Laugh – I'd Rather Cry...

Perhaps you don't feel like smiling right this second. Things are hard, you're feeling stressed, and the last thing you want to do is smile. Cry might be closer to the mark. Well, believe it or not, even in these circumstances, a smile will still help.

Experiments have shown that the very way you arrange your facial muscles and posture can change your feelings. Counterintuitive though it may seem, a conscious manipulation of facial muscles actively generates whatever emotion the face is showing. Appropriating a happy facial expression will lead to not only a increase in subjective emotional feelings of well-being, but also produces many physiological changes in the body associated with a happy state of mind. In addition, adopting happy facial expressions results in the same left frontal brain activity known to correlate to spontaneous joy.

> ***"Sometimes your joy is the source of your smile, but sometimes your smile can be the source of your joy."***
> **Thich Nhat Hanh**

Smile and We Feel Happy

Let me make this point clear in case you haven't followed the facts. You might expect what we think is what affects our facial expression, a simple cause and effect relationship. We feel happy, we smile. We feel sad, we cry.

> ***"Smile, it's free therapy"***
> **Doug Horton**

In fact, the experiments show this relationship can flow in reverse. What facial expression we choose to adopt can affect the way we feel. Choose to smile and you will literally feel better for doing so. We smile, we feel happy.

Don't take my word for it, try it and see. The next time you are sitting at your desk and feel miserable, see what happens if you force a smile for 30 seconds (although you might want to try this alone if you're worried your work colleagues will think you have finally lost the plot!). Hold that smile, and then see how you feel. You might just be pleasantly surprised.

> ***"If a man insisted always on being serious, and never allowed himself a bit of fun and relaxation, he would go mad or become unstable without knowing it."***
> **Herodotus**

Exercise

You Choose

There is a wealth of literature out there trumpeting the benefits of exercise in all its forms. There is no need for us to revisit any of these, nor for me to recommend any one form of exercise over another. You are more than capable, I am sure, of selecting the activity best suited to your own particular interests, free time, location, available funds and so on. However, I will just add that extensive research has shown that the benefits set out below are greatest when the exercise consists of regular short sessions of vigorous aerobic exercise.

> ***"Walking isn't a lost art: one must, by some means, get to the garage."***
> **Evan Esar**

What I want to focus on here is the benefits that exercise in general can bring to the subject of study. It would appear that exercise really is good for you.

Chemical Assistance

One of the benefits of exercise is the production of endorphins, a naturally occurring opiate-like substance. As we have already seen, these are natural painkillers, and they help to give that exercise "high" that many keep fit fanatics rave about. For this alone, exercise is beneficial to those embarking upon a program of study. Endorphins decrease feelings of pain and enhance feelings of comfort and well being.

Allied to the increased production of endorphin is a similar increase in the production of a substance called serotonin. This is a neurotransmitter (remember, this is a type of chemical required for communication between neurons in the brain) which has been shown to have to the potential to combat depression, anxiety, low self-esteem and the like. Similarly, the levels of dopamine, the neurotransmitter involved in feelings of reward, motivation and attention, are also raised during and after exercise. I'm sure you're beginning to see the benefits that exercise can bring – greater feelings of self-esteem, anxiety control, mood regulation, greater motivation and attention. Not bad for starters!

Less Stressed

In addition, those who exercise exhibit a milder stress response. Put simply, these individuals are less stressed than their unfit counterparts, and consequently, less likely to be adversely affected when something goes wrong. They will simply shrug their shoulders and carry on with life. Less stressed is definitely good for exam takers.

"Those who do not find time for exercise will have to find time for illness."
Proverb

Grow Your Brain – Exercise!

Perhaps the most compelling evidence of all however, illustrating the benefits of exercise, comes from recent scientific research. This points to a direct causal relationship between physical exercise and brain cell growth. It would appear that physical exercise promotes the production of a growth factor which plays a critical role in the function and survival of brain neurons. Exercise causes existing neural connections to be strengthened, and new neural networks to be formed. So simply by undertaking regular exercise, not only are we growing our muscles (gaining increased muscle size, mass and strength), but also growing our brain, enhancing brain capacity and potential!

Exercise is good for you – it's official. Make sure you make time for it in your schedule – it really will do you and your brain the world of good.

Nutrition

Media Hype but No Magic Wand

As with exercise, information and advice about nutrition is commonplace. In fact, it fills our daily lives, the latest diet craze reported on morning TV, the latest scientific research about the effect of obesity on life expectancy shown on the evening news. Magazines, books, The Atkins Diet, The Cabbage Diet, the list is never ending. We are bombarded with often conflicting messages about what we should eat, or not eat, as the case may be.

True, I hear you say, but how is this relevant to studying? Is there a particular wonder food that if eaten will somehow increase my chances of success?

Sadly, and despite claims to the contrary by some nutritional supplement manufacturers, there is no edible wonder substance which can take the place of plain and simple hard graft. Popping a pill to increase your intelligence is still very much a thing of science fiction!

Omega-3

Recent research has suggested that taking Omega-3, a fatty acid fish oil, improves memory and general brain function. However, the research was carried out on volunteers with an average age of 70 with' slight memory complaints', and as yet there is no evidence to suggest that there is any positive effect on normal adults. Further research is therefore required before any of the claims made for this latest "wonder" pill can be proven. So by all means take them if you want to, but don't expect miracles!

However, to then discount the subject of nutrition as completely unimportant would be misguided. Nutrition *does* have an important part to play in ensuring you are operating to your full potential. So what do you need to know when it comes to what to eat, and why is it important?

Feed Your Brain

Remember those neurotransmitters, the chemicals that carry messages from once nerve cell to another? They are crucial to a healthily functioning brain. The body has to synthesise these neurotransmitters from proteins, and of course the proteins have to come from somewhere. From what you eat.

"Mental power cannot be got from ill-fed brains."
Herbert Spencer

Which is why a healthy, balanced diet, with regular meal times, is paramount. Without the necessary raw materials to make the neurotransmitters, your body is going to struggle to keep the brain functioning at its highest levels. So make sure you adopt a common sense approach to what you eat, and avoid fasting if at all possible, at least during those periods when you need to be on top mental form.

Study ACE

Another advantage of adopting a healthy diet will be the increased certainty that you are getting sufficient quantities of all the vitamins and minerals your body needs. In particular, the vitamins A, C and E (often know as antioxidants) which, it is believed, help fight the effects of free radicals. These free radicals are responsible for damaging and destroying cells in the body, including brain cells. So ensuring you have enough of the antioxidants can only be good news for your study program.

Blueberry Juice

Another recent piece of research has shown that two cups of blueberry juice a day for 3 months improved memory and recall in a series of tests. As with the Omega-3 research though, this related to a group of pensioners with signs of dementia, and so there is no direct evidence at this point to suggest the same improvements would be gained by normally functioning adults. Nevertheless, as blueberries are packed with 'superfood' ingredients including vitamin C and other antioxidants, a cup or two a day won't do you any harm!

Sleep

Getting Enough

If I were to make the statement that it is important to ensure you get enough sleep, you would no doubt think I was stating the blindingly obvious!

"Sleep deprivation is the most common brain impairment."

William C. Dement

Well, to an extent, I am. It is, of course, common sense to assume that a lack of sleep, if repeated over a number of nights, will eventually have an adverse impact on your well being. General tiredness leads to an inability to concentrate and a related increase in mistakes, whatever tasks you might be undertaking. Nevertheless, obvious common sense or not, there are many out there who, although they instinctively know this to be true, still persist in getting an inadequate amount of sleep.

The Required Amount

The perceived wisdom is that on average we should be getting seven to eight hours sleep a night, and in this case, the perceived wisdom appears to be

> *"The best bridge between despair and hope is a good night's sleep."*
> **E. Joseph Cossman**

valid. This is not to say that if you are getting less sleep than this you are not going to pass your exam, because this would clearly be wrong. However, if on a regular basis you are getting substantially less shut-eye than eight hours, the chances are your lack of sleep is having some detrimental effect on your studies. In such cases, you need to think carefully about how you might find more time to take to your bed.

By including sleep in the factors contributing to your Success Factor, however, I do not have in mind merely the *amount* of sleep you get. As we have seen, this does have an effect. But perhaps even more important is the *quality* of the sleep you get, more specifically, the amount of REM sleep you manage.

Quality, Not Just Quantity – REM Revealed

For those of you who don't already know, the body goes through various stages as you sleep. One of the best known of these is the period during which we encounter dreams. During this stage the eyes move rapidly behind closed eyelids, hence the term Rapid Eye Movement, or REM. Where REM is exhibited in an individual, you can be certain they are in the process of dreaming.

REM Helps Us Learn

So, what relevance is this to study? It is this – scientific research has produced evidence to suggest that REM sleep helps the brain to process and learn from what it has experienced during the day. Those dreams are necessary for the brain to reinforce the lessons learned, and to store them for future use. Miss out on REM sleep, and you adversely affect your ability to learn.

The Proof

This claim has been proved by experiments carried out where the subjects are given a complex set of tasks to learn. If the subjects are tested on the tasks after a night's unbroken sleep, they do better at the tasks than they did the night before. Thus there has been some sort of learning effect overnight whilst they slept. (Interestingly, too, the proportion of REM sleep to total sleep time goes up where these complex tasks have been given to learn, which would again suggest a strong link between learning and REM sleep.)

> *"Without a dream you'll get nowhere."*
> **Kofi Annan**

However, if the subjects are woken during their night's sleep, when it is their REM sleep that has been interrupted, the overnight learning effect normally demonstrated the next morning largely disappears. This is even though the subject's remaining sleep cycle has been allowed to continue without interruption. (This proves it is not tiredness that is causing the reduction in learning.)

You might perhaps be thinking it is the interruption itself that causes the loss of learning, not the fact it happens to be during REM sleep. However, this can be shown not to be the case. Where the subject's sleep is interrupted during a *non*-REM period, and the remaining sleep cycle is allowed to continue without interruption, the overnight learning effect *remains* the next morning, and is not lost.

The Inescapable Conclusion

There would seem to be only one conclusion that can be reached from this. *REM sleep is vital to learning.*

Applying What You Know

How can this knowledge be useful to you? Above all, remember the importance of sleep. It is not something inconvenient to be traded wherever possible for a few extra minutes of study, TV time or whatever. In fact, faced with the choice of less sleep/more study or more sleep/less study, it may well be the latter which is actually better for your long-term success. (Although this doesn't mean I'm giving you carte blanche to give up on study and spend all day in bed instead – eight hours sleep is enough to give you the benefits you need!)

Above all, remember to get a good night's sleep, not just in the days or weeks before your exam, but throughout the entire study process. An increased Success Factor will be the result. And what better argument could there be to go to bed and take it easy than that?

> ***"Take rest; a field that has rested gives a bountiful crop"***
> **Ovid**

Stress – The Invisible Enemy

Is It Really Bad for You?

Not All Bad...

Stress. Arguably an overused word these days, some would say that stress is part and parcel of being human. And indeed, we shall see later in the book that a little stress can be a good thing when it comes to exam performance. So it's not all bad.

.... But Not Good

But overall, stress is most definitely not good for you. The physical symptoms of stress are many – headaches, butterflies in the stomach, skin rashes, chest pain, palpitations, breathing difficulties, diarrhoea,

> ***"Stress is an ignorant state. It believes that everything is an emergency."***
> **Natalie Goldberg**

constipation, sleeping difficulties, indigestion, tiredness, drug/alcohol abuse, speeded up speech, overeating, dry mouth, loss of appetite, poor memory, inability to concentrate, trembling hands, fidgeting, grinding teeth. I could go on! Suffice it to say none of these symptoms are going to be helpful to your studies or in the exam hall.

All of these symptoms can really be attributed to the fact that stress is a reaction to a perceived threat. The body reacts to the threat unconsciously, the adrenal glands producing adrenaline and epinephrine hormones. It is these chemicals that lead to the physical symptoms listed in the previous paragraph.

Fight or Flight – The Redundant Response

Evolutionary Necessity

The commonly used term to describe this reaction is the "fight or flight" response. In evolutionary terms, it is what has developed over the millennia to allow us to survive as a species, the hormones putting the body in readiness to either fight for survival with additional speed and strength, or to run for survival with the same benefits.

No Longer Required

However, modern man has little use for such a response, as thankfully not many of us are put into situations these days which are literally life or death. Instead, we exhibit the response to a wide range of both general and specific threats. (The recently seen phenomenon of "road rage", where normally mild mannered people turn into raging animals because of some perceived wrongdoing to them or their car, is an example of this.)

> ***"Stress is the trash of modern life – we all generate it but if you don't dispose of it properly, it will pile up and overtake your life."***
> **Danzae Pace**

No Release

The problem is that, whereas our ancestors would make use of these hormones to fight or run, and in either case, use the hormone for its intended purpose, modern man is unable to do so. Thus, he remains in a heightened state of anxiety with no immediate form of release. This is the cause of stress.

More Bad News – Cortisol and Brain Damage

We have seen above some of the immediate adverse physical effects of stress, and these in themselves can have a bad enough impact on your immediate well being and your studies.

Introducing the Bad Guy – Cortisol

But recent scientific research has found that the problem goes far deeper and is potentially far more serious than this. Along with adrenaline and epinephrine, stress also produces other chemicals, one of which is called cortisol. In small quantities, this is beneficial. But it has been shown that higher stress-induced levels of cortisol not only have an inhibiting effect on memory, but also are actually toxic to neurons.

This is very bad news! You need those neurons in the brain, working hard, firing electrical impulses along the brain's pathways. The more neurons you can recruit, the more connections you can make between them, the better. Cortisol is the enemy of your neurons. It interferes with brain's neurotransmitters, preventing both the laying down of new memory pathways and the retrieval of pre-existing memories from memory storage.

> ***"Stress is poison."***
> **Agavé Powers**

Longer Term Effects of Cortisol

Now, as long as the stress-induced levels of cortisol last only for say, a matter of weeks, the damage caused to your brain is reversible. But note – long term (and by long term we are talking about months or years) raised levels of cortisol lead to an irreversible loss of neurons. Proof of this can be found in sufferers of PTSD (Post Traumatic Stress Disorder), who have been found in severe and chronic cases to have a shrunken hippocampus. Indeed it is has even been shown that long term high levels of cortisol correlate with Alzheimer's disease.

The Need to Manage Stress

From what you've just read, you should be able to see how damaging stress can be, both in the short term and the longer term. On that basis, we need to find ways of managing it down to more acceptable levels if we're to help your studies.

> ***"I try to put aside an hour a day for myself, except when I am busy, when I put aside two."***
> **Gandhi**

Countering Stress through Relaxation Techniques

Soap Operas Don't Count as Relaxation

For many people, relaxation consists of sitting in front of the TV, catching a five minute cigarette break outside the office, or going down to the local bar to have a few drinks and forget their troubles.

But none of these can be said to be true relaxation. To counter the effects that stress may have on you, and to therefore minimise the adverse impact on your memory and cognitive abilities, we need something more substantial and focussed.

Myriad Relaxation Techniques

There are almost as many different relaxation techniques out there as there are stars in the known universe. Some of them have strong followings, such as tai chi and yoga (in all its various forms). Other examples include meditation techniques such as Transcendental Mediation (known as TM).

If you can find the time to attend a class for one of these tried and trusted techniques, that's great. Alternatively, you could peruse the Self Help or Personal Development section of your local bookshop or internet bookseller and you should find many titles full of advice on the subject.

Do-It-Yourself Relaxation Techniques

However, there are a number of simple techniques you can use in your own home, requiring no prior knowledge or training, which will allow you to achieve the same ends. I have set out below a couple of these for you to try. Give them and go and see what you think – if for some reason neither really works for you, try one of the other sources listed above.

Method 1 – Progressive Relaxation Technique

Preparation

Find somewhere comfortable to lie (this technique can also be carried out seated or semi-reclining, but generally beginners will find the lying position the easiest). If you find music helps you relax, put some on now, although make sure it is suitably relaxing – nothing too loud or discordant. Classical music often does the trick. Alternatively, try one of the many self-help relaxation tapes or CDs available. Some of these consist of natural sounds, such as waves gently lapping onto the shore, or the sound of the rainforest, which can help induce a state of calm.

Place pillows under the head and knees. Take off your shoes, loosen any tight clothing such as neckties, lie down and shut your eyes. Make sure you're completely comfortable – if you're not, you'll find it more difficult to relax and maintain that state of relaxation. You're now ready to begin your self-relaxation routine.

The Routine

Start by concentrating on your breathing. Breathe slowly and rhythmically, with each breath being long, smooth and even. Concentrate on the air going in and out of your lungs, feel your diaphragm rising and falling, notice the air moving through your nostrils. Tell yourself you're falling into a nice relaxed state.

When you feel ready, begin to concentrate on your toes. Imagine a tingling sensation in them. Your toes feel warm as the tingling continues. Then feel that tingling sensation gradually subsiding as they begin to go numb. Feel them getting heavier as they get more and more numb. Eventually your toes feel very heavy and very numb.

Imagine that numbness and heaviness spreading up your body. First to your feet. Repeat the same process. Imagine a tingling, a warmth, then a gradual numbness and increasing heaviness. Continue to concentrate on imagining these feelings. If your attention is distracted for a second, simply bring your attention back to the tingling and numbness, and don't berate yourself for losing concentration momentarily.

Then onto your ankles, your calves. Imagine the tingling, the warmth, the numbness. Imagine the muscles becoming more and more relaxed as the tension in them dissolves. Continue with the process and move up the body as each body part you work on becomes heavy, warm, totally relaxed. Calves to thighs, thighs to buttocks.

With the lower half of your body now completely relaxed, repeat the same thought processes on the upper half of your body, using your imagination to go through the same tingling-warmth-numbness-heaviness routine. Start with your fingers, your hands, move up past your wrists to forearms, elbows, upper arms, shoulders. Then across from your shoulders to your chest, and down to your abdomen.

Finally, move up to your neck, your face, your scalp. Eventually leaving all tension in your body behind as you feel warm, relaxed and tension free. Continue to concentrate on your breathing and feeling your body completely at peace, heavy and limp. Lie there for as long as you want to, enjoying the sensations and feeling good about simply doing nothing other than relaxing. When you do finally get up, do so slowly, then gently stretch out all your muscles.

Once you've mastered this technique you can use it in a range of situations, places and positions, even sitting down outside the exam hall. You'll find that practice makes it easier and quicker to reach that fully relaxed state, and that muscle tension becomes a thing of the past.

Method 2 – Tension-Relaxation Technique

Preparation

Preparation for this technique is exactly the same as for the progressive relaxation technique shown above. In other words, take off your shoes, loosen tight clothing, lie down somewhere comfortable and put on some quiet music. In addition, make sure you don't try this technique immediately after a meal, because the digestion process diverts blood flow away from muscles and this could cause muscle cramps.

The Routine

The idea here is to train yourself to distinguish between tensed and relaxed muscles. In so doing, you end up acquiring the ability to detect when even a small amount of tension is present in your body and can then act to do something about it.

Start with your feet and toes, and tense the muscles up, clenching your toes tightly and pushing your feet down as far as they go. Really feel the tension within them. Hold for at least 10 seconds, then *slowly* release the tension. Let your toes and feet relax and become very loose. Repeat the process three times, each time making sure that during tension you continue to breathe normally, and that the release of tension is a gradual process, not a sudden change.

Then move up to your calves and carry out the same "tension for 10 seconds then gradual relaxation" process on these muscles. Repeat this too three times. Then onto your thighs, buttocks, abdomen, back, shoulders, arms, hands, neck, and facial muscles, in turn, for each one clenching the muscle (or muscles) to introduce tension, holding for 10 seconds, and then slowly releasing the tension into a relaxed state.

You may find it easier to practice the tension-relaxation technique on each individual body part first in isolation, and then combine all of these together when you have mastered the technique. Once you have become familiar with the applying the technique to your whole body in one session, you may find that eventually the tension part of the routine can be eliminated because the relaxation phase will have become a conditioned response.

DIY Relaxation Techniques Concluded

Hopefully, one of these techniques works for you. But don't panic if they don't – everyone is different.

And anyway, don't make the mistake of thinking it's only techniques designed specifically to bring about a state of relaxation that you can use. Other more straightforward methods can bring about the same results too. We'll take a look at these now.

Other Methods of Countering Stress

Physical Exercise

We've already covered the benefits of exercise in an earlier section, and indeed we noted that those who exercised demonstrated a milder stress response.

Hopefully, now you have seen just how corrosive stress can be, you can begin to really appreciate the benefits of a regular exercise program. Within reason, whatever activity you most enjoy will have a beneficial effect on your stress levels, whether it be aerobics, step classes, gym work or a game of tennis. As long as the activity involves at least a moderate degree of physical exertion over a minimum 20-minute period, you will be reaping the benefits. (For this reason, some activities clearly cannot be classed as exercise, such as a game of darts in the bar!)

Walking

Really just another type of physical exercise, it is nevertheless worth singling out walking for attention in its own right, particularly as many might not realise that it is so beneficial.

> ***"Of all exercises walking is the best."***
> **Thomas Jefferson**

Walking is the ideal exercise. It is low impact (thereby creating less stress on the joints, unlike for example jogging) and can be undertaken pretty much anywhere, thereby costing nothing. No special kit or uniform is required to get started. No training need be undertaken before one gets started. All in all, a winner.

It is also interesting to note that one of the commonest things people do when they get anxious or stressed is to get up and pace around. Could it be that this is because walking is nature's way of providing a great antidote to stress, using up those fight or flight chemicals? I like to think so.

So, what advice would I give with regards to that walking program?

- Firstly, *make it regular*, preferably three times a week for at least 20 minutes each time.
- Secondly, *walk at a brisk pace* (no ambling!) and try to maintain a good posture – head up, shoulders back, back straight.
- Thirdly, if at all possible, endeavour to *walk in uplifting surroundings*, such as by the sea, the side of a river, or in a park. If you can't manage this, imagine such a place and hold the images in your head as you walk wherever it is your route takes you.

Acting as if You are Relaxed

You Can't Hide the Way You Feel

Next time you have a few minutes, take some time out to do a little people watching. You might notice a difference, a noticeable physical difference, between those who are calm and those who are stressed.

Those who are stressed tend to speak more quickly, move around or fidget a significant amount, and exhibit more rapid, shallow breathing. They simply *look* stressed.

On the other hand, those who are calm exhibit very different physical signs. Their breathing will be deep and slow, their speech rhythm will be slow and relaxed, their mannerisms languid. These people may even look like they are a little lazy!

These outer physical signs are simply a manifestation of how they feel inside. But, just as with smiling, where we have seen that the direction of the process can be reversed, a smile making you feel happy as well as happiness making you smile, so it is with these other physical manifestations of the person's inner state. Acting *as if* you are relaxed can actually have that effect.

Getting to Laid Back

What should you do? Firstly, focus on your breathing, trying to ensure it becomes deeper and slower. Use the advice shown in the Progressive Relaxation Technique shown above to do this. Having done this, make a conscious effort to speak slower and to move your limbs around more slowly and purposefully. Avoid folding your arms, constantly crossing and uncrossing your legs, along with all the other movements such as scratching, twitching and so on that characterise a stressed person. Although it might feel strange at first, try to slow everything down so that it is even slower than appears natural.

> ***"Sometimes the most important thing in a whole day is the rest we take between two deep breaths."***
> **Etty Hillesum**

After a while, you really will begin to feel the benefits of acting as if you are calm. Practise this on a regular basis and eventually it will become second nature to you. Your natural countenance will changed from stressed-out to calm without you having to consciously make the change at all.

And that can't be bad news!

The 60-second Breather

This technique is useful for situations where you are particularly stressed and become aware that your breathing is especially rapid. It lends itself well to those situations where you may be on the verge of panic and need to control this panic quickly, in so doing returning to a more relaxed state conducive to whatever it is you are trying to do. Done properly, you should feel an immediate reduction in tension.

To the count of eight, breathe in slowly through the nose. Ensure that as you breathe in your abdomen rises and fills first, followed by your chest afterwards. This will ensure you fully inflate your lungs. Having done this, hold your breath for as long as it is comfortable to do so, then breathe out slowly, again to the count of eight, this time expelling the air from your lungs through your mouth.

Having fully emptied your lungs, do not take another breath until you begin to feel uncomfortable, then repeat the process again twice more.

The Calming Touch

As with the 60-second Breather technique shown above, this one is perhaps most useful in fire-fighting particular situations where you might be feeling more than usually stressed.

The basic idea is that applying touch to certain areas of the body can have a calming effect. This technique is one which has been shown to provide maximum comfort to children with special needs who have become significantly disturbed or upset, so its efficacy is as a method of relaxation has been proven beyond doubt.

The method is simplicity itself. With one of your hands, rhythmically stroke with a medium pressure (neither too light nor too firm) one of the following areas of the body

- Your forehead.
- The inside of your arm where your elbow bends.
- The back of the other hand.

That's it! Try all three areas to see which works best for you.

Physical Changes in Conclusion

Many Ways, Many Advantages

You've been shown that there are a large number of ways in which making physical changes to your lifestyle can have a positive effect on your overall well-being, often with a direct correlation between the change itself and your ability to perform come the exam. For example, we've seen how physical exercise can actually have an effect on brain cell growth, and how getting enough sleep is paramount in maximising your learning potential.

> ***"Never hurry. Take plenty of exercise. Always be cheerful. Take all the sleep you need. You may expect to be well."***
> **James Freeman Clarke**

Easy to Implement

Most of what has been suggested is relatively easy to implement, and I urge you strongly not to dismiss the suggestions without at least trying some of them first. Remember the Success Factor – the higher the percentage, the more chance you have of obtaining the pass mark you so desperately need. And remember that, to raise the Success Factor, we needed to focus on both attitudinal and physical changes.

Make the Change Today

So don't ignore the physical changes – if you're really serious about achieving examination success, they should be an integral part of your whole approach to study.

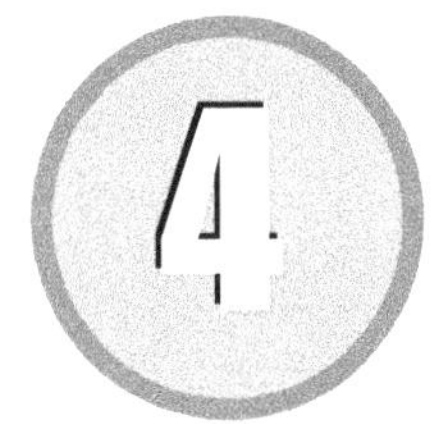

Success Factor Theory into Practice – Attitudinal Changes

Positive Self-Image – the Key to Success

In a nutshell, making attitudinal changes is all about changing the way you think about *you*. The state of your self-image is fundamental to the success or otherwise of your endeavours. Have a poor self-image and you will live up to that view, repeatedly failing when it matters most. Hold instead a positive self-image in your mind and the world is literally your oyster.

In part, we have already seen examples of the power of positive thought. Remember the basketball free throw experiment, where simply imagining throwing successful baskets actually led to a significant improvement in real-world performance? This was astounding proof of the innate power of imagination and positive thought.

> ***"Take charge of your thoughts. You can do what you will with them."***
> **Plato**

But experimental proof is one thing, putting the ideas into practice another. How can we actually use the evidence shown to really improve our own performance in the exam hall? What are the practicalities? This is what you will want to know.

Attitudinal Changes – The Basics

Two Types of Change

Although there are any number of methods which you might decide to use to achieve a more positive self-image, the majority of these methods can be classified into one of two groups. These are

> ***"We must become the change we want to see."***
> **Mahatma Gandhi**

- Visualisations
- Verbalisations

Whichever group a particular technique belongs to, and we shall see details of these shortly, its aim is the same. To improve your self-image. More than that, underlying pretty much every method of self-improvement there is lies one basic premise.

The Basic Premise

And the basic premise is this –

> ***The only person holding you back is YOU***

If you wanted to, you could visit your local bookshop or internet bookseller, bulk buy from the Self-Help and Improvement section, read extensively and learn the same thing. Each book will boil down to this same underlying message. So I make no excuses for repeating it again!

The only person holding you back is YOU

Hold that idea in your head for a while, kick it around and really try to understand it. I'm not joking when I make this statement. I know that even now some of you will find this a difficult one to believe. Surely there are other factors which will affect your success, things outside of your control? Am I really suggesting that literally *anything* you want to do you can do, simply by imagining it?

Anything Within Limits

No. In reality, there are limits. Take the example of the Feel the Fear experiment that we saw in Chapter Two, where statements made by the individual affected the strength of their arm held out at ninety degrees to the body. The statements "I am a strong and worthy person" and "I am a weak and worthless person" are general in nature. There is nothing within them which would be in direct conflict with the individual's subconscious, even though they might not be in complete harmony. As a result, whether they were believed or not, the statements had an impact.

"All things are possible to him that believes."
Mark 9:23

Imagine instead telling yourself the statement "I am a strong and worthy person who will now be able to lift a 500lb weight off the floor without a problem". Do you think that you would then be able to lift the weight?

Of course not. This is because what you are telling yourself is in direct conflict with what your subconscious knows about you and your limitations. So unless you happen to be an Olympic weightlifter, the chances are that such a suggestion would not have the desired effect.

As we will see therefore, when we are looking at visualisations and verbalisations, at all times what we are doing is *persuading* the subconscious that what we are telling it is true. We use suggestions which, whilst not in complete harmony with our self-image, do not contradict what we know about ourselves directly.

Using this method, gradually, with repetition, the subconscious begins to believe what we are telling it, and our self-image changes as a result. And once our self-image has changed for the better, our Success Factor percentage goes up.

Visualisation

So what is visualisation? Visualisation is, if you like, the use of the imagination, the mind's eye, to see in visual form what you desire, with the aim of bringing about the realisation of that desire.

The power of visualisation is both well documented and well used throughout the world. Perhaps one of the areas it is used most extensively is in sport.

Use in Sport

For example, Tiger Woods carved out for himself an immensely successful career in golf at a young age. He has made no secret of the fact that he has used visualisation extensively to help his game. His father Earl taught him early on to use mental imagery when training and playing. When Tiger is hunched over the ball on the green, staring at it fixedly, he is literally creating a mental image of striking the ball and seeing it dropping into the hole.

> ***"Projecting your mind into a successful situation is the most powerful means to achieve goals. If you spend time with pictures of failure in your mind, you will orchestrate failure."***
>
> **Estee Lauder**

Top athletes too use visualisation extensively. Look at any world class 100-metre sprinter as they line up on the blocks. See the way they are staring ahead of them, down the track, mentally rehearsing their start and the race. Athletes in other events too can be seen to carry out this mental rehearsal. They say that using this mental imagery is vital for building up their performance.

And who would argue with them? If a man in the street can improve his basketball skills by simply imagining being better, who is to say a sprinter cannot shave a tenth of a second off his time by using the same technique of visualisation?

In fact, many consider that at the highest levels of sport, where only the elite compete, and where ability levels are pretty much on a par, it is as much a battle of the mind as it is a battle of ability amongst the competitors. Those who win the mind game are likely to be the ones who win the game itself.

Use in the Treatment of Phobias

But sport is not the only place where visualisation has been used to help the individual. Take the treatment of certain phobias. For example, arachnophobia, the fear of spiders. At its worst, a sufferer would not even be able to be in the same room as a spider, let alone physically touch one, whatever the size and type of the spider.

The recommended treatment for such a condition would generally involve the gradual and phased introduction of the feared object (in this case, the spider) to the sufferer, which over time should lead to a desensitisation of the panic mechanism which kicks in when faced with the fear.

But one cannot simply give an arachnophobe a real spider to hold, or likely even an imitation one, at the early stages of treatment. This would be too much for the sufferer, overloading their senses and bringing about a phobic reaction. So in these cases, the subjects are merely asked to *imagine* a spider, perhaps first in a container in the room, and then perhaps outside of the container. This is a form of visualisation.

So again, we can see that it is the power of the mind and the use of visualisation which is harnessed to bring about a change in the behaviour of the individual.

Use in Times of Adversity

Let's have a look at some more examples of the power of visualisation, this time where it is used to successfully overcome difficulties faced in times of extreme adversity, most of which are probably beyond our understanding.

Nelson Mandela spent 27 years in prison in South Africa because of his opposition to apartheid. Throughout this period he used visualisation to help him remain positive. Then there is Terry Waite, a hostage negotiator of international fame who worked as special envoy to the Archbishop of Canterbury. After gaining the release of hostages in Libya, he himself was then held hostage by a militant Middle Eastern group in Beirut for five years, four of which were spent blindfolded in solitary confinement in a darkened cell. He too used his powers of imagination and visualisation to help remain sane during the worst privations.

"Adversity is the first path to truth."
Lord Byron

If you think about it, visualisation is all about using the right side of the brain. (You will remember that it is the right side of the brain that is largely responsible for such things as imagination, spatial awareness, daydreaming, colour and dimension.) In this sense, learning to use the right side of the brain through visualisation allows you to more fully utilise the power of your brain.

And in case you're still not convinced by the power of visualisation, let me give you one more example to think about. In this example, visualisation is not used merely to achieve a more positive frame of mind, but much more than that. It is used to harness that untapped potential the brain has in abundance, just waiting to be used.

Use by the World's Greatest Minds

Einstein. Possibly, arguably, the greatest scientist the world has ever seen. Most famous perhaps for his Theory of Relativity, in reality he achieved far more than this during his lifetime.

Now, you might have imagined Einstein would have worked almost exclusively with the left side of his brain, the side responsible for logic, reasoning, language & communication, maths skill, organisation and so on. After all, it seems reasonable to assume he would use these skills to arrive at his theories and their scientific proofs. Science is seen very much as an academic, logical activity, using reasoning and logic to come up with a scientific conclusion.

But you would be wrong. Einstein himself reported how he came up with the Theory of Relativity whilst imagining travelling down a sunbeam, or light wave. He used his right brain to create a scientific leap which at that time defied logic, and then came back and used his left brain to translate that leap into hard logic. He used *both* sides of the brain to come up with his groundbreaking theories, theories which literally changed the world.

> ***"Imagination is more important than knowledge. Knowledge is limited. Imagination encircles the world."***
> **Albert Einstein**

But enough of the background. Let's now get stuck into the detail. What are the techniques we can use to introduce visualisation into our lives and our studies? The next section will show us.

Visualisation Techniques

The examples given above about how visualisation is used are of course interesting in their own right, and parallels can be drawn from them.

However, the bottom line is that you want to maximise your chances of success in your professional level exams. To do that, you need to understand how to use visualisation to help you in your cause. So now we need to look at some of the techniques you can use, and how they can be applied to improve your Success Factor.

Practice Makes Perfect

Right Brain Inactivity

First, though, it's worth noting that, like all skills, these techniques will need practice if you are to fully master them. In our modern world, and particularly in our educational system, the focus is very much on left brain, precise, logical thinking. The right brain and its creative, imaginative power, tends to be largely ignored, and therefore our ability to use this power atrophies over time.

> ***"The soul... Never thinks without a picture."***
> **Aristotle**

In practice, this may mean that the first time you attempt any visualisation you find it difficult to focus on creating the imagery required. Your attention may wander and you might not be able to conjure up the pictures in your mind's eye that the particular technique requires.

Awaken Your Inner Child

Take heart, however. The imaginative skills required may have atrophied, but they are still there. You're just a little rusty. After all, you had those skills by the bucket-load when you were a child. Children use their imagination all the time without guilt or concern. To them, it seems natural to pretend that a tennis racket is really a guitar, that a toilet roll tube is really a telescope, or that an empty jug is really full of water. It's only as they get older and the educational establishment gets its claws into them, instilling the importance of common sense logical "scientific" thinking, that things change.

Once, you would have run across the park with your arms held outstretched like wings, imagining you were a plane, or a bird, flying freely through the sky.

> ***"Hold a picture of yourself long and steadily enough in your mind's eye, and you will be drawn towards it."***
> **Harry Fosdick**

You can learn to fly again. It just takes a little practice. And with practice, in time, you will be able to awaken that child-like imagination once more.

Practice Visualisation

Preparation

The likelihood is that you are one of those unused to using your imaginative powers to any real degree. If this is you, then you need a gentle introduction (or perhaps I should more correctly say reintroduction, since you had these skills once) to the subject.

This exercise is best undertaken in a place without distractions or other possible intrusions. Find a room where you can be alone, close the blinds, and turn off the TV or radio. Do so now.

The Technique

Close your eyes (some may find that keeping their eyes open but unfocussed gives them better results. Try both methods if necessary and do whatever feels most natural to you). Now, imagine yourself on a sandy beach. See yourself sitting there on the sand, facing the sea, the beach stretching out into the distance on either side of you.

Create that picture in your mind's eye in full colour. See the azure sea in front of you, waves gently lapping onto the white sand, white froth left as they advance and then retreat. Look up and gaze into the deep blue cloudless sky, see the hot sun beating down.

Now feel the touch of a breeze on your face, coming off the sea. Smell the salt in the air, taste that salt in your mouth as you breathe in. Feel the hot sand under your feet; imagine the roughness of the grains of sand between your toes as you wiggle them. Experience the sun's rays on your bare skin. Hear the loud cries of sea birds above you, and the gentle rhythmic sound of the surf. Create whatever other images in your senses that you associate with such a place, maybe boats out on the water, maybe children playing in the sand. Whatever works for you.

Really believe you are there, in that place. Focus entirely on the sensations, take yourself out of the place you are in and become that person sitting there.

Practice with All Five Senses

You may find the exercise difficult at first. You might find the visual images relatively easy to create in your mind's eye, but the other senses less so. This is because our primary sense of vision is the one we rely on most, and the one we are most conscious of. But stick with, and repeat the exercise, say every day for 5 to 10 minutes a day. Gradually you will find that it becomes far easier to create the images and the sensations linked to them. You will be honing your visualisation skills.

And do notice that visualisation is not just about the visual – it is about engaging all five senses in the process of imagination. The more fully you are able to recreate those sensations, the more fully rounded the image, the better.

A Stress Buster Too

Note too that, although this exercise is useful in its own right as a way of reawakening you imaginative skills, a useful side effect should result from undertaking it regularly. Taking yourself to that calm place in your imagination, you should also feel calmer once you have done so. In other words, this is a good way of managing levels of stress.

Once you are happy with the practice visualisation, you are ready to try some of the other techniques available. These are set out below.

Wannabe Visualisation

What it's About

This is about visualising where you want to get to, where you want to be. It might be a place, it might be a situation, it might be a process you need to go through to get to where you want to be. Whatever it is, there is a gap between where you are and where you want to go that needs to be bridged.

The Technique

To carry out this visualisation, close your eyes and imagine the room you are in is a darkened cinema. There are two framed screens in front of you, and onto each screen is projected a moving picture.

Look first at the left-hand screen. This is showing a film of where you are now, and the problems you want to rid yourself of. But this film is a black and white silent movie. Although you can see the problems you have, the image is flickering, scratched, and there is no sound.

> ***"I saw in my mind hundreds of McDonald's restaurants in all the corners of the land."***
> **Ray Croc**

Now switch your attention to the right-hand screen. This image is in full-blown Technicolor, and as you focus your attention on the screen, you are subjected to the full surround sound cinema experience. Imagine the image showing what you want it to show, that is, you achieving your aims and objectives. Where you want to be.

Once the image is firmly fixed centre screen, imagine getting up and stepping into the image itself. It is no longer merely a two dimensional picture, but a living, three-dimensional world, fully real, and you are in it. Everything seems brighter, more colourful. Experience the show with all five senses; use your imagination to really be there in that world. Play the film through from beginning to end, and enjoy the spectacle of your success.

Helpful Examples

I've deliberately not given examples of what your own films should show, because these will be different for each person. However, let me give you some examples in general terms to help you understand what you might use this technique for.

Difficulty Getting Down to Study

Perhaps you have difficulty getting down to studying. Everything is an excuse to distract you, the phone ringing, the tap dripping, anything. You want to get over this problem to allow you to study effectively.

In the visualisation, your left-hand screen would show a black and white silent film of you sitting at your desk, constantly using distractions as an excuse to jump up and stop studying. Your right-hand screen would show a bright colour image of you studying effectively at your desk. You would imagine this situation in every detail – the feel of the chair you are sitting on, the desk your arms rest on, the feel of the pen in your hand, perhaps the smell of a highlighter pen as you read through your text book, marking relevant sections.

> ***"If you paint in your mind a picture of bright and happy expectations, you put yourself into a condition conducive to your goal."***
> **Norman Vincent Peale**

You get the idea.

Difficulty with Exam Time Allocation

Perhaps instead, you have trouble being strict with time allocation in exams (a subject we will cover at much greater length later in the book). You tend to overrun when answering questions, thereby leaving you with insufficient time to fully answer the rest of the paper.

In this case, you would use your Wannabe method to visualise your right-hand screen showing you dealing correctly with this problem in the exam. Perhaps you might imagine looking at the clock as you approach the deadline you have set yourself for producing an answer, and then writing the last concluding paragraph of your essay as the clock reaches this point. You then imagine yourself starting the next question immediately after this, and the good feeling it gives you to know you're still on target to finish the exam paper.

Exam Phobias and Visualisation

Phobias Can Lead to Failure

A note on exam phobias in the context of visualisation. You might be unlucky enough to be one of those who suffers a bad panic reaction to exams, even to the mere thought of an exam. These bad reactions can be anything from a faster heartbeat or palpitations, to sweating, dizziness, feelings of nausea (sometimes even actual nausea), uncontrollable shakes and beyond. In other words, you suffer a bad physical reaction. Your chances of passing will no doubt be severely reduced by such a response.

> ***"Fear is a darkroom where negatives develop."***
> **Usman B. Arif**

Focus Externally, Not Internally

Visualisation can help in these situations. However, when using your imagination to create the images, you need to avoid focussing on the *internal* feelings you would have in the exam hall. Continually visualising the things that one is afraid of will actually strengthen the link between stimulus (the exam) and response (panic attack), making the actual experience even worse than if it had not been continually imagined. Clearly this would not be progress!

Instead, you need to focus on the *external* scene in a positive way, on what is going on around you, the exam hall, the desk, the chair, the pen in your hand and so on. Do not focus on the internal scene, the reactions and sensations that the exam might give you.

Use a Staged Approach

Furthermore, you should build up your use of imagery slowly. Instead of starting with a full-on image of the exam and imagining how and what all five senses might be experiencing, break the process down. Reduce the situation in some way until it does not bring about that sense of panic.

Maybe imagine doing only a practice or mock exam, instead of the final exam. Or imagine just answering a single question instead of an entire paper. You could also introduce each of the five senses one at a time to avoid sensory overload. So just imagine a picture of the exam the first time you carry out the visualisation, and only then add sound when you feel you are happy with the silent image.

Avoid Known Triggers

Or maybe you are aware there are specific triggers which set off your exam phobia. It might be the sight of the endless row upon row of desks which greet you as you first walk into the exam hall, or perhaps the feeling of all of the other delegates crowded around you, seemingly all answering the exam questions so much better than you are.

If so, simply remove that trigger from the mental picture you create, and only add it back in once you are completely calm and happy with the picture you have been working with. Remember, you can do whatever you like in your own world of imagination – simply remove all the other desks from the picture and carry on. It's all under your control.

Frame Your Fear Visualisation

Mild Fears Only

This method should *not* be used where the fear you wish to deal with is phobic in intensity. As we have seen, for fears of this proportion a more indirect and softly-softly approach is required, and advice on this is set out in the section above. However, for those fears of a more general nature, which may produce mildly uncomfortable feelings but nothing more, this is an ideal technique.

The Technique

Imagine the thing you fear on a screen in front of you. Now imagine a frame being placed around this screen, to create a fixed picture. Then imagine this framed picture shrinking in size until it is only the size of one of those miniature portraits sometimes seen in antique shops, no more than a couple of inches high. If you want to, you can also imagine taking the miniature picture down off the wall and placing in a closed drawer, out of sight and mind.

Repeatedly doing this will have the effect of making the fear seem small, trivial and harmless. Eventually you will fear it no more.

Zoom Up and Out Visualisation

Time, Distance and Perspective

This is another technique which is very useful in reducing the perceived importance of problems you may be experiencing. It is based on two ideas – firstly, that something viewed from a different perspective often looks very different, and secondly, that distance and time give greater perspective, or objectivity.

The Technique

Imagine yourself experiencing the particular problem you're having trouble with. Perhaps you are having trouble understanding a particular part of the textbook you are studying. Imagine that you are looking at yourself through a camera from above. See yourself at your desk in your study with the open textbook and a look of discomfort on your face. The view you have of yourself is detached, through the lens of the camera.

Now imagine the camera moving higher, widening its perspective, zooming out to see the entire room you are in, table, chair, walls, windows, door. The camera continues to zoom out and move higher still, now above your house so that you can see the entire house in the frame.

Still the zoom out continues. You can see your house in relation to the road you live in, then this road as part of the village or town you live, then this town in relation to the country around it. The camera moves inexorably higher, as if it is a satellite orbiting the earth, and now you can see the country you live in relation to the rest of the world.

The process continues, the earth now seen as just one of the planets in our solar system, then our solar system as part of our galaxy, then our galaxy as part of the entire universe.

The Result

By this point, your problem will seem insignificant, trivial, unimportant in the grand scheme of things. This visualisation will not solve the problem itself, but it will give you a better perspective on it.

With this perspective, you will be able to move past whatever the problem is, recognising that it is but a very small part of the overall whole within which you work.

Retreat Visualisation

Your Ideal Place

In part, we've already encountered this technique when we ran through the Practice Visualisation. If you remember, I asked you to imagine yourself on a beach. This is, for many, the archetypal retreat, a place that creates pleasant feelings, feelings of peace, warmth, safety and security.

The Retreat Visualisation is about creating a place for yourself where you can go to during visualisation to experience these feel-good feelings. The retreat you use in your imagination can be a real place, or it can be imaginary, a pastiche of what you like the most. It might be from your past, your present or your future. It's entirely up to you.

> ***"There is no need to go to India or anywhere else to find peace. You will find that deep place of silence right in your room, your garden or even your bathtub."***
> **Elisabeth Kubler-Ross**

It could be a warm, tropical beach. Or it could be the top of an alpine mountain in summer. Perhaps it could instead be a verdant glade set in a beautiful ancient oak forest. The list is endless. You choose.

But whatever you choose, create in your mind's eye as vivid a scene of it as you can. Remember to involve all five senses in the visualisation. Really live it, as if you are really there.

Available for a Quick Fix

With practice, you will be able to recall this place to mind at short notice. As such, this technique lends itself not only to relaxation after a hard day at the office, but also to calming the mind during stressful moments. For example, you might employ it to help you maintain as relaxed a disposition as possible whilst sitting outside the exam hall waiting to enter the exam.

Physical Triggers and Visualisations

Immediate Relief Required

Sometimes, you might need to access the benefits that a particular visualisation exercise gives you, without having to actually perform the visualisation itself. Perhaps you can't find the time or place to allow you sufficient peace and quiet to carry out the exercise effectively.

For example, you are driving your car to your exam, concentrating on road and traffic, whilst simultaneously working yourself into a panic about the exam. What can you do to rid yourself of these negative feelings? If you allow them to continue, you will send yourself into a real tailspin from which you may not sufficiently recover in time for your exam.

Clearly, you can't close your eyes and start one of your visualisations. This might prove more than a little dangerous given the circumstances! So what can you do? Is there a method you can use to deal with these ad-hoc situations?

Yes, there is, but a little preparation is required up front, so that when you need to access the positive feelings brought about by visualisation, you can do so.

The Technique

Advance Preparation

Imagine a place, an event or a time (or a combination of these) where you felt completely happy, calm and at peace. If you can't think of one, you could instead use the place you used (or created) in your mind's eye during your Retreat Visualisation.

Replay this experience (time, place, event or whatever) in your mind's eye in detail, again, remembering to take notice of what all five of your senses are feeling. Now, when a feeling of calmness spreads through you, apply a distinctive and memorable pressure to a part of your body for around five seconds with the fingers of one hand.

I would suggest, as an example, applying pressure with the thumb and forefinger of one hand to the triangle of flesh between thumb and first finger on the other hand. But do whatever feels most comfortable and natural to you, as long as whatever you decide works can be carried out quickly, easily and without causing attention to be drawn to you should you be in a public place (applying pressure to some areas may raise a few eyebrows!).

You will need to practice the process a few times to allow the link to be made in your mind between the calm, serene feeling of happiness and the self-applied pressure. Around three or four times should be sufficient.

Access On Demand

After this, all you need to do to access these calm and positive feelings as and when required in the real world is to apply the pressure as you have practiced before. And hey presto, you'll suddenly access the same relaxed, happy state you originally experienced during your advance preparation.

This deceptively simple technique should not be underestimated. Not only is it that, i.e. simple, but the fact that it can be used pretty much undetected whilst you are being observed by others makes it very useful for those situations where perhaps you would rather not make it obvious you are experiencing any sort of difficulties.

So How and Why Does Visualisation Work?

Appeasing the Sceptical Left Brain

At the beginning of this chapter, we said that we needed to make attitudinal changes in order to improve our self-image. We then went on to look at some of the visualisation techniques available to help achieve this change.

But you might well be left pondering an important question. *Exactly how is it that these techniques work?* Your left brain will want coherent logical reasoning to back up the claims that have been made in this book. The sceptic in you will not want to believe the New-Ageist claim that positive thinking really is the key. After all, it all seems just a little too easy!

The Explanation

The logic is this, and it applies not only to the visualisation techniques set out above, but equally to the experimental evidence given earlier in the book which demonstrated so well the power of positive thought (those basketball free throw again).

Visualisation Creates Neural Pathways

When you mentally rehearse something, whether it be an event, a process, a feeling, whatever, you are firing a certain number of brain cells, or neurons, in a particular way. A pathway of neural connections is created as electrical signals are passed from one neuron to another in furtherance of whatever mental task you are undertaking.

Repetition Strengthens These Pathways

With repetition, these new neural pathways are strengthened over time, as a result making them easier to remember and easier to access. Thus, the process of mental rehearsal and its repetition first creates a memory and then cements it into place within the brain.

New Pathways = New Self Image

Self-image comes from accessing a store of memories and feelings you hold about yourself. It follows therefore that creating new positive memories via these techniques will gradually change your self-image. By using visualisation you can literally change what you think and believe about yourself.

Mental (Internal) Practice = Real-world (External) Practice

Interestingly, as well, in the context of performance, it has been shown that whether you are simply imagining an event, say, throwing that basketball at the hoop, or you are actually undertaking it in the real world, the same set of neurons will fire. As the same set of "machinery" is used within the brain, whether the activity is internal (imagined) or external (real world), the brain is literally unable to differentiate between the two. The neural messages are the same. The effect of practice is the same.

This leads to an inescapable conclusion. Not only can you improve the way you think about yourself through positive thought, you really can also improve the way you perform a given action in the same way. The logic speaks for itself.

Visualisation – A Valuable Member of the Team

You've seen the benefits that visualisation can offer, and now you've seen why the techniques work. The explanations are hard science, not airy-fairy wishful thinking. Visualisation really does work – I hope I've persuaded you of that now.

So do make sure you include visualisation as part of the study process. Along with all of the other techniques and advice contained within this book, it really can make the difference between pass and fail.

Verbalisation

Verbalisation versus Visualisation

Verbalisations are Powerful

We've already seen the potentially massive impact of verbalisations (sometimes known as *affirmations*). "I am a weak and worthless person" said just ten times had a significant effect on a person's strength levels in the "Feel the Fear" experiment noted in Chapter Two.

Verbalisations, then, are not to be underestimated. They can be as powerful in their effect as visualisations are.

Which is Better?

So which method should you use? Visualisation. Or Verbalisation? Is one better than the other?

The answer is no. They each have their uses. *Both* methods should be used in tandem for maximum benefit. What you will find is that visualisations are great for those things you can easily create an image for in your mind. Verbalisations, on the other hand, are better for those concepts which are more abstract in nature.

Verbalisation for Abstract Concepts

For example, how would you easily visualise an image to reflect the statement "I am a strong and worthy person"? You might be able to imagine perhaps an image of you lifting heavy weights with ease, but the "worthy" part of the statement might prove more difficult to easily visualise in any concrete way.

In such cases, verbalisations will do the job better.

Easy to Start

One big advantage of verbalisations is that they are easier to get started with. Visualisations require you to use your right brain skills, your imagination and creativity, to create images in your mind's eye. This can sometimes prove difficult if you're out of practice.

Verbalisation, on the other hand, can be started immediately. All you have to do is decide what to say to yourself and then say it.

Experimental Proof

By the way, as with visualisation, there *is* experimental proof that what you are told about yourself, or what you tell yourself, really does have an effect on your self-image. So if you remain a little sceptical, here's some more detail to help persuade you that positive talking really will increase your Success Factor.

> ***"Affirmations are like prescriptions for certain aspects of yourself you want to change."***
> **Jerry Frankhauser**

Watch What You Tell Yourself

In an experiment, researchers asked the subjects to read pre-prepared statements to themselves. The subjects had their brain activity monitored and were also asked about their subjective feelings during the experiment.

When given around twenty or so negative statements to read, such as "Looking back on my life, I wonder if I have accomplished anything really worthwhile" and "There are things about me that aren't very attractive", the subjects not only reported a subjective deterioration in their mood, their brain activity changed significantly, indicating that they were depressed.

On the other hand, given twenty positive statements, the subjects reported feelings of elation and this was backed up by the changes in their brain waves.

It's easy to miss the significance of this evidence if you skip over the detail, but stop for a second and understand just what it means. *What you tell yourself really can affect your self-image.*

What This Means For You

As a positive self-image leads to improved performance, you need to be employing positive self-statements to ensure you take advantage of this reality. In the next section we shall look at the techniques involved.

Verbalisation Techniques

What exactly should you be doing then to introduce verbalisations to your repertoire of self-help techniques? Here's the what, how and when.

The Basic Technique

The Requirement for Positive Self-Statements

The first thing you need to do is come up with some positive self-statements. They should be

- Short, simple and to the point.
- Memorable.
- Positive.
- Couched in the present tense, not set in the future or the past.
- Active, not passive.
- In harmony, or at least not in direct conflict, with beliefs you already have about yourself.

Identify Your Problem Areas

I would suggest initially taking half an hour to carry out some self-analysis. Be honest with yourself. What do you think are your problems and weaknesses when it comes to the study process? What areas could you improve in?

Turn a Negative Into a Positive

Once you have done this, take one of the problem areas you have highlighted and restate the negative as a positive in the form of a statement.

> ***"Sometimes life's Hell. But hey! Whatever gets the marshmallows toasty."***
> **J. Andrew Helt**

For example, maybe you feel that you will fail your exam because you aren't doing enough work. If so, your positive self-statement could be "I have every intention of passing my exam and I'm doing everything I can to make it happen".

Or perhaps you have a tendency to spend hours worrying about the future, working through possible scenarios in your head, and so have less time to concentrate on what you should be doing right now. In the case, your verbalisation could be simply "Stick to the here and now".

Repetition is the Key

To start with, come up with a couple of these verbalisations. Practice them regularly. The key to getting the maximum benefit from these is *repetition* – you need to repeat them so many times that they filter down to your subconscious and are eventually taken as the truth. The more you tell yourself these positive things, the more likely you are to believe them. I would suggest 10 repetitions per verbalisation, twice a day.

Talk to Yourself

And if possible, try to say them *out loud*. For some reason, this seems to give them added weight. But if you can't manage this, don't worry. Repeating them silently to yourself will still have a positive effect. And this silent method allows you to carry out the exercise anywhere, and at any time, on the train, in the office, or even in bed.

The End Result

When you have been practising your chosen verbalisations for a while, you will find that what you are telling yourself becomes believable at the conscious level. Simply repeating the statements will somehow feel right. You should experience a feeling of resonance when you repeat the chosen words of your affirmations.

Tackle Other Problem Areas

Once you have mastered your first few statements therefore, consider whether there are any more areas that you feel might benefit from positive verbalisations. Create verbalisations for these too.

Enhancing the Basic Technique

The Rhythm Method

Depending on the individual, you may prefer to create your verbalisation in the form of a short rhyme. Be creative here – do whatever feels natural.

Using rhythm can help to make your affirmations more "catchy", so that they are easier to remember and easier to chant to yourself. If you like, your affirmation rhyme is a little like the mantra that practitioners of meditation use to gain a meditative state. The very rhythm of the mantra, repeated again and again, helps the person meditating tune out the external and focus on the internal. In the same way, using affirmations with a rhythm can help you really concentrate on the words and meaning so that they fix themselves into your psyche more quickly than they might otherwise do.

As an example of a positive verbalisation, when I was studying for my accountancy exams, my partner made a rhyme up for me, which went

Stay calm,
Take a deep breath
Show them that you can be one of the best

I used to chant this to myself in time with my footsteps as I walked down the road! I would practice it and then use it on the way to sitting my exams. Silly it may be, but its very repetition did indeed calm any panic or fears I might have been suffering from.

Again, I make no excuse for repeating it; don't underestimate the power of the mind. Use it to your advantage. And if that means making up silly rhymes that you can remember, and that make you feel more positive, so be it. Use whatever works for you.

The Stop Method

Are You Being Hard on Yourself?

Often, those who are habitually negative about themselves are not even aware that they are telling themselves negative things. It has become such a habit that it just feels like normality.

To judge whether or not you fall into this category, you need to carry out a little more self-analysis. Take a particular day, and for that one day, really listen to what you are saying, both to others and to yourself. In other words, look at both external and internal dialogue.

> ***"Shut up, Brain, or I'll stab you with a Q-tip!"***
> **Homer Simpson**

Try to reach a judgement about whether, on balance, the statements you make about yourself are positive or negative. Are you constantly criticising your behaviour, wishing you had done something differently, chastising yourself because of the way you behaved, putting yourself down?

When you really sit down and listen to yourself you may realise that in fact you are being very negative about yourself. If so, you need to do something about it.

Stopping Negative Thoughts

Become aware of your thoughts. Whenever a negative thought appears, imagine a sign appearing in your mind's eye.

The sign says "Stop" in big letters. Say the word to yourself as well; "Stop", in a firm voice. (Or if you're not alone, imagine yourself saying it.)

Having recognised the negative thought and stopped it in its tracks, you need to replace it with a positive one. Again, keep the positive statement simple and to the point. It doesn't have to win prizes for originality, literacy or eloquence. Just as long as it is right for you.

An Example

Let's take an example. Perhaps you're in the middle of a study session and have come across a particularly complex and difficult passage. As a result, you've lost your concentration, leading to a feeling of hopelessness and panic. You catch yourself saying "I just can't concentrate when things get tough, I'm never going to get through these exams".

First, you stop the existing negative thought by saying and seeing the Stop sign. Then, you reinforce this by saying out loud to yourself "I'm learning to improve my concentration daily and this will help me pass my exams". Repeat this statement say five times when you experience the panic, and add it to your list of general verbalisations you are practising daily.

Gradually, you will find you have to stop yourself less and less for negative thoughts as the positive affirmations begin to have an effect on your self-image.

Using Quotations as Verbalisations

Throughout this book I've used a number of quotations which I think are particularly relevant to the subject at hand.

There is nothing stopping you using some of these quotations for yourself, as positive affirmations, or as reminders about what *not* to do. Many are ideal for these purposes. Why struggle making up your own ones when you can simply borrow the ones someone else has already spent the time creating?

My favourite is Douglas Adams' immortal line from The Hitchhikers' Guide to the Galaxy

Don't panic!

Never a truer word spoken!

Attitudinal Changes in Summary

Attitudinal Changes for a First Time Pass

We've seen in this chapter just how important self-image is, how the way you view yourself has a direct way on the way you behave, and in the context of your exams, the way you perform.

You've also seen a number of techniques which aim to help bring about the shift in self image away from the negative to the positive end of the spectrum.

Hopefully, I've given you enough ideas for you to take away and experiment with. Because experiment is what you need to do – some of the techniques listed will work for you, others won't. You need to find the ones that have the best fit for you as an individual, and then work with these to achieve the maximum benefit.

"They conquer who believe they can."
Emerson

Attitudinal Changes for Life

One last thing. Although we are most interested in the positive effect that making these attitudinal changes will have on our studies and exam performance, do realise that all of the techniques we have seen described can be used to benefit your life as a whole. They can be applied wherever and whenever you have a problem.

So don't simply discard them once you have gained that first time pass. Add them to your Life Skills Toolbox and they will serve you well in the future!

The Success Factor Revisited

The Story So Far...

Let's quickly remind ourselves about the story so far.

The Success Formula

First, in Part One of this book we defined exam performance in terms of a formula. Remember the Success Formula? It went like this.

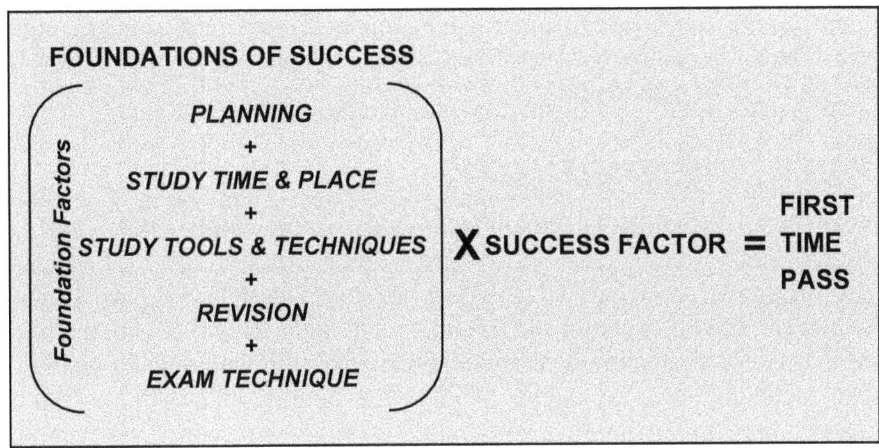

Looking at the formula, we saw how our ultimate chances of success, of achieving that sought after first time pass, are affected not only by the basics that we might expect, such as adequate revision, decent exam technique and the like, but also by something more fundamental.

The Success Factor

This "something more fundamental" is the Success Factor. And as we have seen in Part Two, its effect is indeed profound. Deal with the Success Factor badly and you can deal your chances of an exam pass a mortal blow.

We've now seen the changes we can make to improve our Success Factor score. These changes are both physical and attitudinal. Of course, ultimately it's up to you which of these techniques you use. I suggest you try a number of them and see which works best for you. But whatever the changes you make, remember this. The *more* changes you introduce, and the *more* areas you focus on, the *better* your chances of improving your exam performance. What have you got to lose by at least giving them a go? Get started today if you haven't already done so.

Being in Control

It's worth noting at this point one other benefit gained from implementing the changes we looked at. Taking an active approach in this way gives us a feeling of being in control of ourselves and our life in a way that a purely passive approach never could.

And being in control reduces the feelings of helplessness that are often otherwise present when we're attempting something new, something which is outside of the boundaries we have previously set ourselves. In other words, being in control reduces stress levels and increases confidence levels. This can only be a good thing.

Onto the Foundations of Success

However, to feel fully in control will take more than just a focus on the physical and attitudinal changes we talked about. Because thus far, we have only looked at one part of the Success Formula, the Success Factor. Remember, the other part of the formula, the Foundations of Success? These are the processes and areas normally associated with studying for exams – study technique, revision and the like. Well, to be fully in control we need to focus on these too. After all, a wonderful Success Factor score is never going to make up for a lousy Foundations of Success score.

For example, assume the following Success Formula scores

Situation 1 –	Success Factor Score	20%
	Foundations of Success Score	0
Situation 2 –	Success Factor Score	90%
	Foundations of Success Score	0

Zero times 20% gives the same result as zero times 90%, i.e. zero. In other words, you can be as positive as you like, but sooner or later you're going to have to actually *do* some studying! And *how* you do that studying is very important too.

So this is what we must concentrate on now. The actual study process itself, and the factors which go to make it up. The remaining parts of this book will deal with each of these factors in detail. So read on.

Part Three

PLANNING

Background to Planning

Planning – the Neglected Discipline

Planning – Only One Part of the Success Formula

The definition of the Success Formula has already shown us that a number of contributory factors go to make up exam success. Whilst each of these factors is important in its own right, the formula also demonstrates the interdependency between these factors, the reality that no one thing alone can be responsible for pass or fail. As such, planning is no more important in the grand scheme of things than study technique or revision, or any other of the factors included in the formula.

But the Most Often Ignored

However, if there is any one factor which is most often neglected or ignored completely when an individual undertakes a course of study leading towards examinations, it is planning. Time and time again I have seen students plough straight into their studies without any thought as to planning whatsoever, simply picking up the relevant textbook and reading from page one.

So Is It Really That Important?

You might even be asking yourself right now, what planning is *really* necessary when studying for an exam? Isn't it just a case of picking up the text book, making notes and going from there? Isn't it just common sense? Isn't time spent planning up front, before any books or pens and paper are picked up, just a waste of valuable study time?

> ***"Good plans shape good decisions. That's why planning helps to make elusive dreams come true."***
> **Lester R. Bittel**

To answer these questions, I'll pose one of my own.

Learning is a Journey

What Would You Do?

If you were about to set out on a long expedition to some far-flung foreign land, a journey which would take you across huge oceans, over towering ice covered mountains, through baking inhospitable deserts and dense impenetrable jungle, would you go without a map and compass?

No, of course you wouldn't. To do so would be tantamount to suicide.

By the same token, do you really think it is sensible to undertake a course of study without first having produced a plan of where you want to go and how you're going to get there? After all, during your studies you really will feel at times like you are climbing a huge mountain, wading through a morass of information, and just trying to stay afloat in a vast sea of unknown size called Knowledge. Without any sort of guidance from map and compass, you are very likely to fail.

The Conclusion

Learning is indeed a journey, and the better prepared you are for it, the more likely you are to reach your destination.

Many Routes

Of course, as with all journeys, there will be a number of different routes you can take to get to where you want to go. The exact route depends on you, your strengths, weaknesses, preferences, prior knowledge and so on. No two people are exactly alike, and neither will their journeys be. Your plan will be adapted to best suit your particular situation.

It's Your Journey

As with all journeys, there will be ups and downs. There may be well-worn paths which you choose to follow, or you might decide an alternative route best serves you. But whatever the detail, one important point remains – it is you, the traveller, who has ultimate responsibility for getting you where you want to be. It's no good blaming a slow train for not getting you to your destination on time – you need to remember to factor in contingencies for such unforeseen events!

Your Map and Compass

So what are your map and compass on this fantastic voyage you are about to undertake?

Well, your map is your study timetable. This shows you how you are going to get to where you want to go. And your compass? This is the ongoing review process you will be undertaking, if you like, plotting co-ordinates and map references to compare your actual position to your planned position, and then making adjustments to your plan as necessary.

Let's now look at these areas in more detail.

The Study Timetable

Why Have a Study Timetable?

In part we've already answered the question of why having a study timetable is so important. We likened it to having a map to guide you on your journey.

We'll look at exactly *what* a study timetable is and *how* to produce it in the next chapter. But for the moment, let's answer the question of *why* it's so important to have a timetable in a little more detail.

The Benefits of the Study Timetable

Having a study timetable leads to a number of benefits, which are as follows.

Target Setting

Setting yourself targets has two benefits. Firstly, when you achieve those targets, you gain a sense of real satisfaction, a "Feel Good Factor". This is important. It helps you gain confidence in your abilities, and leads to a feeling of greater control.

Secondly, where you don't manage to achieve your targets, perhaps because of problems you have encountered, you are aware that further work is necessary. Without a target set, it would be easier to sweep these problems under the carpet.

> ***"A goal a day keeps the future okay."***
> **Dina Glouberman**

And if you haven't reached your targets simply because you haven't done enough work, you're likely to feel a certain sense of guilt, which in turn should have the effect of getting you back to work sooner than you would without targets. Conversely, where you *are* achieving your targets, you can take guilt-free time out from your studies, which is important. Otherwise, having no plan may lead to a permanent sense of unease whenever you aren't studying, which isn't healthy either. Leisure and relaxation time are important too.

Put it another way. Having targets to reach gives you both the carrot (the sense of satisfaction from achieving your goals) and the stick (the knowledge that you need to do more work to achieve your objectives). An ideal way to ensure you continue to move forwards!

Focus on Difficult Areas

Without a study timetable, it is far easier to avoid those areas of the syllabus you find the most difficult. You are likely to gloss over these areas and spend more of your time on those you find most comfortable. This is basic human nature after all – to keep yourself in the comfort zone and avoid, if at all possible, any action which leads to feelings of discomfort.

But with a timetable, and the targets it contains, it becomes far more difficult to kid yourself in this way. Your targets, both easy and difficult, are down in black and white. Suddenly, avoiding that difficult topic isn't so easy.

Allows Review

Without a timetable, there is nothing to review your overall progress against. And this review process is vital to your success. Because things will change over time. An area of the syllabus might be far harder than you imagined at the outset, and so take far longer. Your review will identify this and allow you to adapt your plans for the future.

Even Spread of Effort

Most people, when faced with a task they would rather avoid if at all possible, tend to leave most of the work to the last minute, the point at which panic sets in. This is far easier to do if you have no timetable, no targets, to work to.

With professional level exams, however, such last minute "cramming" is simply too little, too late, as these exams require far more than just a regurgitation of knowledge. Instead, they look for proof of your ability to apply your new-found knowledge to sometimes complex situations.

> ***"Continuous effort, not strength or intelligence, is the key to unlock our potential."***
> **Winston Churchill**

On the other hand, producing and then using a study timetable will allow you to ensure that you spread the work as evenly as possible over the period of time you have before the exam. Peaks and troughs of activity will be avoided, and you'll be more likely to work in the most efficient manner. Because, to get the best result, you need to be aiming for *a steady, continuous flow of effort throughout the study period.* This ensures you neither waste precious time, nor burn yourself out during a peak of activity.

And as we shall see later, this continuous study effort is far better in aiding retention and recall of information than irregularly spaced study periods of varying time-lengths.

Optimum Study Mix

Better planning through a study timetable also means that you can create a study plan which builds an optimum mix of study elements. For example, as part of your plan you can ensure that you

- ♦ Alternate study periods between different subjects, ensuring subject variety.

- Alternate between easy and harder areas to ensure you don't get too bogged down and depressed with the difficult stuff.
- Alternate between different study methods, such as reading text books, making notes, answering questions, reading linked publications and so on, to ensure boredom doesn't set in.
- Give more time where required to computational subjects, which often require more effort than narrative subjects due to the necessity to undertake practice exercises to ensure understanding.

Without a plan, working in an ad-hoc way, simply deciding what and how to study as you sit down to your desk, means that it is unlikely you will be able to introduce the variety necessary to maintain your attention.

Breaks the Journey Down

At the start of your studies, the task ahead of you may seem daunting. There is so much to do, so much you don't know. You may fell overawed by the enormity of the task. It is easy in these circumstances to fail prey to overwhelming panic.

> ***"Our plans miscarry because they have no aim. When a man does not know what harbour he is making for, no wind is the right wind."***
> **Seneca**

Having a study timetable, however, allows you to break the task down into more manageable parts. Focussing on each part in turn removes this sense of panic as your concentration is taken up with the task immediately in hand. Only over time do you become aware that the accumulation of tasks dealt with has taken you a long way towards your overall objective, and suddenly the whole thing seems a lot more achievable.

Parallel Journeys

To illustrate this idea, let me draw a parallel with my own experiences. When I was a child, summer holidays were spent 350 miles away on a campsite next to a lake in idyllic surroundings. But whilst I very much wanted to be there at my destination, the seven hour car journey necessary to actually get there was always a daunting proposition. (After all, when did you last come across a kid who on a journey didn't ask "are we there yet?" at least every five minutes? I was no different.)

> ***"You don't have to see the whole staircase, just take the first step."***
> **Martin Luther King, Jr.**

But there was no avoiding it. To get to where I wanted to be, I had to suffer the pain of travelling there. Nevertheless, the thought of all 350 miles in one go was simply too intimidating, too overawing to a child. So what I used to do to make the journey bearable was, instead of focussing on the end destination, and getting depressed when the next road sign told me it was still 300 miles to go, I would set myself intermediate targets along the way. I would literally *pretend* that I was only going to the next large town along the road, say 60 miles away.

> ***"The secret of getting ahead is getting started. The secret of getting started is breaking your complex overwhelming tasks into small manageable tasks, and then starting on the first one."***
> **Mark Twain**

Then, reading the road signs seemed easier, as each in turn told me there was only 50 miles to go, then 40, then 30 and so on. Pretty soon I had reached my next target "destination". Only then would I look ahead along my route and identify the next goal, another manageable distance away. I continued in this way, breaking the journey down into chunks, until almost before I knew it, I was there at the campsite. Somehow, the journey always seemed a lot less daunting when approached in this way.

The Message

The similarities between my car journey and your studies are hopefully self-evident. Breaking down your studies into smaller parts makes the whole thing easier to cope with, and leads to a sense of achievement as each milestone is passed.

A Sense of Control

All of the above advantages can really be simplified to this – a study timetable introduces a sense of control into your studies. You control your work, your work doesn't control you.

> ***"Let our advance worrying become advance thinking and planning."***
> **Winston Churchill**

And this sense of control leads to a reduction in stress levels. Remember, we've already seen in the Success Factor chapters that you want to avoid stress as much as possible – the more stress, the more your brain is likely to not work to its full potential.

So the greater your feelings of control, the better.

Convinced Yet?

You should now be able to see just why having a study timetable is so crucial. Without one, you are leaving everything to chance. Do you really want to do that? I think not. Quite rightly, you want to give yourself every possible advantage, take every possible opportunity to increase your chances of passing those professional level exams. That's why you're reading this book after all.

So let's now move on. However, before we look at the actual mechanics of producing your study timetable, we need to understand some background theory relevant to the study process itself, and to the linked area of memory.

Learning Theories and Memory

There has been a great deal of scientific research over the past hundred years or so concerning the human memory. And some of it is even quite interesting! But, for our purposes, we can simplify the findings of this research down into a few fundamental guidelines which we can follow when designing our study timetable and actually undertaking the study itself.

Individual Study Period Timings – The 45 Minute Rule

The Optimum Time Length

It is generally agreed that the optimum period of study is around 45 to 50 minutes. No more than that.

Are You Sure?

This may seem too short a length of time to you. After all, the image of the haggard student, burning the candle at both ends, labouring long into the night to complete his studies is a commonly accepted one. But, please believe me, all the research suggests that studying for long hours without any break is most definitely *not* the most efficient way of working. Even if it feels like it is to you.

In reality, you will encounter steadily diminishing returns for your labour after your 45 minutes are up. Your recall of what you have studied will start to decline markedly after this time, and not only that, you may actually adversely affect what you have already learned as you try to fill your head with more and more information. Your attention will start to wander. Less definitely is more in this case.

So What if I Have Two Hours to Study In?

This is not to say that you can never work for longer than 45 minutes at any one sitting. If you have two hours available to study one evening, you don't have to stop and go and watch the TV after 45 minutes (although you might like the excuse to if things aren't going well!).

Instead, what this means is that you should break your two hour session down into parts, with short breaks between these parts. Perhaps, for example, you could study for three lots of 30 minutes with a 5 minute break in between each period. (The mathematical amongst you will no doubt point out that this still leaves us 20 minutes short of two hours but the reasons for this seemingly free time will be become apparent later when we consider the importance of including a process of *review* into our studies.)

Five Minutes is Enough

The break only needs to be a short one, five minutes is ideal. Just enough time to get up, make yourself a drink, stretch your legs and disengage your brain from the study process. But even just five minutes will dramatically improve your ability to recall what you are learning.

Little and Often – Study Period Allocation

The Best Method of Allocating Study Time

We have seen above that individual study periods should be broken down into sessions of not more than 45 minutes or so. Short and sweet is what gets results.

Leading on from this is the idea of how these individual study periods are spread across the time you have available to study in between now and the exams.

To illustrate, there are any number of ways you could allocate your study time. For example, you could work only at weekends, but put in lengthy study days, leaving all of your weekdays study free. Figure 6.1 demonstrates this approach.

Figure 6.1

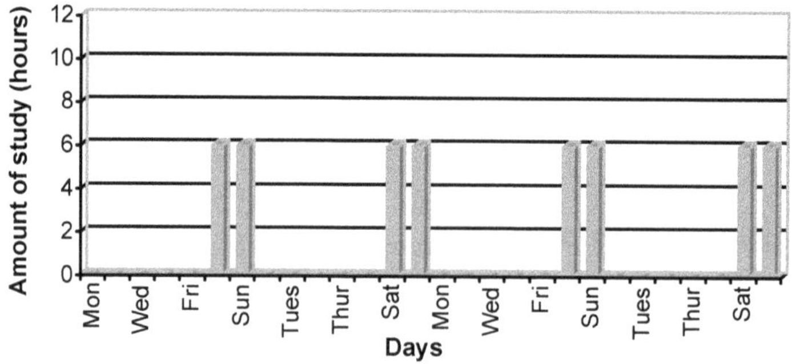

Or instead, you could take this approach even further, and leave all of your study to the last possible minute. Figure 6.2 shows this approach, where all the study for one month is concentrated at the end of the period in a marathon 12 hour a day, four day study session.

Figure 6.2

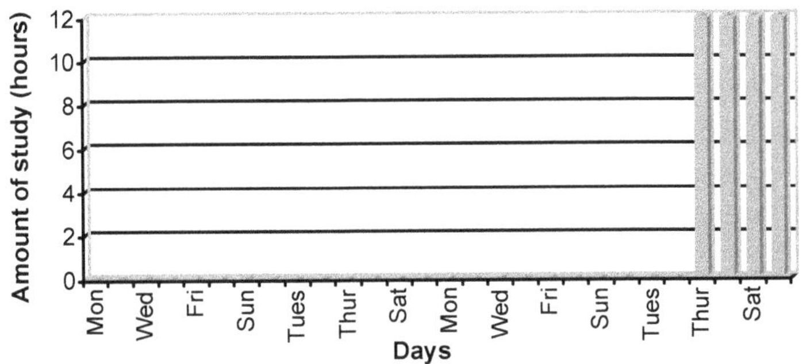

Perhaps you could adopt the approach shown in Figure 6.3, where variety certainly is the order of the day, with large gaps between study days and no real pattern in terms of the number of hours studied per session.

Figure 6.3

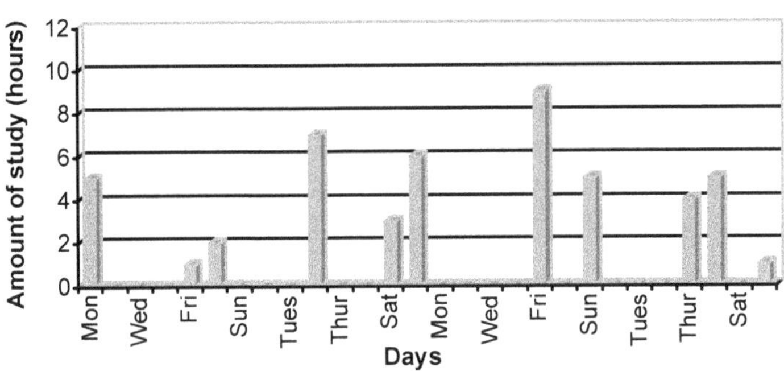

Or lastly, you could study consistently throughout the study period, with each study session lasting a relatively short time, as shown in Figure 6.4.

Figure 6.4

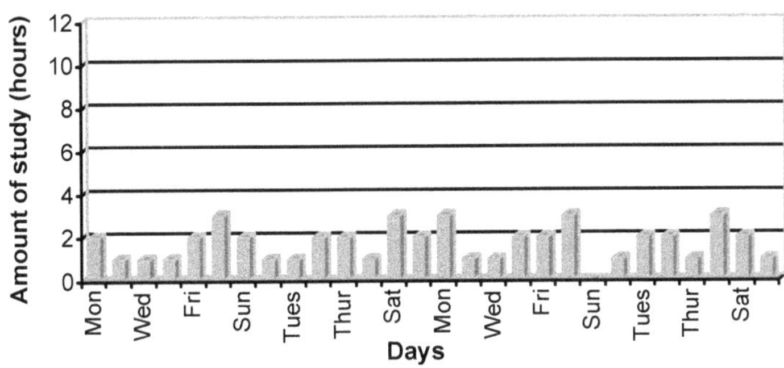

Which do you think would be the best method? Well, it might help if I tell your that the basic premise you should always work towards when designing your study timetable should be *"Little and Often"*. That is, the situation described by figure 6.4.

Why Little and Often Makes Sense

If you think about it, this is really just common sense. Studying for short periods on a regular basis means that you avoid the burnout and boredom that comes through overwork. It also ensures the maximum coverage of the syllabus when compared to leaving all the effort until the last minute (seen in figure 6.2), which is most likely to result in much of the syllabus being missed. Furthermore, short study sessions over the entire period enable you to maintain subject variety and aid retention (these concepts are covered in greater detail below).

> ***"It's the constant and determined effort that breaks down all resistance, sweeps away all obstacles."***
> **Claude M. Bristol**

The Best Advice

I strongly believe that the idea of "Little and Often" is an extremely important one. In fact, when I was fortunate enough to be placed 2nd overall for my performance during my final accountancy exams, I was interviewed by a student magazine, who asked me what advice I could pass on to struggling students. My answer was to simply quote this phrase, "Little and Often". It is one of the best pieces of advice I can give.

Subject Variety

Variety is the Spice of Life

Allied to the 45 minute rule and the idea of little and often, is the principle of maintaining variety during your studies. As we've already seen, the human mind really does start to become less efficient after a relatively short period of 45 minutes studying one subject. Boredom sets in. The mind craves variety in all areas of life.

Different Subjects, Different Activities

Use this natural human trait to your advantage and make your studies as varied as they can be. Why study for 1½ hours on one subject when you can study two subjects for 45 minutes each? And when studying for one particular subject, don't simply plan to spend the whole study period just reading the textbook. Break the period down into different activities wherever possible, perhaps reading, then note taking, then reviewing what you've learned, perhaps attempting exercises too. We shall cover the whole area of study techniques and methods later, but at least bear this principle in mind when creating your study plan.

Different Difficulty Levels

Variety not only means varying subjects or varying study techniques and methods. It also means varying difficulty.

If you're part way through a series of exams linked by a common subject, for example accountancy, you may already have some feeling for the relative difficulty of a particular subject area when compared to others. And even if you're right at the start of your studies, when you may not be able to make such a judgement, this information may be available to you via the examining body, a tuition provider or the textbook you are working from.

Where you do have some feeling as to the relative difficulty of subject areas, if at all possible you should be trying to *vary this level of difficulty as you study*. For example, make sure you cover a relatively easier topic immediately after finishing the study for a more difficult one. This will stop you getting stuck and avoid the loss of confidence that can come by following one failure with another.

> ***"Our minds are like our stomachs; they are whetted by the change of their food, and variety supplies both with fresh appetites."***
> **Quintilian**

The Three R's Equation

The ultimate objective you are all working towards is passing those exams.

And to pass an exam, we need to *recall* information we have learned during our studies, and for professional level exams at least, show that we can *apply* that knowledge to the problems we are given. (This can be differentiated from lower level exams where often we are simply being asked to regurgitate facts we have learned.) Somehow we have to take information into our memory banks and store it so it is available for use at a later date.

Notice that recall is *not* the same thing as understanding – it goes one step further. You may well understand something as you read it in your textbook, but it doesn't follow that you will necessarily be able to recall it when asked the next day.

The question is, what can we do to maximise our recall? I'd suggest that there are two crucial elements you need to build into your studies to achieve this. These I've included in the following equation, which I call the Three R's.

R + R = R

That is,

Repetition + Review = Recall

Now I know that mathematically this might not make much sense, but indulge me here – it's the principle that's important!

And that is this – the use of both repetition and review are a crucial part of storing and retaining information in our memory for later recall and use. Without them, you're going to have a hard time recalling very much at all come the fateful day of your exam.

Repetition

The Multiplication of Memory

When you were a child, no doubt you were taught your multiplication tables (or times tables as they are often called) through rote learning and repetition. You were literally made to chant them audibly, day after day, week after week, one two is two, two twos are four, three twos are six etc. until you had memorised them.

And so well did you manage to memorise them that even decades later you can still recall the answers to these calculations without conscious effort. I don't need to think in any conscious way to know that seven times eight is fifty-six – it's just there in my mind, ready to use.

> ***"Any ideas, plan, or purpose may be placed in the mind through repetition of thought."***
> **Napolean Hill**

This is a fantastic example of the effect of repetition. After all, if instead of making you recount your multiplication tables countless times until you knew them, your teacher had instead asked you to merely read them once or twice and then move on, do you think you'd still remember them today?

No, of course not. It's common sense after all, isn't it? Well, judging by the way some students study, it seems not. They expect to have full recall of material they have studied simply by reading the textbook once over and making a few notes. But this just isn't a realistic approach.

The Science

There is sound scientific basis behind the idea of repetition. A particular task undertaken by the brain recruits a certain set of neurons firing together in a particular way. However, if the task is only undertaken once, the weak link that exists between these neurons will soon be lost as the brain recruits them for other activities (the idea of "use it or lose it", or if you like further evidence of the idea of brain plasticity – the constant adaptation of the brain to new inputs).

If on the other hand, the task is repeated a number of times, the links between the neurons are strengthened over time. The greater the number of repetitions, the greater the strength of bond. Eventually, the links will be effectively hardwired into the brain, there for use whenever required. Hence our ability to still recall the answer to 12x12 years after learning it, and without resorting to a calculator.

> ***"Men acquire a particular quality by constantly acting in a particular way."***
> **Aristotle**

Recreating Lost Memories

Further evidence of the value of repetition can also be found in the study of those people unfortunate enough to suffer brain damage at birth through lack of oxygen to the brain. In some of these cases, the person's hippocampus is damaged, the part of the brain heavily involved in memory. As a result, often these people have a very poor long term memory, and can literally only remember what happened to them for the past half an hour or so. After this the memory is lost. This can lead to a real sense of dissociation as the subject has very little history around which to base his life.

And yet, even in these cases, it has been shown that the use of repetition *can* improve memory. For example, a family occasion can be videotaped and then later replayed many times by the subject. Eventually, the subject will be able to recall at will the details of the event, albeit from a different frame of reference from his original one. The use of repetition has literally created the memory.

Again, repetition is the key to memory.

Review

Review = Long Term Repetition

If repetition is what you undertake to get the facts stored in your memory, review is what you do to make sure they stay there over the longer term. If you like, this is the test your primary school teacher gave you at the end of every month to make sure you still remembered your multiplication tables.

Review is necessary because even where repetition has strengthened the neural bonds to the extent you can recall a particular piece of information, these links can still fade over time unless renewed. Put another way, review is like long term repetition.

The Classic Forgetting Curve

Were you to go out and buy one of the many books on improving memory, you would no doubt find impressive looking graphs illustrating how much you forget over time after study, such as the one shown in figure 6.5.

Figure 6.5

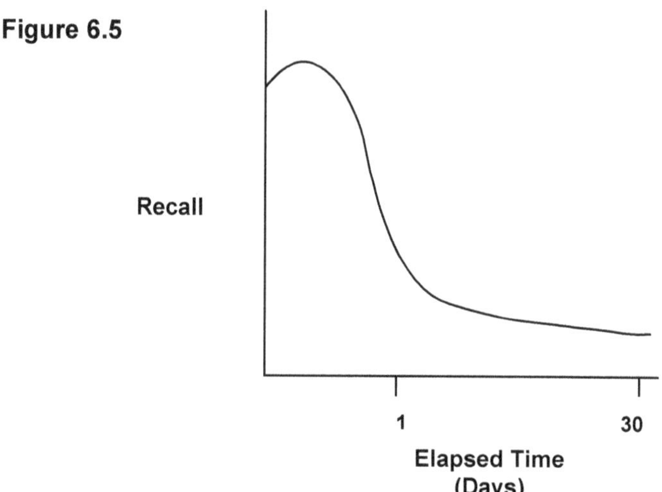

The graph shows that initially, immediately after a study session, recall of the material studied improves slightly, but this recall very quickly starts to decline at a rapid rate so that by 24 hours after the study ended a large proportion of the material can no longer be recalled. This "forgetting" effect then continues at a slower pace the further into the future one goes.

In fact, it is often suggested that 50 percent of all material is forgotten after 20 minutes, 80 percent is forgotten within 24 hours, and over 90 percent within one week. Frightening stuff! You'll also be presented in these books with some pretty hard and fast rules on exactly how often you should revisit subject areas as part of the review process.

Advice Concerning Review Offered by Other Books

The oft-delivered advice is that to stop this memory loss we should adopt an intensive and systematic review process. For example, a review of the material covered should take place immediately after the study session, and then further reviews of the same material should be carried out after 24 hours, one week, one month, and three months after the end of the study session.

Why Such Advice is Flawed

Such advice however, is both misleading and probably unachievable. Firstly, the curve presented in the graph relates to experiments testing the recall of strings of meaningless syllables, where there is no underlying meaning below the surface form of the information. In reality, the information you will be endeavouring to commit to memory will have some underlying meaning and structure, making the memorisation process somewhat easier. In other words, the downward slope on your forgetting curve won't be anywhere near as steep as the one presented above, although it is certainly true that there will still be a loss of recall over time.

Secondly, if you really were to try and formally review *every* study session you undertook immediately after, then 24 hours later, then one week, one month and so on later, imagine the administrative nightmare of trying to keep track of where you were at any one time. Assuming only one study session for one subject per day, after just 30 days you would be reviewing the information from four historic study sessions a day! That's a lot of paperwork on top of an already busy study schedule!

So What Do You Take From This?

So why present all this information to you about the forgetting curve and review if I then point out its weaknesses? Well, simply this. Whilst you need to be aware that the advice concerning review given in many popular books on memory is overdone and unduly onerous, the principle remains – *ongoing review is important in maintaining recall.*

We therefore need to make sure that we build in time for regular and continual review when producing our study timetable, albeit not in quite as regimented a manner as most other study books recommend. We will look at this issue in more detail in the next chapter, where we learn how to produce the study timetable itself.

Study Timetable Production

Producing the Study Timetable

Having looked at some of the important theories behind learning and memory, we can now apply these to the process of producing the study timetable. Before we do that however, I think a health warning is in order!

Don't Panic! It's Not as Bad as It Seems!

If you flicked through this chapter, you might be forgiven for thinking that the whole timetabling process seems to be an incredibly long and complex one; after all, this chapter is one of the longest in the book and appears to contain a lot of detailed instructions on timetable production.

But that's not the case at all, promise! In reality, the concepts contained in this chapter are straightforward. What we're really talking about here is very simple – first, identify how much study time you have available, and then second, allocate your studies to that time via your timetable. There's really nothing more to it than that.

What I have done though in this chapter is make sure that the process of producing timetables is made completely clear by including detailed instructions and a fully-worked example to help you understand what you're aiming for. That's why at first sight the chapter might seem a little daunting.

So fear not – it's not as bad as it seems!

Constant Change Means More Than One Timetable

That said, although we've talked about a study timetable singular, in practice you will need to produce a number of timetables over the study period. At the start of your studies, you need to produce a long term plan, or timetable, which covers the entirety of the study process i.e. from now until you have taken the exams. There is an investment of your time therefore in producing this plan. However, this should be no more than a few hours if you have read this chapter, and it's important to note that this is a one-off up front investment, not an ongoing one.

> ***"It is a bad plan that admits of no modification."***
> **Publilius Syrus**

Clearly, such a timetable cannot be fixed in stone. Circumstances will change, difficulties will arise, unforeseen events will occur. That's a given. Which is why in addition to the long term plan, you will need to produce weekly timetables which contain the detail behind what you will doing on any one particular day of the week. It is these weekly timetables that will really drive you forward on a day-to-day basis. Do note however that you should need to spend no longer than half an hour a week on this, so once again the investment of your time is minimal.

Time Spent Planning is Not Wasted

And just because you have to update and change your plans, doesn't mean that time spent producing the initial long term plan is time wasted. It is not, for the reasons we have already seen in the last chapter. The process of producing the plan gives you the chance to recognise up front any potential difficulties there might be, and plan corrective action accordingly. Forewarned is forearmed, as the saying goes. Far better to consider these issues and difficulties now than to ignore them until it is too late to do anything about it.

In addition, the long term plan acts as your map, guiding you through difficult times, pointing the way in the right direction. It is, if you like, a world map as opposed to a county map, allowing you to get that overview, that perspective, on the journey in its entirety.

In the next section, we will look at the process of producing this initial long term timetable. Separate to that, we also need to look at the ongoing use of the timetable and its adaptation, through the production of detailed weekly timetables, but we'll deal with this a little later in the chapter.

Study Process Overview

In very broad terms, your studies should be broken down into two parts.

Actual Study

The first part will be the actual study process itself, where you will be getting to grips with the material you need to know for the exam.

Revision

The second part will be the revision period immediately before the exam, in which you will be honing your question answering skills, whilst ensuring there are no gaps in your knowledge (or at least as few as possible!).

In reality, this is an oversimplification, because as we've already seen, there should be an ongoing review process throughout your studies if you are to maintain maximum recall. In a sense therefore, the review, or revision process, is a continuous one which starts almost as soon as your studies do.

Decisions Concerning the Revision Period

How Long Should the Revision Period Be?

Nevertheless, the ongoing review process noted above aside, at some specific point during your studies you will need to end the process of "learning" and start the formal process of "revising". The main question to address at this point is *how long* should the revision period last for, and therefore what date should revision start?

Circumstances Will Decide

There's really no hard and fast rule here, and it's difficult to generalise, as everyone's circumstances will be different. You might be able to get one month off of work for revision purposes (although this is unlikely in today's pressurised work environment), or you might only be able to get one day (if that). You might be attending formal revision courses provided by third party training companies, or you might be studying completely on your own. You might be taking exams in one subject or you might have to face four subjects.

The only guidance I can really offer here therefore is to *give yourself as long a revision period as possible*. The longer the period set aside for revision, the better. In any event, it's difficult to imagine a period of less than one week being sufficient, so aim for something greater than this. The decision doesn't have to be final at this stage anyway, so to some extent whichever date you pick for the revision period to start is arbitrary, and can be changed. Having a date just gives us a basis to factor into our timetable production.

A Personal Example as Guidance

Having said the only guidance I can give you is to allocate as much time as possible to revision, let me just give you the benefit of my own experiences. When I was studying for my accountancy exams, my nominal revision period was one month. Given that there were always a minimum of three subjects to be taken at any one exam sitting during my studies, this gave me enough time to deal with all of the subjects, and allowed me a gradual build up of effort over the month. In this way I hoped to be as fully prepared as possible for the exams, whilst at the same time ensuring that I didn't "peak too early".

Producing the Initial Study Timetable

The process of producing the initial long term study timetable can be broken down into two stages and a number of discrete steps.

Stage 1 – Definition of Study Time Available

The first part of the process aims to identify how much time is available to be allocated to studying. Some study skills books suggest at this point that the budding student keeps a diary of how their time is spent, minute by minute, over a number of weeks. From this diary, the theory goes, it is then possible to arrive at a number of free hours available.

The problem is, you simply don't have long enough to use this approach. You need to get started, straight away. For this reason, I strongly recommend using the method below and then getting stuck into your studies immediately. The figure arrived at for free time only needs to be an estimate, as we can amend our plans further once we're into our studies and we've gained some experience.

Step 1

Define your ultimate top-level objective. In your case, this will be the exam or exams you wish to pass. (I'm assuming you've already made the decision as to which exams to take. For some professional qualifications it is possible to select *which papers* you wish to take at certain levels, as well as *when to take* them, within set parameters. Guidance as to how to arrive at these decisions are outside the scope of this book, and are best dealt with by talking to the examining body concerned, who can normally give help on the best approach and route to take.)

Step 2

Most professional exams are sat either yearly or at best once every six months, although occasionally other periods between sittings apply. Take or draw up a calendar planner which covers the period relating to the exams you are taking. You can do this on paper or if you prefer on computer. If using a computer, use an application you feel comfortable with, such as a spreadsheet application like Excel, or perhaps a calendar application like Outlook.

An example format of a blank timetable is shown in Figure 7.1.

Step 3

Add the exam date or dates to your planner (the examining body will provide this information), and then add any other study milestones which must be met to the planner. This would include, for example, revision course dates if you have booked on them.

Step 4

Add the arbitrary date that you have decided your formal revision period will start. Bear in mind that this may change, but putting this date in now at least gives you something to work towards.

Step 5

Add other known or foreseeable events to the planner, such as holidays, family occasions, course dates, and any other regular activities you undertake.

Step 6

Mark on the plan the time you will be required to spend at work as part of your employment commitments. Generally this time will not be available for study, although you may be able to find time during lunch or coffee breaks for some work.

Step 7

Remember too to build in time for exercise and relaxation i.e. leisure time. Maybe you visit the gym twice a week. If so, put these visits down on the timetable. It is important not to omit these – remember the importance of these elements in terms of your Success Factor. And don't forget to build in time for sleeping! Your rest is important too.

Figures 7.2 (a) and (b) show how the first and last pages of your study timetable might look once you've followed steps 1 to 7 above.

Step 8

Identify Free Time Available for Study

Looking at the planner you should now be able to identify the amount of free time you have available for study, and also your busy and quiet periods. Only you can make this calculation, as only you really know what your life entails. Note that at this point you're only interested in identifying the time you can spend on *study*, not the time you're going to spend on *revision*. We'll deal with the revision phase later in the book.

Be Realistic

However, you need to be realistic at this point, and set yourself goals which are challenging, but at the same time achievable. Set your goals too low and you won't be working to your maximum potential (in other words you'll end up frittering away valuable time on non-study activities). Set them too high and you will soon dent your self-confidence, possibly with mortal consequences, when you don't manage to reach your time goals.

Think Laterally

At the same time, look carefully at your schedule. Is there any way you could free up some more time? Perhaps you could get up earlier twice a week? Perhaps you could get a seat on the train and study whilst commuting to and from work? Try to "think outside of the box" here. Remember also you have to build in time for all those mundane day-to-day housekeeping activities that can't be avoided, such as cooking meals, cleaning the house and paying domestic bills.

How to Treat Holidays

With respect to any holidays built into your plan, I would strongly recommend not treating them as completely non-study time. Instead, you should aim to carry out at least some tasks over the holiday period, even if they are for a reduced length of time. A couple of hours a day should be manageable if all you're planning on doing is lie on a beach!

Work When You're Up, Not When You're Down

And lastly, it might be worth trying to take account of your natural circadian rhythms. If you know that you are not a "morning person" i.e. that you struggle to get out of bed in the morning, even after your third snooze of the alarm clock, and that you're not really fully awake until your second double espresso, then don't assume you can allocate study to these dead periods. Be sensible, and be pragmatic. Only you know whether you are being honest with yourself here.

Arriving at the Number of Hours Available

As an example, let's say that, having taken all the other calls on your time into consideration, on a weekly basis you calculate you have 25 hours free left available for study (you have remembered to build in time for sleep haven't you?!). It this case, it might prove more sensible to take say 20 hours as being available rather than 25. In this way you have set a challenging but achievable target.

Best Estimate Only

Do keep in mind that the number you come up with is just your best estimate. You really won't know until you get stuck into your studies just how realistic you have been in your assumptions. That's not a problem. Your plans can and will be adapted. But at least you have something to work with, a target to aim for. Without that target, it's difficult to know whether you're heading in the right direction or not.

But Surely We're Working Back to Front?

At this point, some of you may be questioning whether the approach set out above is the right one to take. Surely, instead of calculating how much free time we have available for study, we should start with an estimate of how much time it will take to study for a subject, and then work from there, allocating this time across the period between now and the exam?

After all, some examining bodies and training organisations *do* give out this information. For example, one accountancy body states *"we estimate that you will need to devote to study a minimum of 180 hours in total to prepare adequately for the examination"*. If this guidance has been given, surely we should use it when producing our study timetable?

Exam Dates are Fixed

However, you are forgetting one very important fact. That is, the exam will be take place on the dates already set and published by the examining body. They are fixed in stone, and are your top-level objective already placed on your timetable. You are stuck with the exam dates that you are entered for.

As a result, you can't simply decide to study the subject for the requisite 180 hours recommended by the examining body or trainer and then take the exam once you have completed this time (unless you want to postpone your exam entrance until a subsequent sitting). There may not be enough hours in the days you have available between now and the exam date to achieve this.

With this in mind, all you can do is work with the time you have available. Which is why defining this free time now is a very useful exercise.

Figure 7.3 shows how the first page of your timetable might look once you've identified how much time you're going to allocate to study. Notice how week 3 has been adjusted to take into account a planned holiday.

Figure 7.1

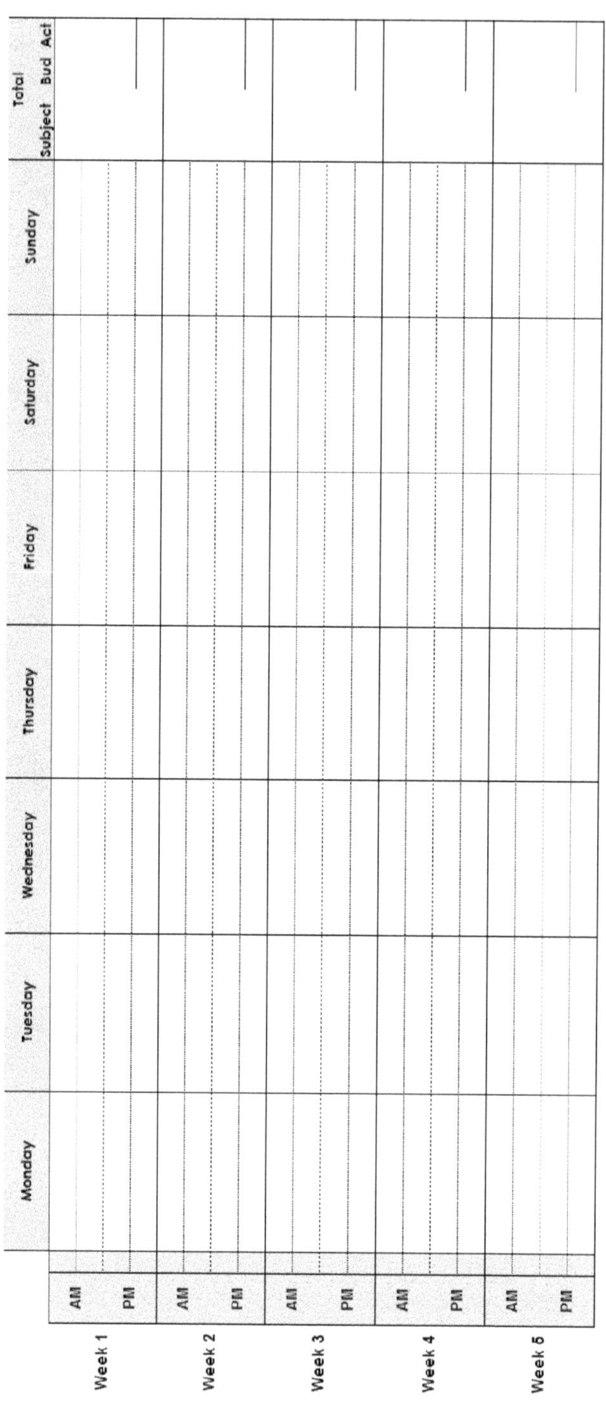

		Monday	Tuesday	Wednesday	Thursday	Friday	Saturday	Sunday	Total		
									Subject	Bud	Act
Week 1	AM										
	PM										
Week 2	AM										
	PM										
Week 3	AM										
	PM										
Week 4	AM										
	PM										
Week 5	AM										
	PM										

Figure 7.2 (a)

		Monday	Tuesday	Wednesday	Thursday	Friday	Saturday	Sunday	Total Subject	Bud	Act
Week 1	AM					G					
		W	W	W	W	W					
	PM	W	W	W	W						
				G		E					
Week 2	AM					G					
		W	W	W	W	W					
	PM	W	W	W	W						
				G		E					
Week 3	AM				H	H	H	H			
		W	W	W	H	H	H	H			
	PM	W	W	W	H	H	H	H			
					H	H	H	H			
Week 4	AM						G				
		W	W	W	W	W					
	PM	W	W	W	W						
				G		E					
Week 5	AM						G				
		W	W	W	W	W					
	PM	W	W	W	W						
				G		E					

Key	
W	Work
G	Gym
H	Holiday
E	Evening class
•	Revision Phase Start
R1	Revision Course 1
R2	Revision Course 2

Figure 7.2 (b)

Week		Monday	Tuesday	Wednesday	Thursday	Friday	Saturday	Sunday	Total Subject	Bud	Act
Week 18	AM	♦ *Revision Phase Start*				G					
		W	*W*								
	PM	*W*	*W*								
				G							
Week 19	AM						G				
			R1	*R1*	*W*	*W*	*R2*	*R2*			
	PM		*R1*	*R1*	*W*	*W*	*R2*	*R2*			
				G							
Week 20	AM				G		G				
		W	*W*								
	PM	*W*	*W*								
Week 21	AM										
			Exam 10am								
	PM	Exam 2pm									
Week 22	AM										
	PM										

Figure 7.3

		Monday	Tuesday	Wednesday	Thursday	Friday	Saturday	Sunday	Total Subject	Total Bud	Total Act
Week 1	AM					G					
		W	W	W	W	W					
	PM	W	W	W	W						
				G		E				20	
Week 2	AM					G					
		W	W	W	W	W					
	PM	W	W	W	W						
				G		E				20	
Week 3	AM				H	H	H	H			
		W	W	W	H	H	H	H			
	PM	W	W	W	H	H	H	H			
					H	H	H	H		12	
Week 4	AM						G				
		W	W	W	W	W					
	PM	W	W	W	W						
				G		E				20	
Week 5	AM						G				
		W	W	W	W	W					
	PM	W	W	W	W						
				G		E				20	

Stage 2 – Producing the Initial Study Timetable

The First Draft

We are now going to create a first draft of our timetable for the entire period of study. I cannot over emphasise however that it is just that – a draft. The timetable will inevitably change and grow over the coming weeks and months. However, the creation of the first draft gives us that all-important starting point. So, use pencil if you're producing the timetable on paper, or if using an application on computer, make sure you can undo anything you input. You'll need to make amendments to the timetable as it takes shape now and throughout the study the process, so it's essential you can make changes with ease.

Step 1 – Obtain the Official Syllabus

For each subject, obtain the official syllabus (and any relevant guidance notes) from the examining body if you haven't already done so. The syllabus is an invaluable guide, and yet one which the majority of students largely ignore to their cost. Although each examining body will produce their syllabi in differing formats, usually there are elements common to all. Each will set out

- The aim and objectives of the exam.
- The format of the examination paper.
- The assessment methods used (for example, the use of 100 multiple choice questions).
- Details of the subject areas, or topics, which the exam will seek to test.

In addition, most syllabi will give guidance on the level of knowledge required for each of the subject areas. This may come in the form of a knowledge level assigned to each syllabus topic from a pre-defined scale, for example

I - Introductory

Basic understanding of principles, concepts, theories and techniques

B - Broad

Application of principles, concepts, theories and techniques in the solution of straightforward problems

F - Full

Identification and solution of more complex problems through the selection and application of principles, concepts, theories and techniques.

Or it may come in the form of what are known as *learning objectives* or *outcomes*, which use words such as list, outline, understand, explain, describe, compare, apply and so on to describe the depth of knowledge required or each topic and sub-topic. For example

> ***Section 2 Performance management***
>
> ***On completion the candidate should be able to***
>
> ***Define the term performance management***
>
> ***Outline a method to establish performance indicators***
>
> ***Illustrate ways of applying performance management***

These types of guidance are useful as they allow you to decide how much emphasis to place, and thus how much study time to allocate, on each subject area.

Step 2 – Identify the List of Subject Areas and Topics

From the syllabus for each subject you should be able to identify a list of subject areas or topics which you need to have covered by the time you sit the exam.

Don't Assume the Textbook Gives Complete Coverage

Taking the syllabus as the primary source of data here and not, for example, a textbook or other study material, is essential. You should not assume that your textbook necessarily covers all you need to know. It is no excuse come the day of the exam to say "it wasn't in my textbook" when you can't answer an exam question – the onus is on you to ensure you have covered all necessary syllabus areas. You can't absolve yourself of the responsibility by blaming the publisher of the textbook, or the training company in question.

So cross reference the syllabus to the textbook to ensure nothing is missing from the textbook.

Step 3 – Create the Timetable

Match Subject Area to Study Time

From the plan already produced (our example was shown in figure 7.3), you've calculated how much study time you have available on a weekly basis, and have identified milestones, deadlines and other factors to be taken into consideration. You've also just identified a list of subject areas you need to cover. Now you need to bring all of these together to create your first draft timetable. In short, you need to allocate the study time you identified as available in Stage 1 to the subject areas noted in Step 2 above.

Use Your Textbooks to Identify Subject Order and Depth of Coverage

Take a look at the textbooks that you intend to use during your studies to find the suggested order that the subject areas should be covered in. It's worth checking this because sometimes the syllabus itself may not present them in a logical, sequential manner and so following the syllabus in a linear fashion might lead to problems during your studies. Also use the textbook to give you a feel for the amount of detail that each subject area appears to entail (clearly, the greater the detail, the more time you'll need to allocate to it).

Guidance on the Allocation Process

Taking these things into account, you now need to allocate each subject area to a study session (or sessions) marked on your long term timetable so that by the end of your study phase you have covered all of the areas on the syllabus. However, it's difficult to be prescriptive here about exactly how to handle this process, as each person's situation will be unique. Do remember though to take into account the following as you allocate the subject areas across your plan.

- The importance of taking time out from studying to enjoy leisure activities, including physical exercise.
- How study sessions are best limited to 45 minutes per session (although you *can* undertake more than one session per study period – just remember to include breaks).
- The axiom "little and often" – five one hour study sessions over five days are better than one single five hour study session on one day.
- How subject variety is important to maintain interest, and how this can be both between subjects and within subjects, by varying the type and methods of study. Also, where you have a feel for the varying difficulties of the subject areas, try to ensure that subject difficulty is also varied during and between study sessions.
- Why repetition and review are crucial in ensuring maximum recall, and so why there must be time built into the plan for these activities. In fact, this area is so important that the section below covers it in more detail.
- How the learning part of your studies needs to be completed by the start of your revision period to allow for adequate revision prior to the exam.
- In general, a computational subject will require more study time than a non-computational one, due to the necessity of completing practice exercises to ensure understanding.

Repetition and Review

We have already seen in Chapter 6 how repetition and review are vital to exam success. But to produce your timetable, you're going to want to know how to build that concept into your plans. Here's how.

- At the start of every separate study session, you should briefly review the notes you produced during the previous study session (we will look at how you produce these notes in more detail in Part Five). This should take no more than five to ten minutes maximum, and can form part of the study session planned that day. There is no need to separately timetable this into your plans as this should part of your normal study procedures.

- At the end of each week, you should return to the notes you produced that week and review them, preferably in a single study session. This "Weekly Review" should be planned and separately identified on your timetable.
- On a periodic basis, you should build in a study session during which you review all of the areas you have covered to date. Your own particular circumstances and timetables will dictate the frequency of this "Periodic Review" but I would suggest a monthly frequency is a good starting point.
- At the end of each week or the start of the next one, you should be assessing your progress to date against plans and deciding your plans for the week ahead. You'll need to timetable in a "Weekly Planning" session in to deal with this. This need take no longer than half an hour at most, so does not need to be treated as part of your study time.

An Illustrative Example

Whilst it's impossible to come up with a model timetable which can be used for any scenario, nevertheless I'm aware that you may still be struggling with actually putting the theories into practice. You need an example to help you understand what the end result should look like.

So let's do that now to make things a little clearer for you. To illustrate what your finished timetable might look like, let's take the example plan we've already seen above in Figure 7.3 and assume you are taking the two subjects whose example syllabi excerpts are shown in Figure 7.4 (a) and (b) overleaf.

Figure 7.4 (a)

COST ACCOUNTING AND QUANTITATIVE ANALYSIS

AIMS

1 To develop an understanding of the nature and environment of cost accounting.
2 To develop an understanding of the classification of costs and cost behaviour.
3 To be able to prepare and communicate costing data.
4 To apply appropriate quantitative techniques in the collection, analysis and presentation of management information.

5% A NATURE AND ENVIRONMENT OF COST ACCOUNTING

1 **The objectives of cost accounting information**
2 **The relationship between cost accounting information and the financial accounts**
3 **Integration of financial and cost accounting systems**
4 **The use of cost information with non-financial information**
5 **The use of computers in cost accounting**

20% B COST CLASSIFICATION AND COST BEHAVIOUR

1 **The reasons for classifying costs and alternative methods of classification**
2 **Understanding and using cost behaviour**
3 **Concept of full cost**
4 **Collection and allocation of prime costs**
5 **Responsibility accounting**

10% C RECORDING OF COSTING DATA

1 **Job, process, service and contract costing**

15% D COSTING METHODS

1 **Absorption costing**
2 **Marginal costing**
3 **Uses and comparison of methods**
4 **Classification and analysis of overhead costs**

15% E PLANNING AND CONTROLLING COSTS

1 **Standard costing**
2 **Introduction to variance analysis**
3 **Forecasting costs**

Figure 7.4 (a) continued

	a	•*The use of regression and other techniques to forecast unit and total costs*
	b	•*Interpretation of results*
35%	F	QUANTITATIVE ANALYSIS
	1	**Basic mathematics**
	a	•*Percentages*
	b	•*Ratios*
	c	•*Discounts*
	d	•*Formulae in spreadsheets*
	2	**Summarising and analysing data**
	a	•*Sources and collection of data*
	b	•*Accuracy and approximation*
	c	•*Presentation of data*
	d	•*Statistical measures: mean, median, mode, standard deviation, tests of hypotheses*
	e	•*Graphical presentation*
	f	•*Variation for grouped and ungrouped data*
	g	•*Index numbers*
	3	**Sampling and probability**
	a	•*Probability*
	b	•*Simple addition and multiplication rules*
	c	•*Expected values*
	d	•*Payoff tables*
	e	•*Sampling methods*
	f	•*The normal distribution*
	g	•*Standard errors and confidence intervals of means and percentages*
	h	•*Problems of sample size*
	4	**Introduction to financial mathematics**
	a	•*Simple interest*
	b	•*Compound interest*
	c	•*Discounting*
	5	**Introduction to forecasting**
	a	•*Simple linear regression*
	b	•*Forecasting*
	c	•*Time series*

Figure 7.4 (b)

FINANCIAL ACCOUNTING

AIMS

1 To develop an understanding of the environment in which financial accounting operates.
2 To develop an understanding of the basic accounting concepts and principles.
3 To be able to prepare, present and communicate simple financial statements from prime documents.

30% A NATURE AND ENVIRONMENT OF ACCOUNTING

1 **The purpose and context of accounting**

a • *The development of accounting and influences on future development.*·

b • *Current role of accounting in society and in business*

c • *Functions of accounting*·

d • *The objectives of financial statements*

2 **Accounting information and users**

a • *The role, responsibilities and duties of the accountant, external auditor and financial manager*·

b •*The use of computing software in financial accounting*·

c •*The nature of financial information in an organisation*·

d •*Users of financial statements*

3 **The framework of accounting**

a • *Introduction to the statutory and professional framework*·

b • *The accounting profession*

c • *Regulation through statute*·

d • *The accounting standards and guidelines*·

e • *Accounting conventions*·

f • *Accounting theories and practice*·

g • *Introduction to accounting concepts, policies and principles and their application to different organisations*

35% B DOUBLE ENTRY BOOK-KEEPING

1 **Accounting for transactions**

a •*The accounting equation and principle of duality*·

b •*Recording transactions using double entry – cash, credit, capital, stock*·

c •*Books of prime entry - day, cash and journal*

d •*Ledgers – general, sales and purchases*·

e •*The trial balance*·

f •*Confirming accounts and corrections of errors*

Figure 7.4 (b) continued

	2	**Reconciliation and control**
	a	*•Bank Reconciliation·*
	b	*•Control Accounts·*
	c	*•Suspense Accounts and correction of errors*
	3	**Other accounting topics**
	a	*•Accruals, prepayments and adjustments·*
	b	*•Accounting for fixed assets – depreciation, disposal·*
	c	*•Bad debts and provision for bad debts*
25%	C	PREPARATION OF FINANCIAL STATEMENTS
	1	**Financial statements**
	a	*•Trading, Profit and Loss Account and Balance Sheets:* *(i) From Incomplete Records* *(ii) For Clubs and Societies* *(iii) For Sole Traders* *(iv) For Limited Companies·*
	b	*•Preparation and use of basic cash flow statements*
10%	D	USING FINANCIAL STATEMENTS
	1	**Evaluating performance**
	a	*•Evaluating and communicating the information contained in financial statements·*
	b	*•Basic ratio analysis*

Following the guidance given above, and incorporating the subject areas included in the example syllabi, your finished timetable might in part look something like that shown on the following page in Figure 7.5. Notice how

- Subject variety has been maintained throughout each week.
- At the end of each week a "Weekly Review" session of an hour has been timetabled to allow a review of the week's studies.
- Each week there is a "Weekly Planning" session to set the timetable for the week ahead (more on this in the next section).
- The study sessions timetabled have been fitted around the other commitments such as work.
- Time for leisure has been built in.
- The budgeted hours for each subject for the week are shown, along with a blank column to allow you to track actual hours against budget.

Obviously your own timetable will be unique to you and your own situation but if you follow the principles outlined above your timetable should prove a valuable guide to your studies ahead.

Figure 7.5

Week		Monday	Tuesday	Wednesday	Thursday	Friday	Saturday	Sunday	Total Subject	Bud	Act
Week 1	AM	Weekly Planning		CAQA A3 1		G	CAQA A5 2		Wkly Rvw	1	
		W	W ~~FA A1a~~ 1	W	W	W	FA A1 c 2	FA A1d 1	CAQA	9	
	PM	W	W	W	W	CAQA A4 2		CAQA B1 2	FA	10	
		CAQA A1 2 2	FA A1a 1	G	FA A1b 2	E FA 3		Weekly Review 1		20	
Week 2	AM	Weekly Planning		CAQA B2 1		G		FA A2d 2	Wkly Rvw	1	
		W	W ~~FA A2a~~ 1	W	W	W		CAQA B3 1	CAQA	11	
	PM	W	W	W	W	CAQA B2 2	CAQA B3 2		FA	8	
		CAQA B1 2	FA A2a 1	G	FA A2b 2	E CAQA 3	FA A2c 2	Weekly Review 1		20	
Week 3	AM	Weekly Planning		CAQA B4 2	H	H CAQA B4 2	H FA A3c 1	H FA A3c 1	Wkly Rvw	1	
		W	W ~~CAQA B3~~ 1	W	H	H	H	H Weekly Review 1	CAQA	6	
	PM	W	W	W	H	H	H	H Weekly Planning	FA	5	
		FA A3a 1	CAQA B3 1		H FA A3b 2	H	H	H		12	
Week 4	AM			CAQA B1-5 1		CAQA C1 1	G CAQA C1 2		Wkly Rvw	1	
		W	W ~~FA A3d~~ 1	W	W	W	FA A3e 1	FA A3f 2	CAQA	10	
	PM	W	W	W	W	FA A3e 2		CAQA C1 1	FA	9	
		CAQA B5 2	FA A3d 1	G	FA A3d e 2	E CAQA 3		Weekly Review 1		20	
Week 5	AM	Weekly Planning		FA A3g 1		FA A3g 1	G FA A3g 1	FA B1 2	Wkly Rvw	1	
		W	W	W	W	W	QACA C1 2	QACA D1 2	CAQA	8	
	PM	W	W	W	W	FA A3g 1			FA	11	
		FA A3f 2	QACA C1 2	G	QACA C1 2	E FA 3		Weekly Review		20	

Using the Long Term Study Timetable

Congratulations – you've followed the process through and you've ended up with a study timetable covering the long term. But where now? What do you do with it in practice? Or having completed it, do you now resign it do a dusty corner of your desk, never to see the light of day again?

No. If that were its fate, I would never have suggested producing it. Time, after all, is a precious commodity, not to be wasted on producing something with no real value. But this timetable *does* have great value – because we can now use it to produce your first weekly timetable, the real heart of the study planning process. It is the weekly study timetable where the essential detail lies, without which your studies will lack both focus and direction.

The Weekly Study Timetable

Not *More* Timetables?

Why more timetables, you might rightly be asking? Haven't we spent long enough already planning? Can't we just get on and do the real work?

Introduces the Detail

Nearly, yes. But whilst the long term plan gives you general guidance on when you will be studying, for how long, and for what subject, it doesn't give you enough detail. This is what the weekly timetable is for.

One Weekly Timetable at a Time

It's important to stress though that at any one time you will only ever have a detailed weekly timetable for the next week ahead. Initially when you first start your studies you only need to produce one weekly timetable for the first week, not one for every week between now and your exam. Then, at the end of the week, during the "Weekly Planning" session you'll recall we've already built into our long term plan, we will review our actual progress to date for the week against our timetables and then factor in the results of this review as we produce the next week's timetable.

Built-in Flexibility

We work this way, producing only one week's detailed timetable at a time, because with the best will in the world, you cannot know exactly how your studies will go over the next week, fortnight, month, quarter etc. Neither can you know what other unforeseen events will conspire to upset your well-laid plans. So the weekly timetable you produce during that weekly planning slot takes account of all that has happened to date. Above all, it introduces the concept of *flexibility* to your study planning.

So, what do you do to produce your weekly plan?

How To Produce The Weekly Timetable

I suggest that the first thing you do is to produce a daily planner to use for your weekly timetable, either on paper or on computer. Figure 7.6 gives an example of how your weekly timetable might be formatted. Use whatever feels most comfortable to you.

You should then follow the steps below to produce your plan each week.

Step 1

Check your long terms plan for the next week – identify any milestones, fixed events and other calls on your time separate from study which need to be factored in. Enter these onto your weekly timetable.

Step 2

Itemise separately all the study tasks which have been bought forward from the previous week (clearly there will be none of these for your first week's timetable). This list should include both "must do" and "could do" tasks that have not been completed (step 4 gives further details on this classification).

Step 3

Add to the list the study tasks included on your long term timetable for the following week.

Step 4

Looking at your list of study tasks, identify which of those you believe are "must do" items and which of those are "could do" ones, which if necessary can be carried forward to a future date. Making this classification will be by definition somewhat subjective. However, as an example your list might contain some subject areas which are central to the syllabus and therefore require a detailed knowledge – these you would probably choose to define as must do's. Your list might also contain tasks relating to peripheral areas of the syllabus which require understanding at an introductory level – you might classify these as could do's.

Step 5

Identify the actual time available for study during the week.

Step 6

Fit the must-do tasks from your list into the time available on the weekly timetable, and then those of the could-do tasks that fit, given the time remaining. Remember to apply all the rules already mentioned in the "Guidance on the Allocation Process" section earlier in this chapter whilst carrying out this allocation e.g. building in variety to short study sessions, including reviews of previous sessions and subjects etc.

You now have your weekly timetable. Using the examples already provided to illustrate the long term timetable, your weekly study timetable might look something like that shown in Figures 7.7 (a) and (b) overleaf.

Figure 7.6

Time	Monday	Tuesday	Wednesday	Thursday
00:00				
01:00				
02:00				
03:00				
04:00				
05:00				
06:00				
07:00				
08:00				
09:00				
10:00				
11:00				
12:00				
13:00				
14:00				
15:00				
16:00				
17:00				
18:00				
19:00				
20:00				
21:00				
22:00				
23:00				
00:00				
Total				

Figure 7.7 (a)

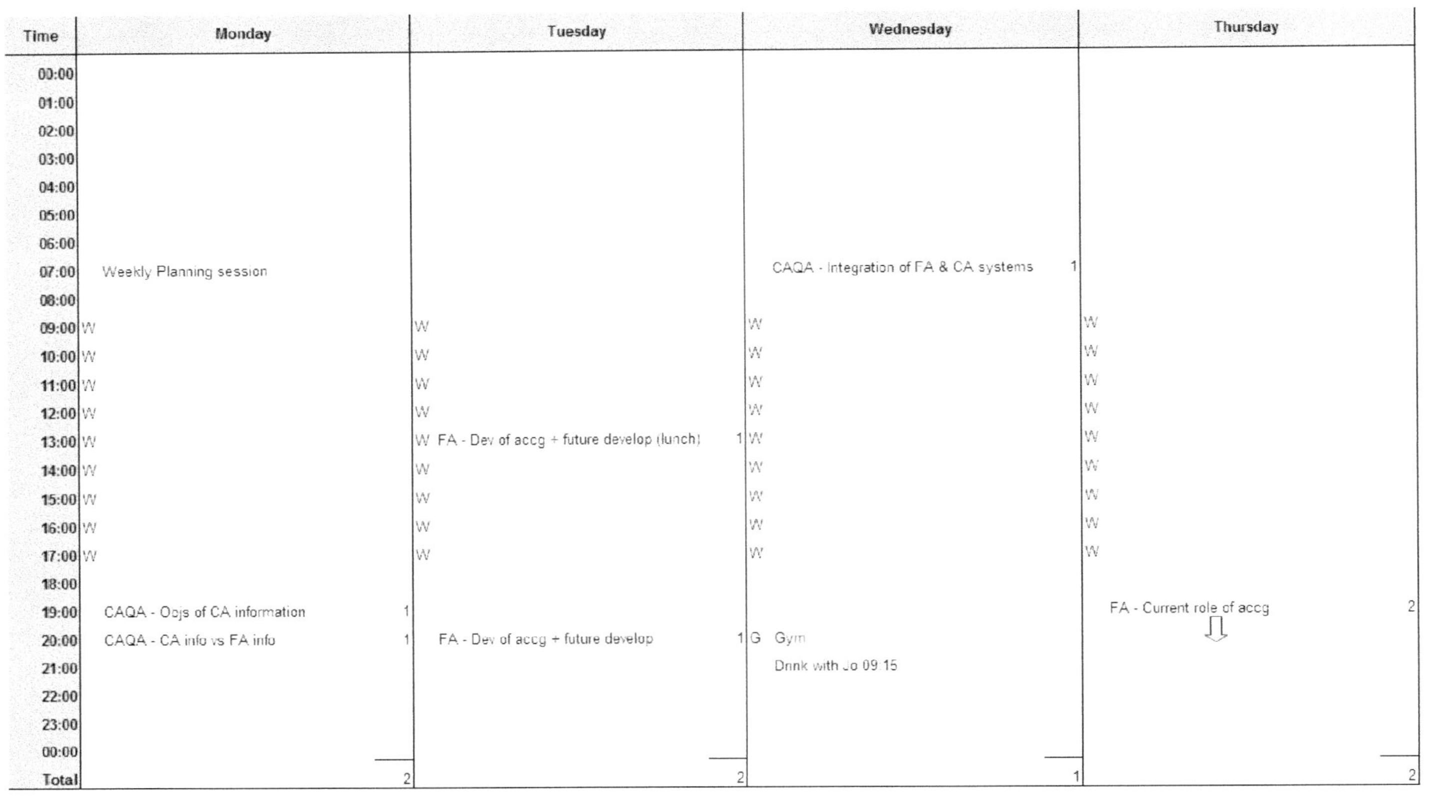

Time	Monday			Tuesday			Wednesday			Thursday		
00:00												
01:00												
02:00												
03:00												
04:00												
05:00												
06:00												
07:00		Weekly Planning session						CAQA - Integration of FA & CA systems	1			
08:00												
09:00	W			W			W			W		
10:00	W			W			W			W		
11:00	W			W			W			W		
12:00	W			W			W			W		
13:00	W			W	FA - Dev of accg + future develop (lunch)	1	W			W		
14:00	W			W			W			W		
15:00	W			W			W			W		
16:00	W			W			W			W		
17:00	W			W			W			W		
18:00												
19:00		CAQA - Objs of CA information	1								FA - Current role of accg	2
20:00		CAQA - CA info vs FA info	1		FA - Dev of accg + future develop	1	G	Gym			⇩	
21:00								Drink with Jo 09 15				
22:00												
23:00												
00:00												
Total			2			2			1			2

Figure 7.7 (b)

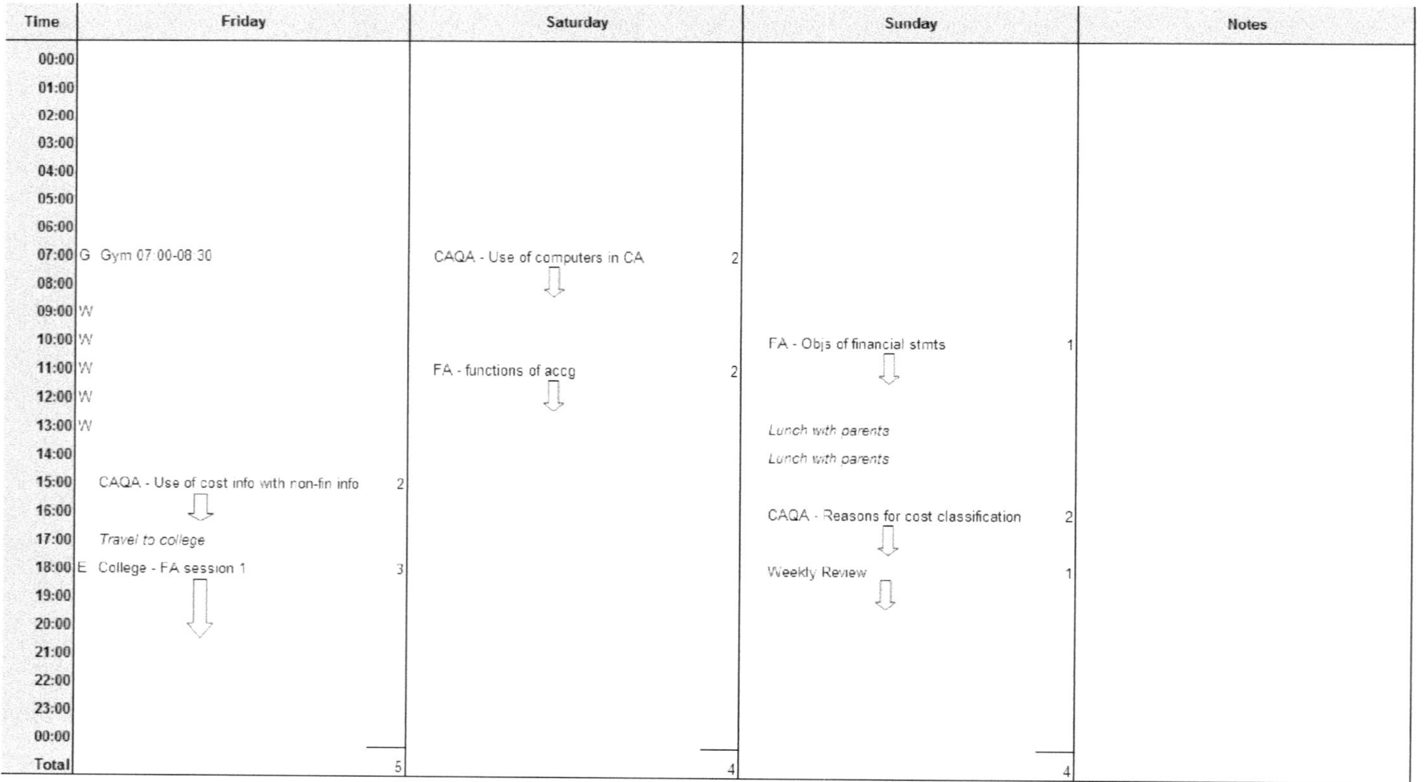

Time		Friday		Saturday		Sunday		Notes
00:00								
01:00								
02:00								
03:00								
04:00								
05:00								
06:00								
07:00	G	Gym 07:00-08:30		CAQA - Use of computers in CA	2			
08:00								
09:00	W							
10:00	W					FA - Objs of financial stmts	1	
11:00	W			FA - functions of accg	2			
12:00	W							
13:00	W					*Lunch with parents*		
14:00						*Lunch with parents*		
15:00		CAQA - Use of cost info with non-fin info	2					
16:00						CAQA - Reasons for cost classification	2	
17:00		*Travel to college*						
18:00	E	College - FA session 1	3			Weekly Review	1	
19:00								
20:00								
21:00								
22:00								
23:00								
00:00								
Total			5		4		4	

Ongoing Progress Tracking on the Timetables

Whilst the purpose of this chapter is to show you how to *produce* the timetables initially, it is worth mentioning now how you will be *using* them over the course of your studies.

We've seen that both long term and weekly timetables allow you to plan out your studies with precision. However, the timetables are also there to track your progress over time, to give you the control you need to ensure that your studies are on course, or if they are not, to recognise that remedial action needs to be taken now rather than when it is too late.

Daily

The easiest way to do this is to print out a copy of your current weekly timetable and, as you go through the week, on the face of the timetable simply mark against each planned study session what you actually managed to do. In other words, write down the actual time spent and whether you completed the study task allocated to that session. Alternatively, mark down the subject you actually spent your time, if different from the one planned. Any further information you might want to add can be written in the notes column.

Weekly

At the end of each week, total up the time spent on each subject and add that to the long term timetable in the "Total – Actual" column. In an ideal world, your actuals will match or exceed your budgeted hours of study!

If they do, give yourself a pat on the back and enjoy the feeling that you're progressing towards your goal. Achievements like this can only add to your confidence levels, which is a good thing. You might also want to consider giving yourself a reward for meeting your targets. We return to the idea of reward setting in Chapter 11.

In addition, you need to identify which study tasks were completed during the period and those which were not, if there are any. The output from this review will be factored into your weekly timetable production session.

If you've not managed to meet budget, or you've got study tasks carried forward to future weeks, don't worry. The whole point of tracking progress in this way is to ensure you are aware plenty of time in advance that you need to adjust your plans to take account of the difficulties you've faced. So again, give yourself a pat on the back for being in control enough to recognise the situation. Remember, whilst you now have the opportunity to rectify the problem, others without a timetable will be sticking their head in the sand and pretending everything is fine. They are the ones who will suffer come the day of the exam.

We'll take a look at how you might adjust your plans in the next section.

Updating the Long Term Study Timetable

The Inevitability of Change

Over time, you may find that there is a divergence between your initial long term study plan and reality. Perhaps a particularly difficult area of the syllabus took a lot longer than expected to cover, and now you have a backlog of work as a result.

> ***"Nothing endures but change."***
> **Heracltus**

Firstly, take heart. Do not panic. This is almost inevitable, and should not be taken in any way as a sign of failure. Circumstances change. The important thing is that you recognise and adapt to these changing circumstances. In other words, that you remain in control of your destiny.

Timetabling Ensures Problems are Dealt With

That is why having both weekly and long term timetables is so important. As part of your weekly timetable planning session, you will be revisiting your long term plan and comparing your actual position to it. If you already have so many must do subjects bought forward from the previous week that you can't deal with those listed on the long term plan for the coming week, it's not possible to ignore the problem – it's down in black and white. If, on the other hand, you had no plan, denial would be far easier.

So, having your long term plan gives you an advantage over your peers who have in their wisdom decided they can do without one. Congratulate yourself on your foresight. You still have time to do something about the problem. Your peers might not.

How & When to Update the Long Term Study Timetable

How often should you update your long term plan, and what action should you take? Well, again, that depends on individual circumstances, but I'd recommend you revisit and update the plan at least once a month. If you're using a paper-based timetable, having used pencil will mean it's relatively easy to update your plans. Or, if you're using your chosen application on the computer, changes should again be pretty straightforward.

As to what changes should you make, these could be in a number of forms, depending on what you decide is right for you. There are no hard and fast rules. However, here are some examples of the changes you might make to your timetable and the reasons why.

- Reallocating syllabus areas over the remaining time before your revision period starts so that full subject coverage is still achieved.
- Where reallocating syllabus areas to gain full subject coverage is simply not achievable in the time frames available, making decisions as to what areas are critical and which will have to be omitted.
- Changing study period timings or dates to better meet your needs.
- Moving the start of your revision period either forward or backwards in time depending on how the study process is progressing. (Think carefully before you reduce the amount of time available for revision though. It's no good having fully covered all areas of the syllabus if you haven't carried out any revision, or attempted any practice exam questions prior to the exam.)
- Reallocating time between different examination subjects to allow more time for the subject you are struggling with. (Again, however, be careful to maintain sufficient time for the other subject. You need to have as even a coverage as possible over *all* subjects and *all* syllabi. Concentrating on one at the expense of others is likely to be counterproductive.)

Whatever the actual changes you make, remember that by making them you are dealing with any problems you may have now, rather than sweeping them under the carpet until it is too late. You're doing all you can to retain that sense of control, and in so doing, you're increasing your chances of success. This can only be a good thing.

> ***Become a student of change. It is the only thing that will remain constant.***
> **Anthony J. D'Angelo**

Learning Approach Options

Decisions Surrounding Your Learning Approach

We've now seen how to produce both long term and short term timetables to help us plan and implement our studies. However, we've been making one major assumption when working through the timetable production process – that you've already made decisions about

- The type of study material you'll be using (e.g. dedicated printed study text, online e-learning materials).
- Whether you're going to study individually at home on your own, or instead within a group environment, such as an evening course at a college.

Not Everyone Has a Choice

It may be that this was a decision made for you. There may only be printed study material available for the course you are taking, with no online course alternative available (although that is increasingly unlikely these days). There may not have been the option available to attend a taught course within your area, in which case you have no choice but to go with the home study route. If that is the case, don't worry, gaining a first time pass using a home study/text book route is perfectly possible.

Where Choice is Available

But, for some of you at least, there may be choices open to you. Your study material may come in a variety of forms, both printed and online, and from a variety of providers. Taught courses may also be available to you, perhaps from local colleges, maybe private training companies, sometimes even the professional institutes you belong to, and these courses may come in various flavours – daytime, evening, block release, revision courses, or maybe blended courses (where some of the training is in a classroom and some via e-learning).

If this is the case, you have some decisions to make as to which approach to learning is best for you – what type of material to use and what method of study/course to go for.

What this Chapter Contains

For those people who have yet to make up their minds, this chapter points out the advantages and disadvantages of each approach. It also gives you some other pointers to help you make your decision as to which method to use. Ultimately, it will depend on your own unique personality and circumstances as to which is the best route for you.

But whichever route you finally decide to take, the results will still need to be built into the production of your timetable. We'll take a look at this after we've visited the methods themselves.

Study Material Types

The Gutenberg Printing Press

There was a time when study material only came in one form – the printed word. The only choice you had back then in the good old days was which particular printed materials you wanted to use – was it the actual textbooks given as suggested reading by your examining body, or was it a more dedicated product such as a distance learning study manual produced by one of the many third party providers ready to sell you their product.

And Beyond...

Now days, with the increasing use of technology in all walks of life, the choice has been somewhat complicated. You may now find that in addition to study materials available in printed form, there are a host of options offering the material you need in electronic form. The choice can even be bewildering, with everything from study manuals which just happen to be in e-book form, but are essentially the printed text offered online, to fully interactive materials, where the learning journey you take will be tailored to you according to your actions, and where content might be not only written words but also multimedia material, such as video clips.

> ***Computers make it easier to do a lot of things, but most of the things they make it easier to do don't need to be done.***
> **Andy Rooney**

Complications Surrounding the Use of Technology

To complicate matters even further, the online material options available may be dependent on you having a certain technological platform to access the material. For example, you might need high bandwidth internet access to view the material, which may actually be stored centrally on a secure server somewhere, rather than stored on your hard disk. Or you might need specific software to read the particular e-book version you are thinking about buying.

Guidance on Which Material Type to Use

Because of the range of potential range of options available to you, it's difficult for me to give you definitive advice about which one is best for you. Added to that, each person will have their own preferences in terms of what form of material they respond to best. Often, this is an age-related thing, with the (ever-so-slightly grey) older generation preferring the written form whilst the younger generation prefer the electronic form, having been bought up on this for most of their lives.

However, there are some common sense guidelines that I can offer you to help you make your decision.

Material Provider

Whichever form of material you decide to buy, make sure that the provider you choose is a reputable one. Many professional bodies actually run accreditation schemes to ensure that you can have access to materials which have been assessed to ensure they are fit for purpose. Make sure you select an accredited provider so that you can be sure the material you are getting actually gives you what you need to know.

Electronic Media

If you have a preference for electronic media rather than printed media then by all means consider the e-learning options available to you. However, do remember to bear in mind the following.

Availability of Hard Copy Material

Make sure that the material can either be printed off in hard copy form, or that at the very least you are able to annotate the material on screen and save your annotations. Some materials are produced in a form that allows you to do neither, severely limiting your ability to study properly. (Yes, I know it sounds strange, but some content providers really will disable the ability to print their material. They do this in an attempt to protect their intellectual property being copied for free, although this is arguably a misguided approach to protecting copyright.)

> ***Computers WORK, people THINK.***
> **IBM Corporation**

Offline Flexibility

Make sure that the materials are available for you to use offline i.e. you do not need to be connected to the internet to view them. Again, only being able to access the materials when you're within range of an internet access point is hardly ideal as it limits any flexibility you might otherwise have to study whenever and wherever you want to.

Technological Platform

This may sound like me stating the blindingly obvious, but do make sure you have the necessary hardware and software to use the electronic material. Check with the providers to see what their minimum technical requirements are (and that you meet them!) and also that any software necessary to access the material is provided to you free of charge.

Provider Support

Because you'll be using technology to access your study material, there are many additional problems you might encounter that you wouldn't were you just studying with a printed book in front of you. Make sure the material provider offers a decent level of support so that you can sort out any issues you have quickly. The last thing you need is to waste valuable study time waiting for days or weeks for a response to a technical query you have.

Printed Media

If you decide you want to study using printed materials, you may have a choice to make as to whether you use dedicated study materials produced by a third party training provider or to simply use the books listed by your professional body as their recommended reading. Unless you are particularly disciplined and feel comfortable using the latter approach, I would recommend using the more structured former approach, where a training provider has done the work for you and produced study materials which directly link to your particular exam subject(s).

Not only will this ensure you cover all of the subject areas you need to, and only those areas, but also you'll likely have access to a more rounded set of training materials such as linked question and answer books, revision cards (more on these in the Part Six – Revision) and CDs. Using a variety of material types like this adds to the learning experience and makes it more likely that you'll understand and retain the things you need to.

But Surely Using Technology Makes Studying Easier?

One myth I do want to dispel is that using technology to study automatically makes the process easier. There's a lot of hype around e-learning and the benefits it has over traditional learning styles, and most of it is just that – marketing hype.

> ***If you don't know how to do something, you don't know how to do it with a computer.***
> **Unknown**

Yes, e-learning can make the learning experience more engaging, yes it can be visually more exciting and yes, it may allow you to collaborate remotely with your fellow students and lecturers. But, ultimately it does not mean that somehow you will not have to work as hard as you would do if you used a traditional text book and classroom based approach. You will still need to do the same work – there are no short cuts.

So when you select your preferred study option, do it on the basis of which way you prefer to study rather than because you think one is easier than another. Otherwise you're going to find out the hard way when you get nearer to your exam that you don't get something for nothing.

Individual Learning Versus Group Learning

We've looked at the study materials you might use but what about the equally important decision about whether we study alone at home or whether instead we study collaboratively as part of a group by attending some type of taught course? Let's look at this now.

Individual Learning – Second Best?

For many, individual learning is the only option. Work commitments, geographic location, family responsibilities – all of these may mean that regular attendance on a taught course (whether delivered physically at a college or real-time online) is simply impossible. But individual learning shouldn't be viewed merely as second best, as a fall back position when nothing else is available. In fact it has many advantages to recommend it.

"One man alone can be pretty dumb sometimes, but for real bona fide stupidity, there ain't nothin' can beat teamwork."
Edward Abbey

Advantages of Individual Learning

- You gain freedom from the straitjacket of the lecture hall. You are not constrained by timetables set by others, or by the abilities of others. You can set your own timetable and adapt it to fit as time passes. This is a major advantage as it allows you to always maximise your free time, instead of, for example, wasting it listening to a lecturer explaining something for the third time to one of your fellow students that you understood the first time round.
- You gain the ability to study whenever and wherever you want to. Instead of having to trek to a college thirty miles away after work, you can return home to the comfort of your own home and study in peace, with refreshments available on hand for free. Should you choose to study at 2am in the morning, you can do so (although remember the benefits of getting enough undisturbed sleep). No college lecturer is going to offer you this flexibility!
- Following on from the above points, you are not bound by the learning pattern of the group, nor are your needs subservient to the needs of the group. You can instead concentrate on the person that's most important in this equation – you!

The Downside to Individual Learning

Nevertheless, individual learning is not an easy ride. It has a number of disadvantages too, and these are worth pointing out.

- There is both an absence of heard language, which when present can make the learning process richer, and also of non-language communication, such as the lecturer's facial expressions.
- There is an absence of feedback from teacher to student and student to teacher.
- There is either a delay in positive reinforcement from the lecturer (where a distance learning approach is used, and you have to send work off to be marked and then wait for comments back) or no reinforcement at all (where you are studying completely on your own without outside help).
- There is no student to student communication, which can make studying seem a very lonely business at times. The social aspects of studying within a group are lost, which can be isolating.
- In attending courses as part of a group, the benefits of collaborative learning can be realised. You can gain access to others' opinions, talents, resources, time, perspectives, and methods of approaching problems. All of this can be valuable in making the learning process easier.

The Decision – Alone or Part of a Group?

The Decision is Yours

Ultimately, only you can decide which method suits you best. However, it is probably true to say that if you decide upon the individual learning route, you will need to work harder in certain areas when compared to those using taught courses.

- You have to motivate, organise, discipline and criticise yourself. As a result, you need to be ruthlessly honest with yourself when it comes to your studies.
- You will need to do your best to banish the self doubt that inevitably comes with the lack of feedback when compared to a classroom environment.
- You will need to work hard at overcoming anxieties concerning the study process (sometimes it helps if you can find someone with whom you can discuss your studies on a regular basis, even if that person doesn't necessarily understand the detail. Friends and family can be invaluable here).
- You will need to learn to cope with distractions at home, such as the phone ringing, someone knocking at the front door and so on.

Without a doubt, it takes a certain kind of person to deal successfully with the above difficulties. Resourceful, disciplined, motivated. Indeed, you might be wondering whether you're really up to the task.

You Can Do It!

Don't be too hard on yourself however; try to remain objective. The very fact you have bought and are reading this book suggests to me that the motivation is already there. You've already been resourceful in looking around you and identifying ways in which you might increase your chances of success. And if you weren't disciplined, you'd be taking a *laissez-faire* approach to your studies, leaving it all to the last minute with a devil-may-care attitude that wouldn't get you through the exam. You wouldn't be at the start of your studies, attempting to find and locate a route through the maze to the ultimate prize – that exam pass.

> ***"The man who goes alone can start today; but he who travels with another must wait till that other is ready."***
> **Henry Thoreau**

So if it's individual learning for you, either through necessity or choice, stick with it. You *are* up to the challenge.

Your Solo Performance

One other fundamental fact to remember when making the decision is this.

The majority of professional level exams are based on the performance of the student (that's you!) in the exam itself. There's no continuous assessment during the course, no course work to hand in which counts towards your ultimate exam grade. It's all about you, performing on the day.

And note that that I said it's all about *you*. Not you and your mates in the same class. Your classmates can't help you in the exam – either you perform, using your own skills, knowledge, and aptitude, or you don't. You can't call on the person sitting next to you to discuss a question you're having problems with!

> ***"We're all in this alone."***
> **Lily Tomlin**

So being able to attend a taught course as part of a group might be a more pleasant experience for you, but it's not going to make it any easier when it comes to sitting the exam. In fact, whether you realise it or not, getting friendly with all of your fellow students is probably more like sleeping with the enemy.

You Versus Everyone Else

Paranoia?

Yes. I really mean it. It really *is* you against the world, and in particular, your fellow students. This may seem to you to be bordering on the paranoid, but really, it's not. Here's why.

Limit Supply – Support Salaries

The vast majority of professional level exams are there as a hurdle you have to jump over. A test to prove you are up to the mark, and have reached a certain level of proficiency in your chosen vocation. But often, they are also there as a control – a control to make sure that the numbers of those professionally qualified remains at a level which ensures there is never an oversupply of qualified candidates for a job.

> ***"Paranoia means having all the facts."***
> **William S. Burroughs**

Make the exams too easy, and numbers of qualified personnel increase. Basic economics suggest that an increased supply (candidates) and the same level of demand (the number of jobs available) leads to a fall in price. In this case, salary.

In other words, not only do professional institutes want to maintain standards, they want to maintain exclusivity. They want to maintain a scarceness of supply. It is, after all, in the interests of their qualified members.

What This Means for Your Exams

How does this translate to your exams? Well, the production of an exam paper is a lengthy process, and the end result should be a fair paper which is of a comparable level of difficulty to all previous papers. The reality is however that sometimes a particular paper set can prove to be far more difficult or far easier than the examining body (the professional institute) anticipated. And as a result, they may have to adjust the marking scheme.

As an example, let's say that on average, 40 percent of all candidates taking a particular exam gain a pass grade at each sitting. Then, imagine that when the next paper is marked, the percentage of those passing suddenly increases to 70 percent.

Such a huge increase would raise difficult questions for the examining body. Was the population of candidates really so much better than those previously, or was the paper set actually too easy? If it transpires it was too easy, what should be done about it?

Although the examining bodies might tell you otherwise, sometimes in these circumstances the marking scheme will be adjusted, and the papers entered given an adjusted score as a result. The adjustment to the marking scheme will be done in such a way that the overall number of successful candidates will be bought down from 70 percent to nearer the 40 percent.

The Inevitable Conclusion

Think about this for a minute. What conclusion can we draw from this? Simply this. You *are* in direct competition with your fellow students sitting the same exam. What they score *does* matter, it *can* have a direct impact on your mark. Any adjustments to the marking scheme mean that *your* mark will be adjusted accordingly as well. It is not just you against the examiner. It is also you against the rest of those sitting the exam.

> ***"In what concerns you much, do not think that you have companions: know that you are alone in the world."***
> **Henry Thoreau**

So don't fall into the trap of thinking that attending a class means you're all one big happy family trying to pass the exam, helping each other along the way, because you're not. Ultimately, a bit like life itself, it's a competition. You need to remember to look after *numero uno*, No. 1, you! In terms of making the decision whether to study alone or in a group therefore, remember to bear this in mind.

Meeting in the Middle – the Study Buddy

Survival of the fittest it may be, as we have just seen, but even with this in mind there will be some of you who find the idea of studying alone difficult to face. And yet, although you may feel this way, you might not have any choice. There may be no taught course alternatives available to you.

There is a compromise, a middle way, however, which may help. And that is teaming up with another person who is studying for the same exam that you are. A "study buddy", if you like.

The Benefits of the Study Buddy

This approach has much to commend it. You have someone to confide in, to share problems you are facing with, to bounce ideas off, and to get feedback from. When one study partner is feeling low and lacking in motivation, the other can be there, where necessary placing a well aimed kick up the backside. Having a study buddy is also a bit like having a training partner down the gym – their very presence spurs you on to lift heavier weights. Having a study buddy will have the same effect – you're likely to try that bit harder, make that bit more effort than you otherwise would do if you were working completely on your own and able to backslide without repercussions.

Be Aware of the Possible Disadvantages

That's not to say there aren't downsides to having a study buddy. For a start, if one partner is more dominant than the other, it's easier for the more submissive side to get led in the wrong direction. Also, the two of you can convince each other you're right about something when in fact you're both wrong. But in general, assuming you can find someone not too dissimilar from yourself whom you feel comfortable with, the advantages outweigh the disadvantages.

How Do I Find My New Friend?

Where to find your study buddy will, once again, depend on your personal circumstances.

- Your professional institute may be able to put you into touch with fellow likeminded students, or they may run local societies where you can meet others like you.
- If you are planning on attending block release type courses, where for example, you attend an introductory course for a couple of days at a college and then return for a week's revision course close to the exam date, you may be able to make contacts with fellow students during the introductory phase.
- These days, with modern technology, it should also be possible to use the internet's rich capabilities to find your study buddy, using chat rooms, internet forums and the like.
- Ask around amongst friends and colleagues. Someone somewhere, even if it's an acquaintance of an acquaintance, will know of someone who dovetails with your needs.

Effect on Timetable Production of Selecting a Group Learning Approach

The procedures for timetable production we saw in Chapter 7 were largely predicated on the assumption that individual learning would be the primary method of study (although the examples shown did include a small element of college training). This assumption was made because, in many cases, students studying for professional level exams have no choice but to follow a distance learning approach, either because of work commitments or because there is simply nowhere available within a reasonable distance to attend classes.

However, should you be one of those lucky enough to have a choice between individual and group learning options, and should you then select the latter, we need to take a quick look at what effect your attendance on taught courses will have on the timetable production process. It's worth noting now though that the process remains largely the same, so there is no need to scrap all you have learned so far – the only real difference is in the allocation of the syllabus across your study sessions. Let's look at this now.

Effect on Long Term Timetable Production

Set Revision Start Date

The first part of the process is the same as already seen. You decide upon your revision period start date. You map in known dates and time commitments to the long range planner, such as exam dates, holidays, and work.

Add Course to Plan

Then, knowing the course dates you are booked onto, you put these down onto your planner as well, noting the subject and if known, syllabus areas to be covered. (Often this information will not be available until you have started attending the course. If this is the case, simply block out the dates on your calendar for now and come back and fill in the detail when you have it.)

Calculate Time Available for Study

Having done this, you can now arrive at an amount of free time you still have available to allocate to further study. Again, as before, use your common sense when making this decision, and bear in mind you may need to change your target hours once you're further into the study itself.

Build the Syllabus Allocation Around the Course Timetable

It is at this stage of the timetable production process that the main difference in method becomes obvious. Whereas before you took the syllabus for each subject and then allocated the syllabus areas across your study periods, this time you will be covering syllabus areas according to an external timetable i.e. your taught course timetable. In a sense, the allocation has already been done for you.

As a result, your remaining free study time needs to be allocated across syllabus areas in the same way, building your home study sessions *around* the subjects to be covered on the taught courses. The plan should be to allocate some study time for a particular subject as preparation prior to attending the class which covers that subject, and some study time after the course for review of that subject. This approach maximises the benefit of attending the taught course by, firstly, allowing you to better participate in the class and understand the subject matter because of your preparation, and secondly, by ensuring that you review what you have covered during class after the event. (Remember the importance of review in building and maintaining memory.)

For example, if you are attending weekly evening courses and you know you are covering "The Accounting Equation" during your next evening class, ideally you would allocate at least one study session to the accounting equation *before* the evening class, and at least one study session *after* it. This would ensure you extract the maximum value from your evening class.

Other than the difference to the way the allocation of syllabus areas across your timetable is carried out, everything else is pretty much the same. Your long term plan will now be complete and you can concentrate on your weekly timetable, one week at a time.

Effect on Weekly Timetable Production

As shown before in Chapter 7, to produce the weekly plan during your "Weekly Planning" session, you'll review your long term timetable for events and study periods, and add these to the plan. Then you'll identify tasks which must be completed during the week, and those which could be completed, time permitting. From this, you can then fit these tasks into your weekly timetable.

The only real difference when using a group learning approach and attending courses is that because you'll be following a fixed timetable given to you by the course provider, there will be somewhat less flexibility available to you when scheduling. When a particular subject will be taught is fixed in stone, and you will not have the option of moving these dates. This is an inevitable downside to attending classroom courses, and cannot be avoided. However, the advantages gained, such as tutor contact and feedback, should more than compensate for the loss of flexibility you might suffer in planning your studies.

Planning Revisited

Fundamental to Success

We have seen in Part Three just how fundamental to success the process of planning is, both before and during your studies. We looked at the process of timetable production on a step-by-step basis, and then at some practical examples of this to help in your understanding and ultimately your application of the concepts when producing your own individual timetables.

Retain Perspective Though

It's worth making the point that you need to retain some perspective here. Planning is only part of the study process, albeit an important start to it. If you are one of those people prone to making lists and producing Gantt charts for every event in your life, you need to guard against making the planning process an end in itself, as opposed to a means to an end.

In other words, don't get too hung up on it and concentrate on every last detail to the exclusion of actually doing the real work itself – the studying. You're not going to be examined on your ability to produce an all-singing, all-dancing study timetable!

A Competitive Advantage

But, at the same time, never underestimate the power of having a good plan – it gives you an enormous advantage over those of your fellow students who plough straight into their studies without forethought. Remember to tell yourself that if ever your subconscious starts to complain to you that you're wasting valuable time on producing something you'll never use again.

Ultimately, remember that having a plan puts you in the driving seat. You are in control of your studies, your studies aren't in control of you. The feeling of self-confidence that comes from being in control is a priceless one. You're another step closer to achieving your First Time Pass.

Moving On...

You've made your plans, you've got your study timetables. In the Part Four of the book we'll focus on the next Foundation of Success Factor, Study Time and Place. Let's do that now.

Part Four

STUDY TIME AND PLACE

On Your Marks, Get Set…

Can I Start Yet?

You're probably itching to get started. (Notice I use the word "probably" – some of you will be using every excuse in the book to avoid actually having to start your studies. We'll deal with these sorts of procrastination issues shortly.)

Having spent all this time producing a study plan, no doubt you think it's time to actually put some work in, get some targets under your belt. The sooner the better.... You want to hear the starting gun so you can take that first step.

Not quite. We're nearly there, yes, and what's contained within this chapter isn't going to take you any great length of time to deal with, so don't worry. But what we're going to look at is nevertheless important.

Learning is a Journey Part 2

The Importance of the Map

Let me remind you of our "learning is a journey" analogy. Remember it? We said that it would be madness to start a long journey without a map, and similarly it would be suicide to start a process of study without a plan. I think this was a pretty persuasive argument for the importance of having that plan.

But hang on a second. If you were about to depart on a long journey, would you just pick up a map and get started? The risk-takers and foolhardy amongst us might do, and they might be lucky enough to muddle through and finally get to their destination without mishap. Then again, they might not.

Getting the Practicalities Sorted Before You Set Out

Instead, would you not think about dealing with the practicalities such a journey entails first, before your departure? I think you would. Things like packing your bags, selecting a method of transport which will give you the most comfortable ride, and making sure you've filed away all your travel documents safely so that you can lay your hands on them easily when you need them.

The same thing goes for your studies. You need to consider the practicalities now and deal with them *before* your start to study. Starting your journey before doing this is simply a recipe for disaster.

So that's what this part of the book is about. Not the mechanics of study, the tools and techniques you'll be using. We'll deal with those in the Part Five. In this part we'll look at time and place – how to actually get started on putting that all important study time in (the time), and where you're going to study (the place).

The Study Environment

Deciding on the Where

If you haven't already done so, you need to decide exactly *where* it is that you intend to carry out your studies. The place it's all going to happen.

You might think this decision is pretty unimportant in the grand scheme of things – after all, as long as there is a desk and chair you've got everything you need, right?

Wrong.

Studying in the right environment, one conducive to good study, can make all the difference between a pass and a fail. It's that simple. So you need to make sure you get it right. What should you be doing to ensure you get it right, what should you be looking for?

The Ideal Environment

What are the characteristics of the ideal study environment? I'd say they include

Quiet

There should be a lack of any significant background noise. I'm not talking a monk's cell here, but the quieter, the better. Working on the kitchen table whilst your family eat their evening meal and watch TV does not fall into this category.

> ***"In quiet places, reason abounds."***
> **Adlai Stevenson**

Free from Interruptions

Ideally, the likelihood of you being disturbed should be minimal. So working next to the telephone should be avoided (or at least put the answerphone on if this is the only place you can find), as should having your mobile phone with you if it's switched on. And make sure your family or housemates understand that you are not to be disturbed for anything other than the direst of emergencies.

Well Lit

You need to be able to see what you are doing without straining your eyes. Avoid low lighting and conversely bright lighting if that causes dark shadows to fall across your work area. You should aim for an all round bright but diffuse light. If you can make it daylight as opposed to artificial light that would be great, although I realise this may not be possible, particularly during the winter months.

Warm

But not too warm. The ideal temperature is between 67°F–73°F (19.4°C–22.8°C) – anything over this is likely to be too warm and after a long day at work and/or a heavy meal you're likely to find yourself falling asleep at your desk. Make it too cold on the other hand and for sure you'll be awake, but too busy noticing the extremities of your body getting cold to concentrate fully on the work in hand.

Ergonomic and Comfortable

You need a desk at a comfortable height and a chair which is comfortable but upright. The desk and/or chair should ideally be adjustable to allow you to maintain an ideal working position (if not, adjust the desk height by using blocks under the legs). The best position is one where the angle between trunk and thighs is at least 90 degrees and where the upper arms can be kept vertical, the forearms horizontal and the hands at the level of the elbows. In addition to getting the ergonomics right, there should also be sufficient space on the desk to hold all of your study equipment and materials.

All in all, your study environment needs to be conducive to maximum concentration. The greater the focus you can place on the work at hand, and the less your mind is distracted by things around you, the better for your studies.

One Place or Many?

A Bit of Lateral Thinking

Don't assume that you have to nominate one place where you'll study and one place only. Think laterally here. There may be a number of places that you can combine for best effect.

For example, maybe you travel to work every day on the train. Many of us commute to work in this way, and our train journeys might take anything from 20 minutes to 2 hours. What do you normally do during this time? Read the newspaper? Sleep? Browse a trashy novel? Send text messages to your friends? Why not use some of this time for study instead?

Match the Work to the Place

Clearly you'll need to tailor the type of work you're doing to the place you're doing it in. Unless you're lucky enough to be travelling on a train where there are tables between the seats (often not the case on the usual commuter routes, as this reduces the number of passengers that can be shoe-horned into a carriage), you're not going to be able to sit and write notes or answer practice questions.

But that doesn't mean you can't spend the time wisely by reading the next chapter of your textbook, or reviewing notes you've already made. Or perhaps your examiner expects you to keep abreast of current events in your chosen field, for example the latest exposure drafts, discussion documents or "white papers", in which case you could be reading these.

Short and Sweet – Wherever Possible

Don't forget what we've already seen in terms of length of study periods – little and often is best. There's nothing inherently wrong with a study session of only ten minutes, other than your misconceptions that it's not possible to study properly unless you're putting in the long hours.

> ***"Perserverance is not a long race; it is many short races one after another."***
> **Walter Elliott**

So review your average day – where are there gaps you can fill with short bursts of study? Maybe you've ten minutes waiting at the bus stop in the morning. Fine, use this to your advantage. Maybe you can find a quiet area in the office during your lunch break to sit and study. If you can, great, make it so.

Of course, some of these places aren't going to fulfil all the criteria of the ideal environment to study in. But that's not a problem – these other places should be in addition to your main place of study, not a replacement for it. You still need a place which you do the majority of your work in, a place which does fit these criteria as closely as possible.

Primary Study Place – Alternatives

That place is most likely to be at your home, but do bear in mind that this is not set in stone. Maybe your parents' house would be quieter. Maybe your friend's house is always empty during the evenings because they work shifts, and they're happy for you to make use of it in their absence. Or maybe your local library would be the ideal place for you to work – they often have areas set aside for quiet study which will not only be well lit, quiet, warm, and comfortable but also free!

So the moral of the story is think laterally and be creative when it comes to identifying your place (or places) of study.

But I Can't Find My Ideal Place!

Be aware – you'll never find the perfect place. There'll always be something not quiet right – the tap may drip, the neighbours may have their TV up too loud, the lighting may not be quite right.

Don't overplay the significance of these imperfections. It's important not to get hung up on the things that you can't change. Just make sure you've done all you can to get the place you study to be as close to perfect as you can.

Then accept the situation as it is and move on. Once you're really into the study itself, your concentration will be focussed on the task at hand anyway and you'll find these annoyances are likely to fade into the background.

Music Helps Me Concentrate

Music's OK, Isn't It?

Many's the time I've heard this from students. They say they prefer to study with the radio on, or a CD playing, or the TV going in the background. They argue that it provides a more relaxed atmosphere, which in turn leads to a better frame of mind and thus improved study performance.

They might even point to some oft-quoted research which suggests that playing classical music (specifically Mozart it seems!) to unborn and new born babies supposedly increases their levels of intelligence.

In fact, the belief that it's OK to listen to music whilst studying is one of the most common misconceptions I come across. And, believe me, it *is* a misconception.

Why It's *Not* OK

I could quote you countless pieces of research which prove beyond all reasonable doubt that the only effect of having music or any other sort of noise in the background whilst you're studying is an adverse one, but I won't bore you with the details.

> ***"Silence is more musical than any song."***
> **Christina Rossetti**

Instead, just think about it in common sense terms. When you're studying, you're attempting to understand and learn new information and new ideas, with the ultimate aim of being able to reproduce and apply these things in the context of an exam question. We've already seen that memories are formed through repetition, where new links between neurons in the brain are forged and then strengthened to fix them for the long term.

The more single-minded effort you put into the study process, the greater the number of neurons in your brain bought on board to help with the learning process, and the stronger the links and connections will be. Anything which weakens that focus, anything which takes your concentration away from the study and onto something else external, can only be a bad thing. Some of the neurons which should be helping you in your studies are instead recruited to a different task, that of listening to the background noise of your radio or TV.

In short, your attention is divided, even if you are not consciously aware of it. Don't believe anyone who tells you that music helps them study better – it does not.

If You Must...

And if you're still tempted to have music on whilst you work, try instead to build it into your study in a different way. Instead of turning it on *during* your studies, use it as a reward to be listened to *after* you have reached your next study objective. In this way you have a powerful incentive to finish your work and a reward for doing so, adding to your levels of self-confidence in the process.

Alternatively, remember we said that study sessions should never exceed 45 minutes without a break? Well, perhaps you can use these breaks to listen to your favourite piece of music. Or watch part of your favourite TV program. Whatever you prefer. There's no requirement to lie there and meditate during these breaks – just do something other than study and preferably something you enjoy.

But whatever you do, don't listen to music whilst you're studying. Don't. Please.

Time of Day

The last thing I want to say about environment concerns the time of day that you undertake your studies. It might seem strange, but *when* you study can be as important as *where* you study when it comes to getting the optimum conditions beneficial to learning.

We've already mentioned in the section on planning that every one of us is influenced by the circadian rhythms our bodies work to. In practice, this means that some people simply work better at certain times of the day than others.

It's important to remember this when you get to the point of deciding exactly when during the day you're going to fit in the study time you've allocated as part of your study plan. If you know you're no good in the morning, there's little point in allocating a two hour study session to be completed before breakfast. Instead, why not just allocate say 10 or 15 minutes to reviewing a subject area you've already covered, and save the longer session for the evening, when you're at your best.

Everything in its Place – Administration

You've identified the place or places where you're going to study. In a moment we're going to be talking about actually getting started with the work itself. But before we do, one more area needs to be tackled. And that is administration.

Love it or hate it, you need to keep on top of the administration which goes with your studies. It might sound a little far fetched if I told you failing to deal with this could jeopardise your chances of success, but it would still be true. For example, you can produce the most detailed, beautifully presented study notes in the world, but if you can't lay your hands on them when you need to, they're worthless. And if you can't find the subject area you need to review at a moment's notice, how are you ever going to review and revise properly?

So when we talk about administration, what do we mean? Well, there are a couple of areas we need to concentrate on, the first one being the most universally unpopular. And this is the dreaded F-word. Yes, you've guessed it. Filing!

The F-Word – Filing

If you're anything like me, you absolutely hate filing with a vengeance. I'm looking at my office filing tray right now as I write, and it's full to the brim with my filing for the past six months or so! You might be the same. If you are, that's OK for normal work and life. But *not* for your studies – you can't afford yourself the same luxuries here.

> ***"It is best to do things systematically, since we are only human, and disorder is our worst enemy."***
> **Hesiod**

You need to set up a filing system for the notes you'll be producing, and you need to make sure that you file your notes away *as you produce them.* I'm not going to dictate to you exactly how you arrange this. Everyone will have their own preferences as to how best to set up their ideal filing system. But the underlying tenet must be that at any time you can find the notes you are looking for quickly.

Nevertheless, having said I'm not going to dictate to you how to do this, here are a few pointers to nudge you in the right direction.

- The filing should be kept in a safe, secure environment, where it will not be physically damaged. Under the kitchen sink or with a pile of magazines next to the waste paper bin are probably not the best places! And make sure it's one place only, not spread around the house!

- You may need to rearrange the order of your notes – to facilitate this, use ring binders to store your work and pre-punched paper on which to make your notes. Furthermore, when making notes, ensure you use a new sheet of paper for each new major point, issue or area.
- Although this may seem to contradict the above point, make sure you number your pages where they need to be kept together. This ensures that if you're unfortunate enough to drop your notes on the floor and they become disordered, you don't waste too much time getting them back into some semblance of order. (If you need to reorder your notes at some point, you can renumber them when you do so.)
- Keep each subject and area separate and easily identifiable by using colour-coded dividers with tabs in your binders, and consider producing indexes to help you find what you're looking for.
- As we shall see later in the book, the use of colour can aid learning and memory. This can be used to your advantage too in filing. Consider colour-coding pages, maybe with a highlighting pen or sticky coloured labels, to identify the subject.

Timetable Review and Update

We've already covered the timetabling process extensively, so there's no need to do so again here. However, the production of the weekly timetable and study objectives, along with the review of the long term timetable, is in effect part of the administration process.

So make sure you keep this part of the study process up to date, and store all of your timetabling papers together in an easily accessible place. You're going to need to look at them daily after all, to remind yourself what objectives you have set yourself for that day.

The Learning Journal – a Step Too Far?

In many books offering advice on study, I've seen the recommendation to keep a "Learning Journal", in effect a study diary, in which you write everything you can about your study day, what you've studied, how it went, how you felt, how many cups of tea you had, that sort of thing. The idea is that you can then review this journal to identify any patterns or issues that might help you get more from your studies in the future, such as the fact you never get much work done if you try to study whilst eating your dinner (that's a surprise then!).

If you've got the time, great, do it if it makes you feel better. But frankly, I think you've got better things to do. What with trying to hold down a full time job and studying for a professional level examination, I don't think you'll have a whole lot of time left for this type of navel gazing exercise. Use your valuable time wisely!

Computer-Based Learning

We saw in Chapter 8 that these days technology is often harnessed to increase the range of study options and methods available to you. Let's take a quick look at how the decision to use a computer-based or e-learning approach might affect the advice already given in this chapter.

Study Environment

Pretty much everything we've seen above about the environment you study in holds good whether studying using a traditional book and paper-based approach or an e-learning one. You still need to find the right place (or places) to work, with as close to the ideal working conditions as possible – quiet, well lit, free from interruptions, you know the kind of thing.

The only thing I'd add to the guidance already given is that you'll need

- Sufficient space to put both your desktop/laptop computer *and* papers such as study notes.
- A power feed for your computer.
- A printer to allow you to print off materials as required, ideally in the same room as you're located (although if this isn't possible, at least nearby).

Having access to a printer is a necessity because as we have already seen, having the ability to print off your study materials and notes is very important. You can't work effectively by just reading text on a screen.

Administration

The advice already given about filing still holds good for a computer-based learning approach too. You'll still have study notes to keep in good order, whether they be soft or hard copy (i.e. computer or paper-based).

Coherent Folder Structure

If you are using online material, making annotations directly on screen and then saving the amended document on your hard disk, make sure you set up a decent folder structure to store your files in. As with paper-based notes, you should be able to lay your hands on a particular section of your notes without delay. So have separate folders for each subject, and then separate sub-folders as required to split out the subject into its various parts.

Regular Backups

> ***Jesus saves! The rest of us better make backups!***
> **Unknown**

The other very important piece of advice is this – make sure you *regularly* back up your study material and notes – and make sure this back up is stored separately from the computer you're using. This is crucial as computers are so very prone to crashing when you least need them to, and with maximum adverse impact to your work. And by the way, regularly means regularly, not once every few weeks! Ideally set up an automatic daily back up on your machine, and then save that to an external hard drive. You'll be glad you made the effort to do this when your laptop's hard drive fails!

On Your Marks, Get Set, GO!

Ready to Go

You've got your timetable produced, your ideal place of study lined up, and a filing system ready to receive its first set of study notes. You're ready to go!

This can be a daunting prospect. So far you've managed to busy yourself with lots of other tasks, but now it's not possible to hide from the real thing any longer – the work is there, ready and waiting for you to make a start.

> ***"He who has begun has half done. Dare to be wise; begin."***
> **Horace**

So let's look at the process of getting started, and how to make it as easy as we possibly can.

Getting Started

Step 1 – Set Objectives

At the start of each session, you should set yourself your objectives. You'll get these from your weekly study timetable that you've already produced (you have produced one, haven't you?). This is why having a timetable is so important – it gives you targets to aim at, and gives you the direction you would otherwise lack, helping you avoid that fear of the unknown.

And if you've got your weekly timetable right, you'll have already built in some subject variety and varying levels of difficulty to the session. If not, think about how you can do this to avoid boredom setting in.

Step 2 – Organise Your Study Session Environment

Make sure you have everything around you that you need to study – paper, pens, pencils, ruler, study manuals and textbooks, computer (if you're using an e-learning type approach), highlighting pens, calculator, whatever items are needed to get you through the study period.

Then there is no excuse to go wandering off to find something you suddenly need when things get tough during your studies.

And make sure the environment is the nearest to the ideal one that you can manage – turn that TV off!

Step 3 – Organise Your Study Session Timings

Build In Breaks

You already know the amount of time you've allocated to study, because you've just looked at your weekly timetable when setting your objectives. But break this down further, remembering the rules we've already seen (i.e. a maximum of 45 minutes study without a break), so that you have allocated time for your breaks.

Suggestions for Break Activities

In terms of the 5 to 10 minute breaks between each study period, we've seen some suggestions as to what you might do, but here are a few more ideas to help you decide.

- Listening to music
- Resting
- Meditating
- Exercising/stretching
- Short household tasks
- Dancing
- Taking a short stroll
- Doodling/drawing
- Singing
- Playing a musical instrument
- Day-dreaming
- "Just doin' nothing"
- Wandering round the garden

The list is endless. Do whatever feels right.

Set Rewards as Carrots

Make sure as well that you've set yourself a reward for the end of the session *if* you meet your objectives. It might be watching your favourite TV program, or having that drink with your friend. This gives you something concrete to look forward to if you complete your set objectives, and so a reason for not giving up if things get difficult. Associating the completion of a study task with personal celebration and reward makes the whole study process more pleasant, and so increases the probability that you will continue your studies in the future.

Step 4 – Visualisation

We've already explored the power of visualisation at some length. Use it to your advantage now.

Suggested Visualisation

You're at your desk, materials around you, objectives set. Close your eyes, take three or four deep breaths, and then for one minute use your imagination to create an image in your mind's eye of you studying successfully during the study period. Use all your senses to create a vivid picture of you working. See the look of concentration on your face, feel the paper and the pen in your hand, smell the distinctive aroma of a highlighting pen as you mark important areas of your study text. Then imagine a picture of you having successfully achieved your goals for the session, the look of satisfaction on your face as you clear your materials away.

> ***"The beginning is the most important part of the work."***
> **Plato**

A Minute Well Spent

You need only take a minute or two to carry out this visualisation. Hardly a waste of time in the grand scheme of things. Do it every time you sit down to study, and it can help put you in the right frame of mind to start your studies positively.

Step 5 – Go!

At last – you can start! In the next part of the book we'll look at the tools and techniques you can use during your studies in detail. So we'll skip over the detail on this for now.

Don't Panic – The First Few Times Will Be The Hardest

Starting to study is a bit like starting a new diet – at first, it's hard to be disciplined, to know the plan and to keep to it every day. Everything's new and unfamiliar, the end seems a long way off, and there are lots of temptations to entice you off of the path along the way.

Take heart though. As with dieting, getting down to your studies will eventually become second nature and simply part of your life. You need to re-educate yourself to do this in the same way dieters need to re-educate themselves in the way they eat. Eventually it will become habit. Honest!

> ***"A journey of a thousand miles must begin with a single step."***
> **Lao-tzu**

Step 6 – Record Your Progress

When you get to the end of your study session, record what you've done on your weekly study timetable. Remember that your timetable is invaluable in tracking your progress and allowing you to control your studies effectively. So note down the time you've spent and the subject areas you've spent it on.

And remember to give yourself that reward if you've met your objectives!

Getting Started...Again

There will inevitably be times where you find it difficult to get started. Either you can't summon up the enthusiasm to sit down and start studying, or you find every reason under the sun for not doing so. Perhaps you've got stuck on a particularly difficult area of the syllabus and have become bogged down in a morass you're unable to extricate yourself from. You feel yourself slowly sinking into a dark pit of despair.

> ***"No task is a long one but the task on which does not start. It becomes a nightmare."***
> **Charles Baudelaire**

If this is the case, you need something to kick-start yourself, to get you going again. Try one of the following suggestions to help you get back on track.

Review Your Notes From The Previous Study Session

Aids Memory, Removes Performance Pressure

This is often an ideal way to start a new study session (apart from the very first session of course, when there are no notes to review!). Not only does reviewing your notes from the previous study session aid memory, as we have already seen, but undertaking it as the first part of your study session removes from you the pressure of feeling you have to "do" something new, whether it be write notes or read text.

A Reminder of the Foundations

Often, you will be studying a subject syllabus sequentially, getting to grips with the basics of a subject before then using these as building blocks to reach and understand the higher level material. Reviewing the material from the previous session is ideal in these circumstances, as it reminds you about the assumed knowledge you will need to complete the next subject area successfully.

Ten Minutes Only

Spend no more than ten minutes on this review process before moving on to the current area of study. By this time, you will probably already have silenced those voices in your head telling you there's something far better than studying to attend to down at the local bar.

Depriving Yourself of Study

You might be finding it difficult to settle down to your studies. Perhaps you find you can only manage ten minutes without getting itchy feet and feeling the need to spring up and do something else. You can't keep your concentration from wandering.

The following method might help you address this problem.

The Method

The idea is to deprive yourself of study, as the heading suggests. Instead of sitting down to study, knowing that you've set yourself two lots of 45 minute study periods to plough through, instead set yourself just 10 minutes of study. Go further than this and stand up instead of sitting down whilst you're working.

When the 10 minutes are up, stop your studies and do something else instead. Perhaps you could flick through a magazine, or make yourself a cup of coffee. But whilst you're doing this, keep thinking about what you studied during the 10 minute session. Turn it around in your mind, ask yourself questions about it. Do you understand it; do any questions arise from it? If you can't remember something, take just a brief look at it to remind yourself, and then continue reading that magazine or drinking that coffee.

> ***"This thing that we call 'failure' is not the falling down, but the staying down."***
> **Mary Pickford**

After 10 minutes or so more, start another 10 minute study session. And 10 minutes later, return to the other activity. And so on.

The Idea

The idea here is to trick your mind into thinking it's not really studying at all. With only ten minutes to worry about, and with no desk to sit at, the sense of panic induced by the thought of slaving away at a desk for a long study session disappears. Once that panic has gone, you should then be able to sit down at your desk and continue your studies.

Allow Yourself a Warming Up Period

Just as any athlete needs to warm up before they perform to the peak of their abilities, you need to warm up too. You shouldn't expect to simply sit down and be able to immediately place 100 percent of your concentration on the job in hand. This would be unrealistic, particularly in the early stages of your study.

That's why the suggestion made earlier of reviewing your notes from last time's study session is a good one – because it allows you to warm up slowly, gently introducing you to the task instead of making you run at full pace before you're ready, before your mental muscles have warmed up.

> ***"To climb steep hills requires a slow pace at first."***
> ***Shakespeare***

Do remember therefore not to be too hard on yourself when you first sit down to study. You *will* find that your concentration wanders, that thoughts of what you need to buy when you next go shopping, memories of the conversation you had with the next door neighbour as you came in, and so on, impose themselves on you, demanding attention. This is perfectly normal. Simply acknowledge that this is so, and then bring your attention back to the work in front of you. No doubt you'll have to do this a number of times – no matter, just stick with it. Eventually you will be fully focussed.

Aids To Concentration

Some people find that having one or two concentration aids help them achieve the fully focussed state mentioned above. I suggest you experiment with these if you feel the need, to find out which best suit you. Aids to concentration might include

- Sweets to suck.
- Earplugs to filter out extraneous noise.
- Aromatherapy candles.
- A photograph of a scene you find particularly soothing to look at when concentration wavers.
- A symbolic reminder of what your ultimate objective is, i.e. passing your professional level exams first time. Perhaps a job advert aimed at those with the qualification you're studying towards, with a nice big fat salary package attached. Or whatever gives you that reminder. Be creative.

All of these aids really aim to produce a more pleasant environment to work in, inducing a sense of relaxation and calming the panic in your mind. This then leads quite naturally to an increased ability to concentrate.

Shock Therapy – "Terminate" Those Sticking Points

World Famous Bodybuilder to World Famous Movie Star and Beyond

Arnold Schwarzenegger is recognised pretty much the world over. Star of many Hollywood blockbusters, including the Terminator films, he's famous for his muscle-bound physique and action movie hero antics, not to mention more recently his foray into the American political arena.

But not everyone is aware that he first became famous not as an actor but as a bodybuilder. Between 1966 and 1975 he won the Mr Universe contest five times and Mr Olympia six times. He was and is probably the most well known bodybuilder the sport has ever seen, although Lou Ferrigno of TV's Incredible Hulk fame might disagree with that.

Breaking Through the Plateau

Bodybuilding is a tough sport. Intensive training, day after day, week after week, trying to break the muscles down through weight training exercise in order to build them back again, bigger and stronger. What bodybuilders often find is that after a certain length of time with a particular training routine they reach a plateau. They can't increase the weights they are lifting, and there's no muscle growth any more.

What they do to break out from this plateau, to get further improvements in strength and bulk, is to use shock tactics during their routine. Arnold would have done the same thing. Introduce some different exercises, train at a different time of the day, change the duration or the intensity of training. Literally shock the body out of the routine it has got itself into and into a new growth phase.

Do the Same – Introduce Change

You can apply the same principles. When things aren't going well, don't simply carry on with more of the same in the hope that eventually things might right themselves.

Instead, shock yourself out of *your* routine. Try something different. Study in the morning instead of the afternoon, study for longer or shorter periods, study in a different place, use different study methods. Just introduce change.

You should find that using these shock tactics really will help you break free of the problems that have been holding you back. You'll be able to say "Hasta la vista, baby!" to those sticking points and move on.

Hurdling Stumbling Blocks

You're Stuck

Sooner or later during your studies, you are going to come up against a stumbling block. A part of the syllabus you find particularly difficult to understand. It seems to stand in front of you, blocking your path and therefore your way forward. You are stuck, well and truly.

In these situations, it's easy to get into a tailspin, arcing ever downwards through the sky in a spiral until you hit the ground with a large crash. The feelings of depression and failure increase exponentially until they take over your entire being, sweeping away any rational thinking and your ability to continue studying.

Jump Over and Move On

Often, the best way to deal with these stumbling blocks is simply to jump over them. That's right. Ignore them and move on.

This might seem to be avoiding the issue, but it is not. Jumping over the problem area in this way allows you to continue studying. It reduces tension and stops you floundering around like a netted fish on the deck of a trawler. The human brain has a natural ability to fill in the gaps, so take advantage of this. You can use the information gained from the other side of the problem to help you do this, to fill in the blanks.

Often you will find when coming back to the problem area later on, having initially bypassed it, that suddenly you gain new insight to the problem. The difficulties you experienced previously will simply disappear. Sometimes this is simply because you'd got yourself into a stew the first time around and "couldn't see the wood for the trees", whereas the second time around you are calm and collected. Sometimes it's because your brain is working behind the scenes and has made sense of the problem whilst you've been occupied elsewhere.

Give it a go. You might be pleasantly surprised.

Maintaining Interest in Dull Subjects

Sometimes, the areas you have got to study are just plain boring. There's no escaping it – this will be the case for most people at some stage during their studies. Even the most exciting subjects in the world have their less interesting bits. The problem is, it may well be boring, but it's still examinable. You can't avoid doing the work.

This is when the use of rewards linked to study objectives really comes into its own. You may not enjoy the studying itself (in fact you'll probably hate it) but at least you can have something good to look forward to at the end. Imagine if you didn't allow yourself these rewards – there really would be little motivation to get you to complete the work.

So set yourself a particularly nice reward (maybe three pints of beer instead of the usual one), grit your teeth and get through it. Tell yourself it's a necessary evil to get through on the path to examination success.

Knowing When to Call It a Day

Sometimes, you just aren't going to be in the right frame of mind for study. Perhaps it's been a hard week at the office and you're too tired to concentrate. Perhaps, no matter how long you sit there with a book in front of you, the meaning of the words on the page is just not sinking in. Perhaps you suddenly realise that for the past ten minutes you've been off with the fairies without even realising it!

Whatever the cause, accept that sometimes it just isn't going to happen. You're human, not a machine, and humans are by nature fallible. Don't beat yourself up about it – just stop studying immediately and go and do whatever it is that helps you to feel better, whether it's sleeping, relaxing with some soothing music, taking a bath or whatever.

The beauty of having a cycle of weekly study timetable production, after all, is that you can remain *flexible*. Use this flexibility to your advantage and don't force yourself to work when you're really not up to it. It's not slacking, it's being sensible. Tomorrow is always another day.

Rome Wasn't Built in a Day

We've now pretty much covered everything you need to know to get you started, along with a number of techniques to help you through the tough times.

I think it's worth reiterating though a very important point, and one that's easy to forget in the heat of the moment.

As the saying goes, Rome wasn't built in a day. Nothing big can be completed overnight. This applies to your studies as well. You need to allow yourself a lead-in period before every part of the study process is bedded down, until you are familiar with what's required of you. Having planted the seed, you need to nurture it and let it grow – you're not going to have a fully-grown tree overnight.

> ***"Be not afraid of growing slowly, be afraid only of standing still."***
> **Chinese Proverb**

So stick with it and don't lose heart the first time you encounter difficulties. Gradually, over time, both settling down to study, and doing the actual work, will become second nature to you. Eventually they'll be ingrained habits that you're not even consciously aware of. It will happen. Honest. Stick to the principles contained in this book and you'll get there.

Pack Up Your Troubles...and Smile

There's an old First World War song with a jaunty tune and the immortal line "Pack up your troubles in your old kit-bag and smile, smile, smile". I reckon this line summarises nicely the last point I want to make in this chapter.

Once your study session is over and the books are closed, do not spend time thinking, worrying or obsessing about it. Instead, think of other things to do, go out and enjoy yourself, spend time with your family, throw yourself into whatever leisure pursuits turn you on, whether it's line dancing or playing golf. And enjoy it. Put a smile on your face and keep it there (need I remind you the benefits of smiling?).

> ***"Finish every day and be done with it. You have done what you could. Some blunders and absurdities no doubt crept in; forget them as soon as you can. Tomorrow is a new day; begin it well and serenely and with too high a spirit to be cumbered with your old nonsense."***
>
> **Emerson**

Then, the next time you come back to study, you'll be refreshed, relaxed and more likely to be efficient. Wasting your precious time worrying about something isn't going to make it any better. Pack those troubles away each time you finish your study and only get them back out again the next time you're at the desk.

It'll do your chances of success no end of favours.

Study Time and Place Revisited

Study Time and Place

In Part Four we've looked at Study Time and Place, the second of the factors contained within the Foundations of Success.

Relatively Unimportant?

On the face it, most of what is in this part of the book might seem unimportant when compared to say, the revision process, or how to approach exam questions. After all, can where and when you study really be that important?

The answer is a definite *yes*, it is that important. I wouldn't have included it as one of the Foundations of Success if I didn't think it was. So please give some thought to the practicalities involved in your studies.

- Find a place, or places, to study as near as possible to the "ideal" place.
- Think laterally and consider other places to study for short periods, such as sitting on a bus.
- Don't listen to music whilst you're studying. Unless you want to dilute the effectiveness of your effort.
- Make sure you don't ignore the important of setting up a decent filing system.

Organisation

And when you actually get down to studying, be organised.

- Set yourself objectives, and rewards for meeting those objectives.
- Make sure you've everything you need to hand when you sit down to study.
- Remember to build in breaks.

Hard Times

Recognise too the reality that there will be times when you find it hard to get going, or get stuck and unable to continue. This doesn't mean you're not good enough, it just means you're human. Fight off those feelings of panic and despair. Try some of the techniques contained within the section "Getting Started...Again" in Chapter 11 to help you through these difficult times.

Moving On

In the next part of the book, we'll take a detailed look at Study Tools and Techniques, the fundamentals behind the study process. The "How" to do it, if you like.

Some of what you are about to see will no doubt be expected. How to read a study manual, how to make notes, for example. But do be ready for a surprise or two…!

Part Five

STUDY TOOLS AND TECHNIQUES

A Pragmatic Approach to Study

Get Ready for a Surprise

Finally. We're ready to start the work itself, to get down to some hard graft. Everything is in place and we're ready to go.

But stop – here's some earth shattering news. Wait for it…

No One True Way

There is no one "right" way to study, no one particular method which is the "correct" method to use.

That's right, you've read correctly. You haven't gone completely mad! I *am* telling you that there is no one true path to follow to ensure study success. Whatever other books on study might tell you, this is the truth. Do not be fooled into thinking that by slavishly following a particular technique set out in a book on how to study you're assured of that exam pass.

The reality is, everyone is different. We need to adopt a pragmatic approach to our studies, taking the ideas and methods which seem the most sensible to us and then adapting them to meet our own unique set of characteristics, personality and circumstances. Inevitably, it's a trial and error approach.

The Same Goal But Different Paths

A useful analogy to use to illustrate this point would be the eternally thorny subject of religion. Think about all the different religions there are in the world. Each has their own ideas and beliefs, their own rituals and ceremonies. On the face of it, each is very different from the others.

And yet, ultimately, every one of them has the same underlying goals. To improve the self, to become closer to their own particular god or gods. In reality, there are more points of similarity than there are differences.

Any Path is Valid, As Long As It Leads to the Destination

The same goes for study. The ultimate objective is the same, it's just that the approaches might vary a bit from method to method. There is no one True Way, but each path ends up at the same destination. You need to find the path that's best for you and then stick with it.

So What Now?

Given that there is no one single technique which you can use to study, no one single method which if followed will guarantee exam success, what do you do now? Is it all up to you to decide what might work, and just hope for the best that you get it right?

No. Because although there might not be one true way, nevertheless there is a great deal of common-sense guidance I can give you to help you through the jungle. You need to read the advice I have to offer, and then think about how best to apply it given your own unique situation.

The Two Fundamental Principles

However you finally decide to study, whatever specific ways and methods you use, there are two fundamental principles which should underlie *everything* you do during your studies.

> ***"We soon forget what we have not deeply thought about."***
>
> ***Proust***

Notice that I say they should underpin *everything* you do. I'm not exaggerating here – it's absolutely crucial that you seek to build them into your studies at every possible point. Fail to do so and you're reducing your chances of success.

What are these two fundamental principles?

1. Active Learning
2. Multiple Encoding

Let's look at each in turn.

Active Learning

The Majority Get It Wrong

If you gave 100 people a study manual and then asked them to study it, I guarantee that at least 90 of them would sit down at a convenient desk or table, open the book at page one and simply start reading. And they would carry on reading, page after page, from cover to cover, in a linear fashion, with the more conscientious perhaps making a few notes along the way.

In my experience, this is one of the most common mistakes made by students. And it seems to be based on the belief that by simply sitting down and reading a study text, by being purely passive during the study process, that somehow the ideas and information in the text are going to be understood and retained by the brain. It's as if the student thinks that the mere fact the book is open in front of them is enough for the ideas contained in it to magically be soaked up by their brain cells by some kind of osmosis-like process.

A Mistake That Costs You Valuable Time

But this is a misconception. Such a passive approach will never yield you the best results. Sure, if you sit there for long enough and read the book enough times, you might eventually remember at least some of it, but simply ploughing through the material in this way is without a doubt the most inefficient way there is to study.

And time is not on you side, am I right? You've probably got a full-time job to hold down as well as your studies. You need to work smart, you need to work efficiently.

That's why fundamental principle No.1 is Active Learning. Active being the opposite of passive. Don't just sit back, reading your study text, being passive, letting the whole thing wash over you – do something more. Engage with the material. Grab it by the neck and shake it. Make the learning experience a rich one. Studying actively in this way has been proven to not only improve the results obtained from the study, but also to reduce the amount of time needed to get to the required standard. So you'd be silly to ignore the benefits.

> ***"Knowledge must come through action."***
> ***Sophocles***

Applying the Principle of Active Learning

Of course, the idea of Active Learning is fine in principle, but I'm sure you'll want to know how to translate it into practice. We'll see the principles being applied in more detail when we look at some suggested study methods shortly, but here are some examples for now to give you an idea of the approach.

- Asking yourself questions about how a particular area fits into what you have already learned about a subject as you read the text.
- Drawing diagrams to illustrate points you are reading about to help you visualise the problem more clearly.
- Summarising a section of the material using only key words or a single sentence to identify the key point or issue.
- Scanning chapters before you start detailed reading to get a feel for the subject matter.
- Setting yourself "mini-tests" on what you have read to ensure you remember and understand the material.
- Giving a lecture on the subject you're studying to an imaginary class.
- Recording yourself giving the lecture so you can then play it back to yourself whilst sitting on a train or driving the car.

- Attempting practice questions and exercises whenever they are available.

Multiple Encoding

Brain Facts Recalled

Remember how in the Success Factor chapter we looked at the human brain and how memories were formed? You'll recall how neurons firing together created pathways within the brain, essentially storing the memory for future use.

And we also saw how the brain was split into two parts, the right and left hemispheres, and how each side tended to specialise in certain things, or certain types of activity. For example, the left brain dealt with all things mathematical, language, logical reasoning, sequences and so on, whilst the right brain dealt with colour, rhythm and the whole picture amongst other things.

Using Both Sides of the Brain

Scientists have shown that using both sides of our brain together to process information and store memories, as opposed to just one side only, improves these functions. Put another way, the more areas of the brain used to input data, the stronger the ability to recall it.

> ***"The one who thinks over his experiences most and weaves them into systematic relations with each other will be the one with the best memory."***
> **William James**

This is because the more areas of the brain used to store data, the more neural pathways there are created within the brain structure. Instead of just one pathway, there are multiple pathways. This means that if one pathway fails, the others are still available as a back up and so the memory can still be recalled. Not only this, using multiple pathways strengthens the memory trace, so the memory can be recalled more easily.

Using Multiple Encoding to Create Multiple Pathways

So how do we create these multiple pathways? We use the technique of multiple encoding. This involves using methods which ensure we use both sides and/or multiple areas of the brain simultaneously when studying. For example

- Using both written notes (left brain) and diagrams/pictures (right brain).
- Introducing colour (right brain) to written notes (left brain).
- Trying to engage as many senses as possible during study e.g. reading notes and then speaking them out loud into a voice recorder for later playback.

- Using visualisation and your imagination (right brain) to help remember information.
- Wherever possible, trying to introduce some feeling of emotion into the study process. The more emotionally involved you are with the material, the better you will remember it. This is not always easy, particularly where material is dry or boring, but the more you "get into" or engage with the material, the better.

> ***"Learning without thought is labour lost."***
> **Confucius**

Not Yet Convinced?

If you're not convinced yet by this argument, consider the power of advertising in today's world. Advertisers these days are extremely good at making a visual impact, using a combination of words, images, sounds, striking colours and unusual juxtapositions so that a lasting impression is etched into your mind (sometimes subconsciously!). Often a single viewing of a particularly well put together advert can make enough of an impression for you to remember both the advert and the product. That's powerful stuff.

And given that power, wouldn't it be good for you to use similar tactics when approaching your own studies? There really is more to studying than just making written notes.

A Final Thought...

We'll see more about introducing multiple encoding into your work as we look at some suggested study methods in the next chapter, but for now, let me leave you with this.

It has been suggested that we remember 20 percent of what we read, 30 percent of what we hear, 40 percent of what we see, 50 percent of what we say, 60 percent of what we do and 90 percent of what we read, hear, see, say and do. Are you really so sure that sitting there reading that text book is enough to get you through the exam?

> ***"Tell me, I'll forget. Show me, I may remember. But involve me and I'll understand."***
> **Chinese Proverb**

The Pragmatic Approach to Study

We've already seen that there is no one single "right" way to study. Nevertheless, whilst this is undoubtedly true, the bottom line is that somehow you have got to get to grips with the material. There is no getting away from this fact. You have to read the material, understand it, remember it, and be able to apply it to a range of situations the examiner may use to test whether you are on top of the subject areas contained in the syllabus.

And whilst there may not be any one single "right" way to deal with the material, there most definitely are a number of "wrong" ways, things you need to avoid if you are to minimise the level of effort you need to expend and maximise the benefits gained from study.

For this reason, I'm going to take you through a methodology which, if you apply it to your own situation, should ensure you make the most of the time you spend working. Remember, you don't need to follow my ideas slavishly – use common sense to decide which areas feel right for you and adapt as appropriate. But, as you do so, try to keep in mind the basic principles we're going to see in the next section.

Building Your Study Success From the Ground Up

Imagine for a moment the process of building a house from scratch, from empty building site and bare earth through to finished house. We're going to use this idea to help illustrate and understand the way in which you should be approaching your studies, as strange though it may seem, the principles are the same for both.

Elements of a Successful Build

What type of things might you imagine would be required for a successful house build? You might suggest some of the following.

- The right place/site to build on.
- A set of plans to follow whilst building the house.
- The right building materials.
- A suitable set of tools to carry out the build.
- Use of the correct building techniques.
- Control systems in place to monitor the build against plans.
- Plus a lot of hard work!

We'll see in a moment how these elements are also part of the study process.

Variations in Build Technique and Materials

Of course, not all houses are built exactly the same way, or using the same type of materials. For example, in the UK most new houses are still generally built using a combination of block and brick walls, whereas in the US, houses might more often be built using timber frames and panels. In other countries different techniques might be used, for example the use of adobe in hot dry regions, or bamboo in the Far East.

The important thing is that although different techniques and materials might be used, the end result is the same. A stable, waterproof and long-lasting structure is erected on solid foundations. The structure will have walls, doors, windows and a roof.

Drawing Parallels with the Study Process

This is just like the study process – as has already been noted, there is no one single right way to study. Different techniques can be used in different situations, the choice as to which often being dependent on the preferences of the individual involved. As long as the end result is the same. A solid structure built on solid foundations. That's what you need to aim for when building for your study success.

A House called Study Success

Above we saw some of the elements which might go towards a successful build. Let's now have a look at the building itself.

Figure 13.1

ENVIRONMENT

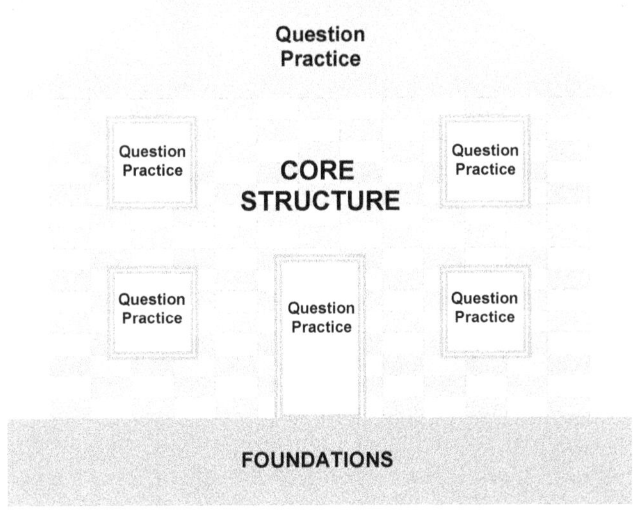

ENVIRONMENT

HOUSEBRICK KEY

Active Learning

Multiple Encoding

From the diagram we can see

Environment

The house sits on a plot of land. Ideally, when building a house, you would want the plot to be in an undisturbed, quiet place, with good natural light and a pleasant environment. This can be likened to the place you study – the requirements are the same. We covered the ideal study environment in Chapter 10.

Foundations

The house is built on solid foundations. These are put in first. No foundations – no stability. The house could collapse at any time.

In the context of study, your foundations are your study timetables. You need to spend the time up front getting these right before you start to study. Start work without any timetable and you're working on constantly shifting ground. There's a strong possibility of failure as the whole thing could collapse around you. So make sure at the base of your studies you have your foundations, or plans, in place. Producing study timetables was covered in chapter 7.

Core Structure

A Strong Core to Build Around

The next thing to be built is the main part of the building, the walls and the roof structure. These are the core parts of the building, around which everything else fits. As such, it is vital to make sure these elements are strong, square and built using the right materials.

At the core of the study process there is the actual studying of the material contained in the exam syllabus. In other words, reading the relevant textbooks, understanding and learning the ideas and information contained within them, and making notes as appropriate. This part of the process is where the real hard work is necessary, and it needs to be done correctly – get it wrong and your core structure won't be sound, in which case you're heading for disaster.

Building in the Fundamental Principles

Notice that I've shown the core of the building made up of two types of brick. One is Active Learning, the other Multiple Encoding. Thus the two fundamental principles we've already seen are built into the very fabric of the building, in the same way you need to build them into every part of your studies.

Question Practice

An Integral Part of the Process

The doors and windows, along with the tiles on the roof of the building represent question practice. Notice how the spaces for the doors and windows have to be built in during the core build itself, almost from day one, and continue to be built in as the walls go up and the roof is added. You don't come back later having built solid walls and then try to cut holes in to fit your doors and windows! (This might be possible, but it will waste you a lot of valuable time.)

Starting From Day One, Not an Afterthought

In the same way, you need to build question practice into your studies almost from day one. Yes, that's right, you've read it correctly. Question practice should *not* just be part of the revision process – if you've not attempted any questions or practice exercises by the time you get to the start of your revision period, it's probably going to be too late. Question practice throughout your studies is *crucial* in ensuring you understand and can apply the concepts you have read about. You need to build it into your study process *now* – it is an integral part of the build, as important as putting up the walls.

Ignore It and Fail

And without windows, doors and tiles on the roof, you can't make the structure watertight. If that's the case, you can't do any of the work needed on the inside, from first fix work such as fitting the electrics through to finishing touches such as decorating the walls. In the same way, if you don't get this part of your studies right, pulling it all together during the revision period and putting it into practice in the exam hall itself is just not going to be possible. The probability of failure will be high. The building will crumble and collapse.

Structural Elements

Ok, so we've now seen the structural elements involved in building a house, and we've drawn the parallels between this and your studies.

Both "Environment" and "Foundations" have already been dealt with at length in the earlier chapters noted. That leaves use with the two remaining structural elements

- Core Structure
- Question Practice

In Chapter 14, we will look at the techniques involved in building the core structure. Question practice will be covered in more detail in Chapter 15.

The Five-step Active Study Technique

Using FAST for Your Core Build

We already know from the section on Active Learning in the previous chapter that simply sitting down with your study text and reading it from cover to cover is not the best approach to use. So, if you shouldn't do this, what should you do?

Follow the Five-step Active Study Technique (or FAST for short), that's what! A technique which is based on sound psychological research and has been used by countless numbers of successful students. In many ways, it's just the application of common sense, so there's nothing fundamentally difficult about it. Let's see what it's all about.

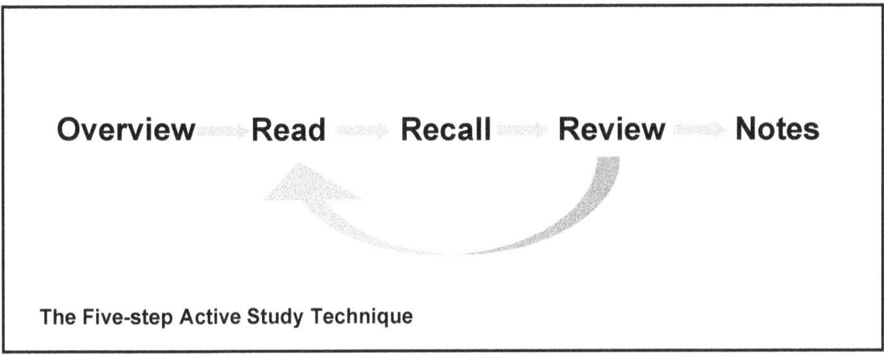

The Five-step Active Study Technique

As the name kind of implies, and the diagram demonstrates, FAST involves five discrete but linked steps. We shall look at each one of these in turn now.

Step 1 – Overview

What is the Objective?

You're at your desk, with the relevant study manual or material in front of you. The first thing to do is *not* start reading page one in detail, but to take a step back and look at the thing in overview mode. What you are trying to do here is to get a feel for the area you're about to study as a whole, without any attempt to look at the detail. If you like, you're going to take a helicopter's view of the landscape whilst hovering above it. In this way, you can get the general drift of the material first.

Why Do It?

Gaining an overview of the problem helps to appreciate its scope, and gives you an idea of how the material is structured. Identifying the key themes of the material gives you a structure, or a set of hooks, on which to hang the ideas you then look at in detail. You can then understand the context within which a particular idea or area fits.

A useful parallel to draw is with completing a jigsaw. How would you approach such a task? Would you simply start picking pieces of the puzzle out of the box and attempt to find two that fitted together? This might work fine for a small child's puzzle with only a few pieces, but for a complex multi-piece adult-sized jigsaw you would probably still be there trying to finish the puzzle come the end of the world!

Instead, you're far more likely to

- Look at the complete picture shown on the front of the jigsaw box.
- Find the pieces of the puzzle with one or more straight edges so that you can build the jigsaw's border first.
- Gradually work your way into the puzzle from specific areas of the border using colour, pattern, shape and the finished picture on the box to guide your work.

The same goes for your studies – at the overview stage you're simply looking at the overall picture, getting a feel for what it contains and what the major subject matter is. This overview process happens *before* you then go on to look at, and work on, the detail.

How to Do It

- Take a look at the contents section for the chapter you're about to study. Notice the hierarchy of headings and sub-headings, and see whether it's possible to identify what the major issues covered are.
- Where a book has them, look at the learning objectives quoted at the start of the chapter, and the chapter summary noted at the end. These will give you a very good indication of the main themes covered in the chapter.
- Flip casually through the chapter, noticing its organisation and structure, things such as headings, charts, diagrams, the general look and feel of the material. You should be able to gain some sense of the relationships between the main ideas contained in the chapter by the time you've done this.
- Having carried out this overview, write down the questions that occur to you as a result of carrying out this initial survey. These will be questions that you might expect answers to when you read the text more carefully. For example, "how does this fit in with what I have already learned?", "what can I do with this information?", and "what types of question might the examiner set on this area?". The idea here

> ***"The important thing is not to stop questioning."***
> **Albert Einstein**

is that by asking yourself these questions up front about the material, you are then able to *read with a purpose*, instead of just trawling through the text word by word with no sense of where you're headed or what the important points you need answers to are.

Step 2 – Read

What is the Objective?

Having taken the helicopter view of the material, now is the time to read it properly at length. The objective should be to read "questioningly" so that by the end of the process you understand all of the main themes of the material and the relationships between them.

Why Do It?

There is no other way to understand and learn the material, unless you are attending lectures, when you have the added benefit of seeing it presented to you both audibly and visually. (Making the most of lectures will be dealt with later in Chapter 15.) This is the hard truth. You've got to do the reading.

> ***"Reading is to the mind what exercise is to the body."***
> **Sir Richard Steele**

But using the correct method of reading, as opposed to just reading without a purpose, will make sure you use your time efficiently and get the most out of your hard work.

How to Do It

You might find the idea of having to be told how to read a little odd. After all, surely it's just the same as you were taught at school – there can't be any more to it than that, can there?

In fact, there is. Let's see what's involved.

Read Smart – Read Actively

We come back to the idea of active versus passive learning again here. There is a big difference between passive reading and active reading, with a commensurate difference in results.

> ***"Reading without purpose is sauntering not exercise."***
> **Edward G. Bulwer-Lytton**

A two-stage approach using active reading techniques will yield the best results.

Stage 1 – Skim Level Read

Generally, written English is structured in such a way that each paragraph holds an idea. The first sentence of each paragraph states and explains the idea, whilst the last sentence often picks up the idea in the first sentence and shows how the rest of the paragraph has developed it. Reading the first and last sentence of a paragraph therefore can be a good way of skim reading.

Taking into account that generally the first and last paragraphs of a specific section or chapter normally act in the same way (i.e. state a theme or idea, and then show how the section or chapter has developed it), an ideal skim reading method presents itself.

- Read carefully the first paragraph or two of the chapter and each section.
- Read the first sentence or two of each paragraph within each section.
- Read carefully the last paragraph or two of each section and of the chapter.

This first stage skim read will give a sense of what the chapter is about, showing you the topics in more detail than you'd gathered during the overview stage. As you carry out this process, try to interact with the material in a positive way. For example, practice second-guessing – try to anticipate what's coming next. Also, try to fit what you learn into what you already know. As with the overview stage, the aim here is to come up with questions for which you need to find answers.

Stage 2 is where you look at the detail and arguments contained in the text in order to find those answers.

Stage 2 – Deep Level Read

You now need to reread the chapter from the beginning, in detail this time, sentence by sentence, word by word. But again, you need use an active approach to your reading. Don't just plough through the material unquestioningly, accepting everything you read at face value and making no attempt to understand how the various ideas contained within the chapter dovetail together.

Here are some pointers in helping you achieve this active approach.

Finding Meaning

When reading, ask yourself "What's the main idea here?". There will be ideas at all levels, from the overall chapter, to sections, to paragraphs and even sentences. You need to tease these out from the text.

> ***"Accumulate learning by study, understand what you learn by questioning."***
> **Mingjiao**

Sometimes it is difficult to pick out the main idea because you are not looking for it – instead you are too busy trying to memorise the *surface details* and not looking beyond these to understand the *meaning*. Make sure you're not trying to remember every last fact at this stage. You need to understand the meaning first so you can put the facts in context. Don't try to put the cart before the horse.

Of help in finding meaning will be finding answers to the questions that you came up with when you carried out your overview and skim read. And from these answers, other questions may arise, which you should again try to find answers to. Again, it's all about reading actively, interacting *with* the material instead of just passively letting it wash over your consciousness.

Using Signposts

To help you pick out the important details and ideas, look for signposts within the material which will help you identify them. For example, visual ones such the use of italics, underlining, capitals, bold text, bullets, boxed text, colour, diagrams and tables, and verbal ones, such as the use of words like "therefore", "furthermore", "for instance" etc.

Highlighting Text

Highlighting or underlining key parts of the text is an extremely valuable way of

- Focussing your attention on the text.
- Making you think about what the key ideas and concepts are.
- Leaving a visual record of the sense you have made of the text, allowing you to return to it more quickly at a later time, and also gaining some sense of motivation as you can clearly see what you have already covered.

Annotating the text, perhaps in the margins, with questions that come to mind as you read, increases the benefit of this approach still further.

Ideally, use different colour highlighters for different kinds of information being read e.g. one colour for reference dates and names, another for key words or concepts etc. This helps harness the power of the right brain in a way that simple underlining cannot.

When the Study Material is in Electronic Form

These days, study texts can come in electronic form (i.e. they exist as a computer file to be read on an electronic device such as a laptop, smartphone or e-book reader) and so you may not have a paper "hard" copy in front of you. Some electronic document formats will allow you to annotate or amend the file you have on your screen, and if that is the case, use a similar approach to the one outlined above, i.e. use the highlight and underline options to mark key parts of the text, and then save the changes you have made.

If however it is not possible to mark the document, which is unfortunately the case with some electronic formats currently in use, then I recommend you print the document onto paper and use that as your primary document. This may seem like a backward step; after all, surely using technology is all about removing the need for paper! However, in your case it is not. You need to find some way of ensuring you can quickly identify the salient points from the text you are studying, both to help understand the information now when you are initially studying it and later, when you come back to review what you have learned. If you have to trawl through the entire document again because you have not been able to annotate it, then you are going to waste your time.

Sometimes, technology is not so much an enabler as a disabler, and the inability to annotate your electronic study text would definitely be classed as the latter. So print out the material onto paper and work in the old-fashioned, time-honoured but well-proven way. Change isn't always progress!

Charting the Main Ideas

Another mistake commonly made by students at this stage of the study process is attempting to produce detailed notes. Partly I think this is due to the fact that no one is ever taught how to study correctly when still at school or college. Somehow, in the mind of the student, reading and making notes are inextricably linked. To sit and read a textbook without making notes makes them feel that in some way they are slacking. The action of writing notes is an almost Pavlovian response to opening the textbook.

So I repeat – **do not make detailed notes at this stage**. There – I can't make it any plainer!

That's not to say you shouldn't be putting anything down on paper though. Whilst you are carrying out your detailed reading, you can be jotting down key words and ideas. And an ideal technique to employ is to attempt to chart the main ideas diagrammatically. Not only does this necessitate you asking yourself questions to understand how the subject fits together, making sure you're actively engaging with the material, but also this introduces the power of the right side of your brain, which excels at shape, form, and seeing the whole picture.

A very simple example of a diagram setting out the main thrust of an idea is the one in at the beginning of the chapter illustrating FAST. Five key words, their order, and the relationship between them are all demonstrated effectively by a very simple diagram. It is this high level overview of the key concepts that you should be aiming at when producing these diagrams. Find yourself writing paragraphs of notes and you can be sure you've gone too far and into too much detail.

A Word on Speed Reading

> ***"I took a speed reading course, learning to read straight down the middle of the page, and I was able to go through War and Peace in 20 minutes. It's about Russia."***
> **Woody Allen**

Many how-to-study books will have you understand that speed reading (the skill of being able to skim-read large amounts of text at high speed) is an ideal technique to employ whilst studying. The idea is that the quicker you can read the book, the more effective your study time is. Some of these books will even suggest that you practice your speed reading techniques on the daily broadsheet newspapers, gradually building up the amount of print you can skim in a given time.

In my view, the idea that speed-reading could be of help in your studies is a triumph of wishful thinking over reality. The quote above from Woody Allen just about sums the whole thing up nicely – sure, you'll be able to get through the textbook in next to no time, but you'll have gained almost nothing from it. Reading is not a race against time – far better to fully understand one chapter completely than to half understand two.

> ***"When we read too fast or too slowly, we understand nothing."***
> **Pascal**

And particularly for subjects of a scientific or mathematical nature, where much of the content is not just written English, but instead complex mathematical formulae, equations and so on, trying to speed read is sheer lunacy. For these types of subjects there is simply no substitute for focussing on the detail.

Steps 3 and 4 – Recall and Review

What is the Objective?

The main aim of these steps, which are inextricably linked, is to find out just how much of the material you remember correctly having carried out Steps One and Two.

Why Do It?

You've now read the text in detail. It may have made perfect sense to you (if you're lucky!). You might think you understand it. The problem is, what you *think* you know or understand compared to what you *actually remember* are usually two very different things. Put simply

Understanding ***is not equal to*** **Recall (Memory)**

We've seen this before in Chapter 6. Just because you believe you understand something when you read it in your textbook doesn't necessarily mean you'll be able to recall it properly the next day, or indeed that you have understood it correctly.

So we need to find out (a) what you remember, and (b) whether it is correct.

How to Do It

Ignore the Advice Given Elsewhere

Again, I take exception with a number of how-to-study books here. Many will suggest that at this stage you write detailed notes without referring back to the study text, and then compare these notes to the material to find out what you have missed. Having done this, you should then rewrite your notes as appropriate.

In principle, this theory is fine, as you do need to find out what, and how much, you remember, and you cannot do this by producing notes directly from the text open in front of you. But spending time writing notes, only then to find that they need to be rewritten to include something you have missed, or something you got wrong, is a waste of time you simply cannot afford.

The Suggested Approach

So, we need to find out what you remember from your reading, and whether it is right, as quickly as possible. I'd suggest the following approach.

- Once you have finished your detailed reading of the text, close the book up and place out of view any diagrams or jottings of key words you have made.
- Try to **Recall** (Step 3) the main points of the section you've just studied. Produce a rough diagram or chart showing these points, using key words, concepts and ideas only. Note down any other facts you recall which are linked to these key ideas, again, in summary form only. DO NOT WRITE FULL SENTENCES AND PARAGRAPHS.
- Once you're satisfied you've got everything down on paper you can remember, return to your study materials and **Review** (Step 4) what you've just written against the text itself. Note the areas you missed completely, and those where your understanding was either partial or

incorrect. Be honest with yourself here – if you tell yourself you've done better than you really have, the only person you're fooling is yourself.

- Having identified your weak areas, you now need to return to Step 2 and revisit these areas. Hence the looped arrow shown on the diagram illustrating FAST. Go back and read again the areas that you need to work on. Then, once you're happy with them, carry out the recall and review process again to check whether you now understand and remember everything correctly.
- Repeat the loop Step 2→Step 3→Step 4→Step 2 etc. as many times as you need so that not only do you *understand* the material, you can *remember* it. This is such an important point it cannot be overemphasised. Understanding is NOT the same thing as recall – and it's recall you're going to ultimately need to pass your exam.

How Much Time Should I Spend On Recall and Review?

You should expect to spend a considerable amount of your study time in the recall and review process. Clearly, exactly how much depends on the subject, its level of difficulty and your own strengths and weaknesses, but an estimate of 50 percent of total study time would not be an overstatement.

This may sound like a lot – but it will be time well spent. Make sure you use your time wisely and don't skip over these recall and review steps.

> ***"An education isn't about how much you have committed to memory, or even how much you know. It's being able to differentiate between what you do know and what you don't."***
> **Anatole France**

Step 5 – Notes

What is the Objective?

By the time you have finished with this step, you should have in your possession a set of notes covering the material you have studied. You will have produced these notes by incorporating the guidance set out below. The notes will be comprehensive yet concise, and presented in such a way as to take advantage of your brain's full potential.

Why Do It?

Notes = Better Results

Ultimately, there is no alternative to written notes. It's as simple as that. Research has shown that those students who produce written notes (and I'm including diagrams and pictorial notes in here too, not just the written word) as part of their study process invariably do better in their exams than those students who have not. This alone should be a good enough reason for you making sure you incorporate notes production into your timetable.

> ***"I can't believe it! Reading and writing actually paid off."***
> **Homer Simpson**

But if we were to go deeper into this and ask *why* does making notes give you this advantage, we would see that there are a number of benefits that come from making notes.

Active Not Passive

Making notes is an *active* process. It tests your comprehension and recall, it highlights gaps in your knowledge, and it focuses your attention. You have to think in order to reorganise the concepts and ideas you have been presented with into your own words. You get none of these benefits from simply reading the material.

Facilitates Review

The notes can be used for the ongoing *review* process you should be undertaking. Remember we saw how repetition and review were essential for recall to be maximised? Well, when you're revisiting material you've already studied as part of your ongoing study program, do you want to have to go back to the original study book every time, or would you rather use a set of summary notes? I rather think you'd choose the latter.

Fundamental During Revision

Summary notes are essential for the *revision* process. By the time you get to your revision period, under no circumstances should you still be working from the textbooks. You simply don't have enough time. Summary notes, on the other hand, will be ideal.

Shows Progress

Another psychological benefit of making notes is that they are *a symbol of your progress*. Never underestimate the importance of self-confidence. Having a written set of notes in front of you covering all you have studied to date gives you a sense of achievement about how far you have come during your studies. You can feel good about yourself and give yourself a pat on the back. This will all help when it comes to facing the ultimate test – the exam.

How to Do It

Get It Right or Don't Bother Trying

Making notes may indeed be an essential activity, with all the resultant benefits we've just seen above, but there's a big "but" here. And it is this. Making notes is entirely necessary, *but* get them wrong, or use the wrong approach, and you'll not only be wasting your time, you'll learn little from them.

The sad truth is that, although a large proportion of students spend many long hours producing detailed notes, they don't then make much use of these notes after this. Often, they never even read the notes they've written again!

There may be a number of reasons for this. Perhaps they simply can't find them (of course, you're not going to suffer this fate are you, as you've already set up a system of filing for your study notes!), perhaps they can't read them, perhaps whilst they seemed to make perfect sense at the time they don't when they come to review them. All of these reasons are the result of using the wrong approach to making notes.

> ***"Our life is frittered away by detail. Simplify, simplify."***
> **Henry Thoreau**

The essence of effective note taking is *selectivity*. It's always best to err on side of taking too few notes rather than too many. Overly detailed notes really aren't a good idea – here are some reasons why.

- They take too long to write.
- They take too long to read.
- They tend to have more information in them than you need.
- They tend to be repetitive.
- Not much thought goes into writing them, so little is learned.
- Finding something specific in the notes can take a long time.
- They will need to be rewritten to be useful during the revision phase.

So, writing notes that you then never look at again really is a complete waste of your time, time that you can ill afford. In which case, let's make sure you get it right.

Characteristics of "Good" Notes

What else can we say about the characteristics of the ideal set of notes, other than that they shouldn't be simply copied verbatim from the study text?

They should be easy to review

You need to be able to carry out a quick review, without having to wade through masses of material to find what you're looking for. The key words, phrases and issues of the subject therefore need to be distilled down to their essence. Also, you need to make sure what you produce is legible. (An obvious point, but one often missed by students. Be honest – how many times have you scribbled down notes only to later find you cannot read your own writing!).

They need to be flexible

They need to be kept in a way that makes it possible to amend or change parts of them as your studies progress. Pages upon pages of closely set text in long paragraphs are not likely to afford you this luxury, which is another reason for not producing notes in this style. Instead, you need to introduce the concept of *space* to your notes.

They need to take account of the way the brain works

We've encountered this idea on a number of occasions already. Making the most of the brain means using both sides of it to maximise results. Thus notes taken purely in linear form using the written word might not be the best approach as this only uses the left side of the brain – the language based, logical side of the brain. Introducing colour, shape, images and patterns to your notes will help you use the full range of the brain's capacities.

Note Making Methods

In very simple terms, there are three styles of notes which can be produced.

Method 1 – Summary using straight prose

Using this method, a summary of the key points and ideas is written in prose i.e. using a normal sentence and paragraph structure. Figure 14.1 gives an example of this.

The main advantage of using this approach is that it encourages having to think about what to write and how to write it. Having to focus attention in this way boosts learning and later recall of the material.

However, there are disadvantages. Firstly, and perhaps the biggest disadvantage, because the notes end up being word-dense (just look at the amount of black text on the example page), it's very difficult to pick up the essential points locked up in the text. To find out all of the pertinent points, you have to read the entire page of text.

Secondly, by their very nature, written notes are linear. One idea follows the other, in a logical order. Because of this, it's more difficult to understand the inter-relationships between the ideas without detailed reading and thought. This is a disadvantage of all written notes.

Method 2 – Outline notes

In this method, instead of full sentences being used, a skeleton structure is produced, showing the hierarchy of ideas dealt with by the material. Full sentences are replaced by key words and highly summarised notes. Figure 14.2 illustrates this method.

Again, one of the advantages of outline notes is in the thought processes required to decide what to actually put into the notes themselves. The necessity of having to understand the material before one can decide how to distil it down to its very essence is an active process, with all the attendant benefits. The big advantage over the summary straight prose method shown above is that this time there are no full sentences and paragraphs to have to plough through when trying to review the salient points, just a list of ideas and key concepts.

This isn't perfect however, because it doesn't allow for additional information to be added, so important details can be missed. Not only that, but once again the form is linear, meaning the inter-relationships between concepts and ideas are not easy to spot.

Method 3 – Patterned notes

Whereas the first two note forms by their very nature present information in a linear form, patterned notes are different. They introduce the idea of using diagrams to represent the ideas contained in a section of text, and the relationships between them, in a non-linear way.

> ***"A picture speaks more than a thousand words."***
> **Confucius**

Although a number of different titles are used to describe the diagrams created when using this type of approach, such as

- ♦ Patterned notes
- ♦ Spider diagrams
- ♦ Spray diagrams, and
- ♦ Mind Maps

in reality they are largely the same thing. They all use the concept of displaying a subject and its ideas pictorially or diagrammatically. Mind Maps merely introduce the idea of using images and colour on the diagram to enhance the use of the brain's right hemisphere. An example of patterned notes is shown in Figure 14.3.

Using patterned notes has some major benefits.

- ♦ They allow relationships between key ideas to be seen easily.
- ♦ They show the big picture on one page.
- ♦ They stop the mind being cluttered with detail.
- ♦ They are easier to revise from.
- ♦ They are inherently flexible (it is possible to add to the diagram relatively easily).
- ♦ They harness the power of the right brain in a way written notes never can. This means that memory is strengthened through the use of additional pathways in the brain.

Clearly there are a number of advantages in using this approach to produce study notes. However, it's not without its disadvantages, the main one being that the level of detail is by necessity low. Where detail is important, these diagrams are never going to be enough on their own.

The other potential disadvantage is that some people simply do not get on with these diagrammatic techniques at all. This is most likely for those who are predominantly left brain thinkers and who have been taught at school or college to produce notes in the traditional manner, that is, using the first two methods above. The time required to master these new patterned note techniques may simply be too much of a drain on resources to make it worthwhile given the time constraints you may be under.

Figure 14.1

STUDY TIME AND PLACE

It is important to consider the practicalities involved in the study process before starting the process itself – commencing your studies without giving any thought to the practicalities could lead to disaster. One analogy to illustrate this would be starting a long journey traveling to a distant place without having first packed your bags and got all your travel documents in order.

The decision on where to study is an important one. Having the ideal place in which to study can make the difference between pass and fail. The ideal study environment should have the following characteristics –

a) It should be quiet – for example, the TV should not be on
b) It should be free from interruptions
c) It should be well lit – a bright but diffuse light is best
d) It should be warm (but not too warm)
e) It should be ergonomic and comfortable – both chair and table should allow you to adopt the ideal working position

It is not necessary to have only one place to study. Consider where else one can study – e.g. bus, train, at work during breaks, at the library, at your parent's house.

Having decided on your study place(s), don't focus on anything that's still wrong with the surroundings. Do the best you can to make things ideal, but then accept the imperfections and get studying.

Despite what students are often heard to claim, listening to music whilst studying does not help your studies. Research has shown that it divides your attention and means neurons in your brain which could be helping you study are instead being used to monitor the music. Instead, use music as a reward to listen to after you've finished studying.

The time of day can have an effect on your studies. Study when you feel you're at your best e.g. if you're not a 'morning person' don't try to study first thing after getting out of bed.

Administration can't be ignored either.

a) A filing system needs to be set up – the underlying principle is that one should be able to find notes on a specific subject without delay.
   - Make sure the notes are kept in a safe and secure place
   - Use ring binders to allow re-ordering of notes
   - Number pages in case notes are dropped
   - Separate each subject and subject area
   - Consider colour coding notes
b) Review and update the study timetable weekly
c) A learning journal can be kept time permitting

Figure 14.2

STUDY TIME AND PLACE

A. Important – consider study practicalities BEFORE starting studies

B. Ideal study environment – the difference between pass and fail.

Characteristics –

a) Quiet
b) Free from interruptions
c) Well lit
d) Warm
e) Comfortable/ergonomic

C. Study place – one place or many. E.g. bus, train, library, work, parents' house

D. Ignore imperfections in study place

E. No music whilst studying – diverts attention and brain cells away from task

F. Time of day – study when you feel best

G. Don't ignore administration.

a) Filing system
   Safe & secure
   Use ring-binders
   Number pages
   Separate subject/area
   Colour code
b) Regular review/update of study timetable
c) Keep learning journal only if time

Figure 14.3

Study Time and Place
Administration
Regular review/update of timetable
Filing
Safe and secure
Ring binders
Number pages
Separate subject/area
Colour code
Learning journal
Only if time
Consider before study
Ideal Study Environment
Characteristics
Quiet
Interruption free
Well lit
Warm
Comfort/Ergonomics
One Place or Many
Bus
Train
Work
Library
Parents
No Music
Diverts
Attention
Neurons
Time of Day
Work to best time

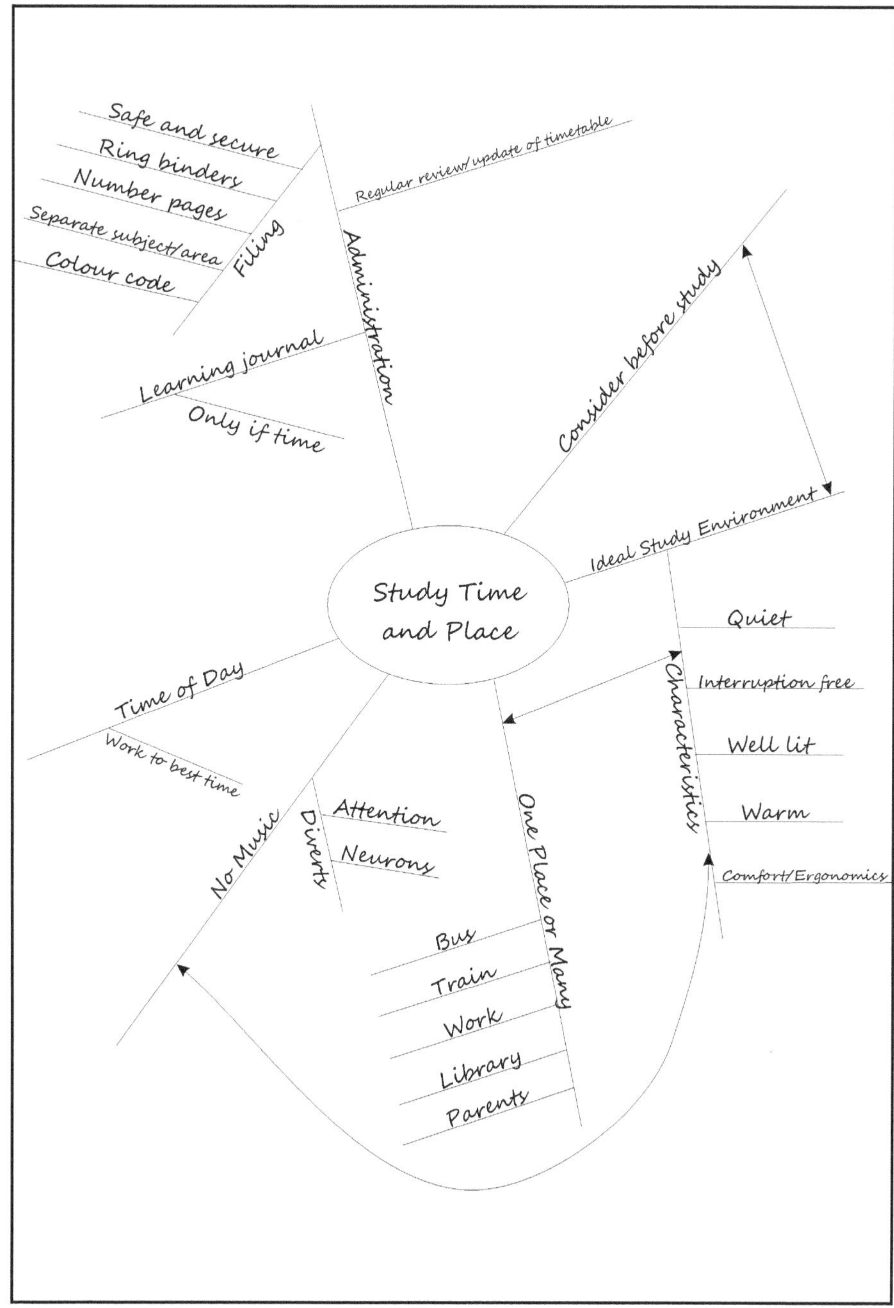

Which One Should I Use?

The simplest answer to this question is "all of them".

There is no "right" or "wrong" approach to use when making notes. Each method has its own unique advantages and disadvantages, and each is the best method given a particular set of circumstances. Sometimes a spider diagram will contain all the information you need to record and remember, sometimes only written notes will do.

Add to this the reality that each person will, as a rule, feel an affinity for one style more than another, and you've got the reasons for my "all of them" answer. As with your studies as a whole, you need to adopt a flexible and pragmatic approach.

What this means in practice is that a *combination* of these three methods is most likely to yield you the best results.

The Combination Method

This method comes with the usual health warning – don't just slavishly follow the techniques described and expect it to fit the way you work. Read the principles, try them out, and adapt them if necessary to best suit your mindset. But do remember to steer well clear of overly detailed notes and make sure the notes you produce do fit the characteristics of "good" notes shown above.

Step 1 – "Brainstorm" the Subject

As part of your initial reading of the study text, you will have already made some initial jottings of key ideas and concepts in your attempt to understand how the material and the ideas contained within it fit together. (See Charting the Main Ideas in Step 2 – Reading.) However, at this stage these will likely only be rough notes.

Reflect further on these notes and the subject material you have just studied. Write down any other ideas, concepts or information you feel is important to record in your final set of notes. Continue to use rough notes only for now, and don't worry about the logical order of ideas or using the rules of English grammar. At this stage you're just making sure you've got everything down that needs to be incorporated into your finished notes, no more.

See figure 14.4 for an example of the type of notes you might end up with.

Step 2 – Capture the Big Picture

You now need to produce a global "big picture" in your mind and on paper which encompasses in a high-level way what the subject is about. This is where the use of patterned notes comes in. In essence, produce a diagram which pulls together all the subject's key ideas you've noted, and draw the connections between them. (An "ideas map", if you like.) You may need several iterations to get this diagram completely right.

Wherever possible, consider introducing colour and images to the diagram. This will help fix the image in your mind's eye so it is available to you during later studies, revision and the exam itself. The more unique and eye-catching the diagram, the easier it will be to remember.

Figure 14.5 shows how the big picture might look for the rough notes produced in figure 14.4.

Step 3 – Write the Story

Unless you're a predominantly right-brained person, producing the big picture in the form of a diagram may help you understand the main ideas and the relationships between them, but it's probably not going to be enough to fix the detail you need to remember into your memory. This is why producing some form of written notes is a necessity.

In practice, you should be aiming to produce notes at a level of detail somewhere between summary prose level (method 1 shown under Note Making Methods above) and outline level (method 2 from the same section above). This will give you the best of both worlds – an idea of the hierarchical structure of the material but with some additional detail where required. Figure 14.6 illustrates how these notes might look.

Here are some important points to remember when producing your written notes.

- Think before you write.
- Keep notes brief.
- Use your own words – do not copy directly from the text.
- Leave plenty of white space throughout the text (this makes your notes easier to review, and easier to add to or amend where necessary).
- Use key words, abbreviations, and phrases.
- Break the text up into manageable parts using headings and sub-headings.
- To maintain the maximum "readability", use lists, numbered/lettered points, capitals, bold text, underlining and the like to help presentation.
- Remember to include diagrams and drawings wherever relevant. Use whatever is best in the circumstances e.g. flow charts, decision trees, bar charts etc.
- Even with all the planning in the world, sometimes you may still end up with messy notes. When this happens, to save having to rewrite your notes, draw coloured boxes around sections of the text to make them stand out, draw a ring round linked sections of text to pull them together, and colour code text to categorise it or link it.

Figure 14.4

Brain – most complex object in universe
Av weight 3lbs
1 – 3% of bodyweight
uses
15-20% of body's blood
oxygen
Fuel
Size – small ≠ less intelligence
Einstein
Structure
Two Sides
Left
Right
Corpus
callosum
200m nerve
fibres
Langauge
Maths
Logic
Analysis
Colour
Dimension – spatial
abilities
Rhythm/Music
Imagination
Q – anything else?
Check text
not as clear cut in reality
→ question of degree
Learning – predominantly left sided – but use RH to enhance

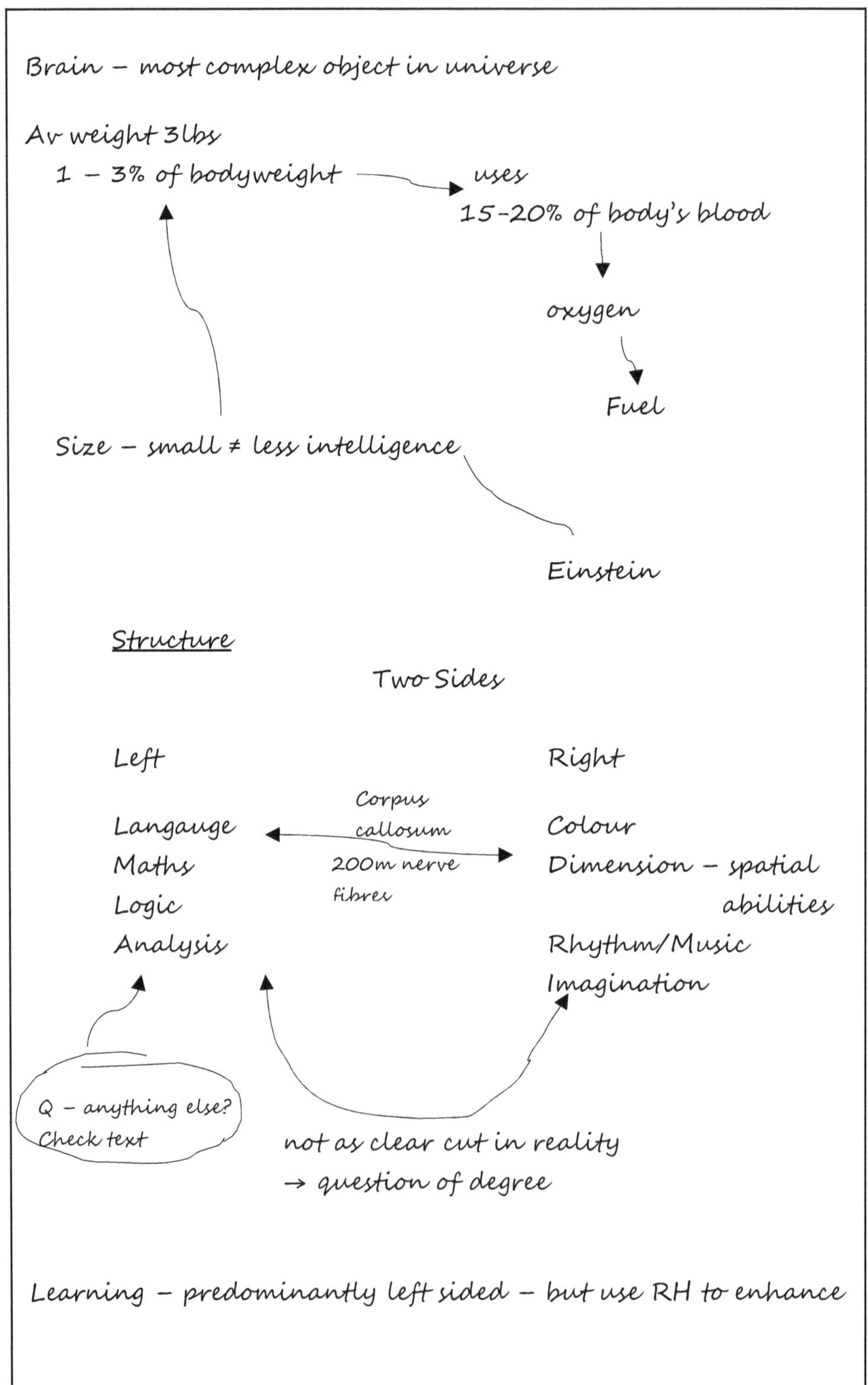

Figure 14.5

3 lbs
= 1-3% of bodyweight
BUT
Uses 1-20% of blood
i.e. very important
SIZE
small ≠ less intelligence
Einstein –
'average' sized
brain
BRAIN
STRUCTURE
LEARNING
Traditionally –
L
To enhance
L + R
Two hemispheres
L
R
Corpus callosum
200m nerve fibres
Language
Maths
Logic
Analysis
Linearity
Sequence
Rhythm
Imagination
Colour
Music
Dimension
Spatial abilities
Overlap – no real clear cut
distinction of function in reality

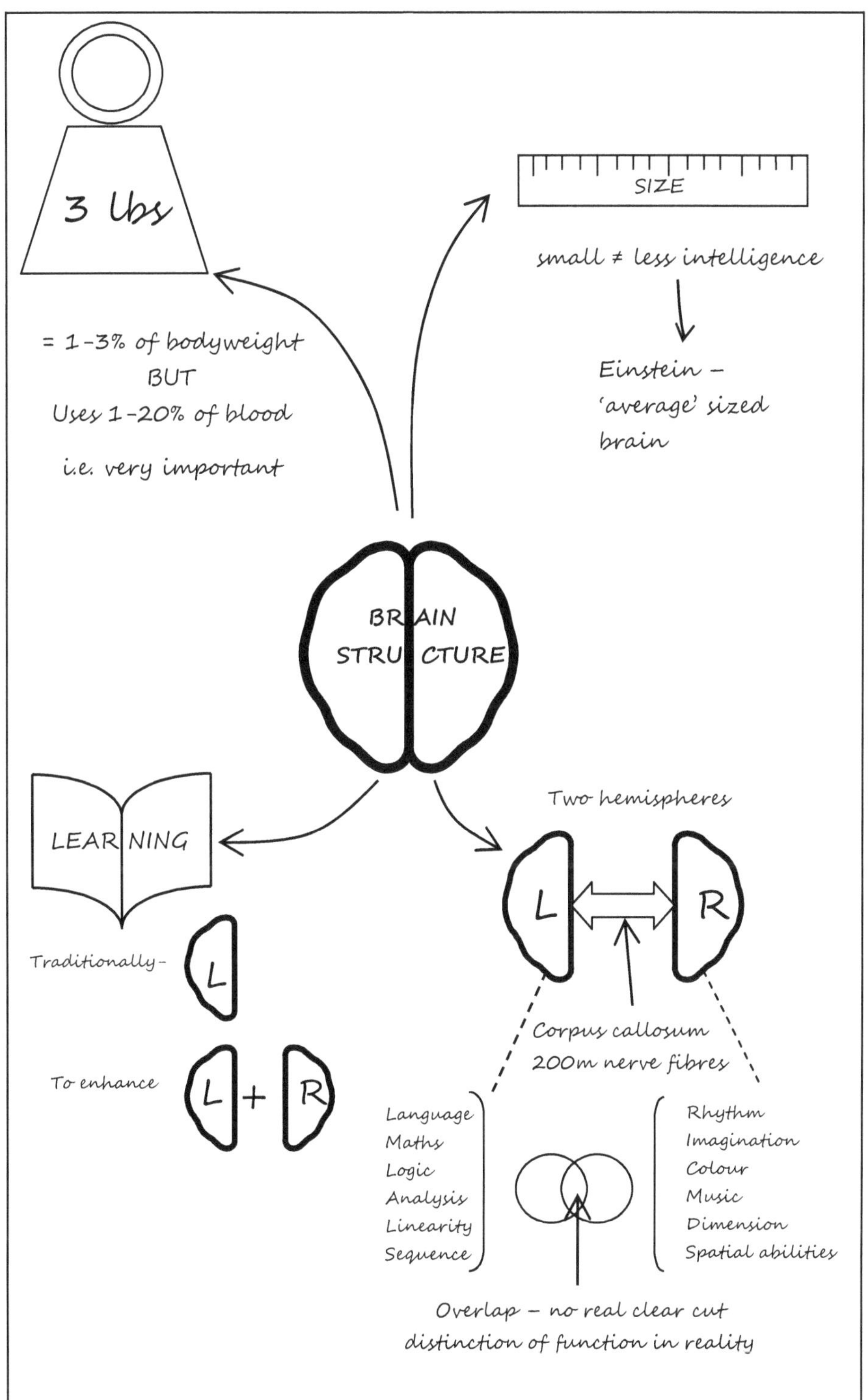

Figure 14.6

Brain Facts

A Complexity

The <u>most complex</u> structure in the known universe

B Weight

(a) The average human brain is <u>3lbs</u> or 1.4kg.

(b) Although accounting for only 1 to 3% of bodyweight, the brain <u>uses 15 to 20% of the body's blood supply</u>. (Blood=oxygen=fuel for the brain's cells)

C Size

The level of intelligence of a person is not related to their brain size. Small does not equal stupid. E.g Einstein's brain was only around average size

D Structure

(a) In simple terms, the brain is made up of <u>two hemispheres, left and right</u>.

(b) These hemispheres are connected by the <u>corpus callosum</u> – a bundle of 200m nerve fibres

(c) Research on epileptic patients has shown certain brain functions are located in particular hemisphere

(i) Left brain specialistions include

Languagem w3222
Maths
Logic
Analysis
Linearity
Sequence

(ii) Right brain specializations include

Spatial abilities
Rhythm
Dimension
Colour
Music
Imagination

(d) Left/right brain distinctions an oversimplification in reality. Work is spread across hemispheres. More a question of which hemisphere is dominant for a particular function i.e. a question of degree and not absolute distinction.

E Learning

Traditional academic learning heavily based on left sided skills. Introducing right brain skills → enhanced learning → greater success

FAST Reviewed

We've now seen the core Five-step Active Study Technique (FAST) in its entirety. Let's just get our bearings and recap before we move on.

The Five Steps

FAST is made up of the five steps shown in the diagram.

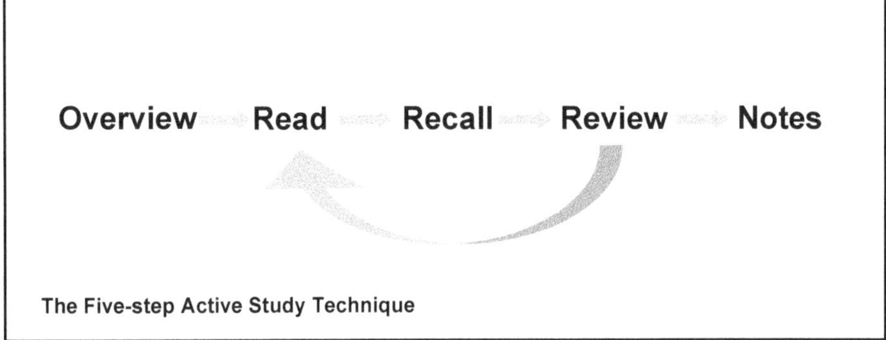

The Five-step Active Study Technique

Active Learning and Multiple Encoding

Each step is undertaken adopting an active mindset, as opposed to a passive one. That's what the A in FAST stands for. We've seen the detail behind each step above. Hopefully you've also noticed how the concept of *multiple encoding* was built into the steps, for example, the use of both words and pictures in making notes. If you're still not clear what makes each step up, make sure you go back and re-read the sections in question until you're happy you understand the techniques involved. It's crucial you get it right.

Understand and Apply FAST to Avoid Disasters

Remember, in our analogy of building a house, FAST is what we use to put up the essential structure, the walls of the building. Without strong walls built on strong foundations, the chances of the building remaining upright are low. And the same goes for your studies. Use the wrong techniques, and your studies are likely to collapse around you.

So I repeat one more time, make sure you understand what FAST involves, **and make sure you apply those lessons**.

Building on FAST – Other Study Tools and Techniques

FAST Plus

In Chapter 13, we saw that question practice was an integral part of the study process, and that it needed to be planned for and built into your efforts pretty much from day one. In this chapter, we will look at the whole issue of question practice in greater depth, building on the core FAST technique you learned about in the previous chapter.

We will also look some of the other tools, techniques and processes that you should be incorporating into your studies to help this building process along. These include the techniques you should be using where, in addition to studying alone at home, you are attending taught courses, as these require a particular approach in order to get the most out of your attendance.

Question Practice

Build It In From the Start

If the first and main part of the structure is the core, or walls, the second part is the doors, windows, and roof tiles, as we've already seen earlier in this book.

A building without these elements is not going to be watertight; in fact, it's not going to be a lot of use at all.

> ***"The more I practice, the luckier I seem to get."***
> **Arnold Palmer**

In the context of your studies, the doors, windows and roof tiles are comparable to question practice. And again, as we've already seen, this means that question practice has to be built into your studies right from its earliest stages. Question practice is not something you leave until the revision process. It's far too late by then.

Questions Aren't Just for the Revision Phase

This is another common mistake made by students. Because of the way they've been taught to study in earlier life, they associate study with simply reading books and making notes, and revision with practising questions. In their mind the two activities are completely separate.

You need to make sure you don't make this mistake.

The Performance of Your Life

Imagine for a second you're learning a script for a play you have a part in. The first thing you do is to read the play to get a feel for it (a skim read if you like), and then you go back and look at each act in detail (the detailed read).

Read the Lines to Yourself?

What would you do then? Would you continue to just read the lines from the book in your head, not actually practising speaking your lines out loud until the play's dress rehearsal? The dress rehearsal is probably going to be just days before your first live performance after all.

I think not! This would be a big mistake – you'd never get to grips with the play fully at such a late stage. Your first night would be a disaster!

Or Practice the Play Out Loud?

No, first of all you'd read each act yourself, and then you'd practice your lines with your fellow actors or willing helpers, at this stage still reading from the play's text itself. Gradually, with enough practice, you'd begin to remember your lines without having to refer back to them, and you'd start to get a feel for the play as a whole. Then, eventually, you'd have learned all your lines off by heart and be able to concentrate on your overall acting performance, and not just getting the lines out right. The dress rehearsal would just be a final run through before the big night, and not the first time you've tried to pull what you've learned together.

Relevance to Your Studies

Your studies are just like learning the part for a play. The same activities are involved, the objective is the same. And that is to make sure that by the time you come to give your greatest performance in the exam hall, you're more than ready for it. Which is why leaving question practice until the revision stage should be avoided. It'll be too late to get it right.

So what does this mean as far as your studies are concerned?

Guidance on Introducing Question Practice

- To start with, you'll be reading through the text at overview level and then at detailed level. You'll produce notes as part of your core FAST build.
- Then you should be introducing question practice into your studies. Attempt any exercises and questions included in the study book. For example, often a chapter will have some relatively simply questions set at the end to test your recall of the main points covered.
- At this stage, don't worry about having to refer back to your notes or the study text when attempting questions. You're not in the exam yet. The important thing is to use the question to test both your recall of the material itself, and perhaps more importantly, *your ability to apply it to a range of situations*.

- Continue this question practice throughout your studies. Don't simply attempt questions on a particular topic when you first study it and then leave that topic until the revision phase. Remember, *repetition* is important in improving memory. Make sure you revisit areas you've previously covered and try some more questions. And begin to try and answer questions without referring back to your notes or the study manual.
- Where possible, try to attempt questions of increasing difficulty as your studies progress. This will ensure that by the time you reach your revision stage, you are ready to attempt exam standard questions.
- If you run out of new questions to try, look for alternative sources. Aren't there any other text books out there covering the same subjects? If you're using a distance learning product, ask your assigned tutor for more questions – they often have some in reserve for students that ask. The same applies if you're attending lectures.
- Go one stage further – write your own questions. This may sound bizarre – after all, if you write your own questions, you know the answers, right? But in fact, it's the actual process of asking yourself the questions that is important. Ask yourself, with your knowledge of the subject, if you were the examiner, what questions would you set? What concepts and ideas would you seek to test, and what novel ways might you dream up to do that? This is the kind of active mindset which will ensure that come the exam, there are no surprises lurking.

> ***"If you don't ask the right questions, you don't get the right answers. A question asked in the right way often points to its own answer."***
> **Edward Hodnett**

- Don't discard questions simply because they are in a format not used by your examiner. For example, your exam might be a written exam, requiring you to write essays. But that doesn't mean that multiple choice questions covering the same subject aren't useful – they are. Merely by attempting them you are again testing your recall and application of the facts.

Dealing with Specific Question Types

Questions can be set in all sorts of different ways, using different styles, depending in part on the subject itself.

Examples of question styles are

- Multiple choice (sometimes called objective testing)
- Essay
- Short written answer
- Fill-in-the-blanks
- Calculations/mathematical

Each question type needs to be dealt with in its own way. How to approach each of these different question types and also some of the others you might encounter is dealt with in more detail in Chapter 21 How to Approach Questions, as it's at this stage that using the right methodology becomes crucial. I therefore suggest that you refer to this chapter when you're ready to start your question practice in earnest.

Other Tools and Techniques

We've now seen the two main elements that you will use to build your study success – FAST to deal with the core study work required, and question practice to ensure that you can recall and apply what you've been learning.

But in the same way as you're going to need to use more than two techniques and tools when building a house, so it is with study where there are other tools and techniques available to you which you should be looking to introduce as part of your study "mix".

Let's now therefore have a look at some of these other tools and techniques.

Self Lectures

One very good way of seeing whether you really understand something is to present it in the form of a lecture to other people. What appears to make perfect sense when it's down on the page in front of you can suddenly become a lot more complicated when you have to explain it to someone else in your own words!

> ***"If you would thoroughly know anything, teach it to others."***
> **Tryon Edwards**

Now I'm not suggesting here that you actually have to go as far as standing up in front of a group of people and make a fool of yourself (although if you can bring yourself to do this and find the people willing to listen and question what you have to say, this will yield you excellent results).

No, what I am suggesting is that you prepare and present lectures *to yourself*. Nobody's going to know if you get it wrong or fluff an explanation, only you. But the benefits to be gained are still considerable.

- Thinking about how to present the material in this way requires you to actively process the information, interpret it and then present it in the way you find easiest to explain clearly.
- Whilst carrying out the preparatory work, new questions are likely to occur to you as you try to make sense of the material and get it into some semblance of a story.

- You can actually record yourself whilst you are carrying out the self-lecture. This will give you another source of study material which uses a different sense (auditory instead of the usual visual) and therefore allows you to follow the principles of multiple encoding.
- Whilst you are presenting the material, yet more questions may well arise as you realise that whatever you've just said doesn't quite make sense, or has a flaw in it. For some reason, it seems easier to spot these errors when actually reading to yourself aloud rather than just forming the words in your head whilst you're reading quietly.

Try this method and see what you think. Find a quiet spot where nobody will disturb you (or can overhear you if you feel particularly shy) and really believe there's an audience out there as you present your lecture. I think you really will find the benefits are significant.

Mnemonics and Memory Techniques

Useful in the Casino but not in an Exam

You've all seen the advertisements in the newspapers – improve your memory 1000 percent with our unique patented memory technique, or your money back. Guaranteed.

And it is true that at least some of these techniques will work. Given enough patience, time and hard work.

But there is one major problem. The type of exam set at professional level is not simply a memory test. Instead, you will have to be able to both *recall* and *use* information and concepts in complex ways. It's all about the *application* of your knowledge, not the mere recall of it. Such memory techniques are therefore of limited value to your studies. They can't give you this deep level of understanding, and never can. Being able to recall the order of all 54 cards from a shuffled deck simply ain't gonna cut any ice with your examiner!

> ***"It is possible to store the mind with a million facts and still be entirely uneducated."***
> **Alec Bourne**

Targeted Use

Nevertheless, these techniques can have a place in your studies, as long as you understand their limitations, and don't assume that because you can regurgitate the reams of data you have memorised that somehow passing the exam is going to be a breeze. These methods are useful, for example, where you need to memorise lists.

There are numerous methods out there, such as memory chains, telescoping, the link system, the Roman room system and the Major system. The main disadvantage of each though is that they require a lot of hard work in essentially reprogramming the brain. This takes time and effort, neither of which you have much to spare.

I suggest therefore that if you still wish to pursue these alternatives, you visit your local library and borrow one of the many hundreds of books available on memory techniques.

For the purposes of this book, let us just look at the simplest of memory techniques, which is both simple to understand and simple to use.

First Letter Mnemonics

Damage Without the G

Some years ago, when I used to teach towards the threshold competency exam used by the Securities industry in the UK, one of the areas we needed to cover was regulation. And one thing students needed to remember about regulation for their exam was the statutory definition of what constituted "investment business".

This was a simple memory exercise, no more than that. But it was examinable, so therefore did need to be committed to memory. The way I taught it was to tell my students to remember "DAMAGE without the G". What did I mean by this?

The items that constituted "investment business" under the regulations were as follows –

D ealing in investments

A dvising on investments

M anaging investments

A rranging deals in investments

G

E stablishing or operating a collective investment scheme

So, as you can see, DAMAGE without the G. This was a simple way of fixing in the minds of my students the first letter of each of the five elements of investment business. I fully accept that the method is somewhat trite, if not a little silly. But that's the point – make it memorable (even if it is slightly ridiculous!) and it will help you to remember what it is you need to know. Of course, the students still needed to remember what the letters stood for, but this gave them a head start!

The Famous Roy G. Biv

Another example of a first letter mnemonic, albeit it used in a slightly different way, is one which every science-studying school child will be able to repeat. This time, the first letters of each word form a list which needs to be remembered and are used to create memorable phrases and names.

The letters are ROYGBIV, being the colours of the rainbow, Red, Orange, Yellow, Green, Blue, Indigo and Violet.

The varying ways of remembering these letters are

- "Richard Of York Gave Battle In Vain", or
- "Read Out Your Good Book in Verse", or even simply
- "Roy G. Biv", if you find a name easier to remember!

These first letter mnemonics are perhaps the simplest, quickest and therefore most useful of memory techniques to apply. In addition, when used with phrases like the examples above, the very creation and use of these phrases allows the creative potential (and memory) of the right brain to be tapped.

However, whilst they do have their place, don't get carried away with them and spend all your time dreaming up acronyms at the expense of the rest of your studies. These techniques used on their own are not going to get you up to exam standard.

Reviewing Progress Against Plans

Constant Review

When building a house, it's necessary to constantly review the plans. Why do this?

- It reminds us what needs to be done next, and in what order.
- It allows us to measure our progress to date against the plans.
- It allows us to see if we have deviated from the original plans, and to what extent.

Of course, the same goes for your studies. Don't forget those timetables of yours. You should be constantly monitoring your progress against these plans. You should be using them to see where you're going, and what you should be doing next.

And remember, you should be updating your short-term timetable on a weekly basis. It's easy to dismiss this as unimportant when you've got your head down working hard.

But just like not standing back once in a while to make sure the wall you're building is straight, leading to a wall that isn't square and that has to be demolished and rebuilt, not stopping when you're studying to review where you are is a mistake you simply can't afford.

So check those plans. And keep on checking them.

But What If Things Aren't Going to Plan?

You may be concerned, because having reviewed your progress against your plans, you find things aren't going according to plan. You're not where you should be in the study process.

Don't panic. What you have to understand is that this is quite normal – you cannot expect everything to happen exactly as you planned it. After all, your plans were in reality built on incomplete information – you did the best you could to produce them, but they are never going to be accurate (unless you have some hidden talent for fortune telling!).

"You always pass failure on the way to success."
Mickey Rooney

Once more, think about the analogy of building a house. It's very rare for a building project to go to plan. There will almost always be delays in completing the project, where some part of the build takes longer than imagined, or where unforeseen events occur. This is considered quite normal by the builder, who simply then adapts the plans to accommodate these changes. You can do the same. So I repeat – Don't Panic.

Mistakes are Normal

On the same theme, I know that a number of you may be perfectionists by nature, always wanting to get everything absolutely right, and feeling disappointed (or worst, depressed) when you can't quite meet your own exacting standards.

If this is you, you need to try really hard to rid yourself of this trait, in your studies at least. Why so?

Because

100 Percent is Not Required

You don't need to get 100 percent to pass your exam. The pass mark for most professional level exams is set at 50 percent, so by that measure you only need to know *half* of everything in the syllabus to get a pass mark. *The examiner does not expect you to understand every single element of the syllabus*. If he did, he'd set the pass mark to 100 percent, wouldn't he!

"Don't be discouraged by failure. It can be a positive experience. Failure is, in a sense, the highway to success, inasmuch as every discovery of what is false leads us to seek earnestly after what is true, and every fresh experience points out some form of error which we shall afterwards carefully avoid."
John Keats

To Err is Human

Making mistakes is the normal human condition. It's the way we learn things. Try something, get it wrong, find the reason why we got it wrong, try again doing something different until we get it right. All humans demonstrate this ability, right from birth. How else do you think you learned to walk and talk as a baby? Do you think you got it right first time, simply stood up and walked perfectly round the room? Of course not!

> ***"Trying is the first step towards failure."***
> **Homer Simpson**

So don't be too hard on yourself and expect to get everything right in your studies first time. You *need* to make mistakes so you can learn from them. This might seem difficult for the perfectionist in you, but making mistakes is in fact *making progress*. I would be more worried if you told me you understood everything and had no problems at all!

And allied to this, try to feel comfortable with the knowledge that you don't need to have covered the entire 100 percent of the syllabus during your studies. Try your best to cover it all, yes, but don't beat yourself up if your plans go awry and you have to skim one or two areas. It's really not the end of the world. You need to remain positive – remember the importance of having the right mental attitude. Focus on your successes during your studies, and not the few minor failures there will inevitably be.

> ***"The gem cannot be polished without friction, nor man perfected without trials."***
> **Chinese Proverb**

Study Techniques for Taught Courses

The guidance on study tools and techniques given so far has largely been based on the assumption that you're studying at home, probably using some sort of distance learning product, possibly in combination with a revision course nearer the time of your exam. The onus is largely on you to make sure you maintain the momentum needed to get you through the necessary work.

If, however, you are attending some kind of taught course on a regular basis during your studies, whether that be evening classes, day or block release, the situation is different. For that reason, you need some specific guidance to make sure you extract the maximum benefit from attending these taught courses.

How to Get the Best out of Lectures

On the face of it, learning by attending lectures seems a whole lot easier than having to learn alone at home. After all, you get to sit there and have the subject presented to you by a knowledgeable lecturer. He or she is likely to not only talk but also present visual material, making the learning process more interesting (well, maybe!). And the lecturer can answer questions on the spot, as they occur, which can never happen in a distance learning situation. All in all, this seems a whole lot easier than working by yourself.

> ***"If all the students who slept through lectures were laid end to end, they'd all be a lot more comfortable."***
> **Unknown**

Yes, certainly attending lectures appears to give the student an advantage over those slaving away in isolation at home. But beware – it's not that simple. There are in reality a number of problems associated with attending taught courses which you need to be aware of in order to deal with them successfully.

Lectures are a Poor Teaching Mechanism.

Yes it's true, they can be. This might be because

- The material is presented *to* you; there is no "learning by doing".
- The lecturer won't necessarily take account of your attention span, so you may lose concentration and miss vital points.
- The large amount of data presented to you in one session (which might exceed the optimum 45-minute time period) may mean you end up forgetting part of it immediately, or find it difficult to maintain interest.
- There may be discipline problems within the class, such as other students talking, which may distract your attention from the lecturer.
- For a number of reasons, the questions you need answers to may not be asked or answered, and visa versa, your time may be wasted listening to question and answers for areas you are already happy with.
- The lecturer may simply not be good enough, or his/her "style" may not suit you.

Psychological and Motivational Issues

Since you're attending the lectures along with other students, there's always the temptation to compare yourself to them. This can often appear disheartening, as it appears that many of your compatriots seem to be finding things a lot easier than you are, and understand the subject far better than you ever could. Such a negative mindset can lead to a downward spiral in confidence and motivation which is difficult to pull out of.

Because of these problems, many students simply don't make the most of the time they invest in attending lectures. In my own experience, I have seen students attend lectures in body but not in mind, taking no part in the lecture at all. This is simply a waste of their time, and if you adopt the same approach, a waste of your time too.

Attending lectures is *not* simply about making sure you turn up on the right day at the allotted hour and then sitting there listening to someone lecturing. It's far more than that. In reality, attending the lectures themselves is only *part* of the overall study process you should be adopting when you are attending taught courses. So let's look at the study approach you should be using in this case.

Back to Active Study

The key to success when using taught courses as part of your study programme is to ensure you remember the importance of *active* learning. If you choose to simply turn up to your lecture having done no preparatory work, and then just listen to the lecturer from start to end of lecture, you're not being active, you're being passive. And as we've already seen, passive is not good when it comes to learning. You're not engaging with the material, you're not processing the information and concepts. As a result, you're going to learn very little for the amount of time you're going to be sitting in lectures.

> ***"Action without study is fatal. Study without action is futile."***
> **Mary Ritter Beard**

So, we definitely need to adopt an active approach to attending lectures. Here's how.

Before the Lecture

Preparation is what's required here. You need to avoid just turning up on the day for your class. Instead, you should be doing the following.

- Checking the topics that are going to covered. Normally you will be provided with this information by the college at the start of your course. If you don't have this, ask for it.
- Knowing which topics are to be covered, ask yourself what you already know about these topics. Think about how they fit into what you've already studied in other topic areas and/or at earlier classes you've attended.
- Skim read the chapters in question (remember, to skim read you look at headings, sub-headings, beginning and end paragraphs and the first and/or last sentences of each paragraph and section). Get a feel for what's going to be covered.
- Prepare a list of questions that occur to you as you read to try to make sense of the material and its context. These are the questions that you hope attending the lecture will answer for you.

If you manage all of the above, you'll have a head-start when it comes to the lecture itself (and on many of your fellow students come to that!). You'll have set yourself up to get the maximum benefit from your attendance.

During the Lecture

Every lecturer will have their own unique style and way of doing things. However, your approach should be basically the same regardless. Once again, the key is being *active*. What does this mean?

Listen actively

Constantly question what you are being told to ensure you understand it. For example – "what does this mean?", "how does it connect?", "where is it leading?", "what's the overall structure?", "what are the main ideas?" and so on. If you merely sit back and think "I don't understand this, I'll look at it later when I get home", you might as well not be there!

Make brief notes

But note carefully – I said *brief.* I've seen many a student trying to write down verbatim what the lecturer is telling them. Even if you're an expert in shorthand (somewhat of a dying art these days), you're still going to miss the point. You'll be concentrating on the words themselves, getting them down correctly on paper, not on their underlying *meaning.*

Do this even if you're given written notes – again, the point is that by making these brief notes you're being active and not passive. And by brief notes, I mean noting down key words and concepts, perhaps using patterned notes to help you see how the big picture looks. If you're writing down whole sentences and paragraphs, you're writing too much.

If you don't understand something, ASK

I know many people find this difficult, being too embarrassed to speak up in front of a group of (often) strangers, but please try to get over this hurdle. The lecturer is there to help you, and expects questions. Moreover, you or the company you work for have undoubtedly paid for the course – so remind yourself you're entitled to get your money's worth!

> ***"He who asks is a fool for five minutes, but he who does not ask remains a fool forever."***
>
> **Chinese Proverb**

You'll find that once you've opened your mouth the first time, you'll find it far easier to ask questions a second time. And you'll probably find that secretly, everyone else in your class is glad you asked the question. If you didn't understand the point, you can be sure many others didn't either!

After the Lecture

Having attended the lecture doesn't mean you can now forget about the subject you've covered until the revision stage. Again, this is a mistake made by many. Merely attending a lecture and seeing a subject presented once isn't going to fix it in into your memory.

It's down to remaining active. This means

- Reading your rough key word notes and any handouts provided in the lecture as soon as possible afterwards, preferably the same day but certainly the next day wherever possible.
- Once you think you understand the issues, put your notes to one side and try to recall the subject covered. Then review your knowledge against your notes. Find out where you still have difficulties or gaps, and focus on these areas. If necessary, return to the source study manuals and/or materials to fill the gaps in your knowledge. Or alternatively, contact your lecturer and talk through the problem areas – they should be able to provide you with additional material or assistance.
- Repeat the read, recall and review steps above as many times as necessary until you believe you understand the material and can both recall and apply it.
- Produce a final set of summary notes which will be used during your revision phase.
- Attempt any practice questions and exercises you are given by your lecturer to test your ability to recall and apply the knowledge.

You may have noticed how the points above really mirror the Five-step Active Study Technique (FAST) you've already seen. In fact, the only realdifferences in approach between self study and attending taught courses is that the "Read" stage of FAST has been replaced with a "Lecture" phase. Other than that the processes are exactly the same.

A Word (or Two) on the Mythical "Natural Student"

I'm Surrounded by Geniuses!

I mentioned above that one of the problems with attending group lectures is the natural temptation to compare yourself unfavourably to other students. Self-confidence and motivation can be severely dented by doing this, and as such, it's something to be avoided at all costs.

> ***"Success is more a function of consistent common sense than it is of genius."***
> **An Wang**

Often these comparisons are unfavourable because many carry round in their heads the idea that the perfect, or "natural" student exists. This mythical student is an absolute natural when it comes to study, demonstrating abilities mere mortal students can only dream of. Not only this, these type of students somehow make up the rest of the class!

Characteristics of the "Natural Student"

- They are always superbly organised, with every minute of every day timetabled in detail up front.
- They can concentrate for long periods.

- They can understand everything they hear and/or read the very first time without any effort.
- They produce in-depth notes with every item fully indexed.
- They find practice and exam questions easy, and always get maximum marks for their attempt.
- They are always brimming with confidence and do not get anxious about exams.

Would This Really Be So Good?

You need to make sure you don't fall into the trap of thinking you should be aspiring to these ideals, and inevitably find yourself coming up short when you make the comparison. The reality is that not only does such a person not exist, but that even if they did, they would be particularly unsuited to studying towards exams.

> ***"Genius is one percent inspiration, ninety-nine percent perspiration."***
> **Thomas Edison**

How so? Well, think about it for a minute. In reality, they would be

- Inflexible (they've already planned every single minute – not an easy plan to adapt when things change!).
- Suffering from information overload.
- Likely to understand material at a superficial level only, not the real underlying meaning (complex subjects cannot be fully understood at the first read).
- Wasting time producing detailed notes when summary notes would serve them better.
- Unlikely to give their best performance in the exam room (as we shall see in the Chapter 23, a certain level of stress is needed to maximise performance).

All in all, maybe the mythical natural student hasn't really got any advantages over you at all.

Comparison is Counterproductive

So cut yourself some slack. Concentrate on getting things right for you, by following the advice contained in this book. And avoid comparing yourself to anyone else in your group, especially the one always asking the difficult questions (you know the type – there's always one in every class. They spend so much time trying to impress their fellow students with their searching questions that they omit to learn the basics they need to actually pass the exam).

You'll have good days, and you'll have bad days. Accept it. Learn from it. And move on. As long as you're moving forwards, and remaining active, you'll be making all the progress you need.

Study Tools and Techniques Revisited

Study Tools and Techniques

The Traditional View of Study

What most people would recognise as the "study process" has been covered in this part of the book, Study Tools and Techniques. That is, the real mechanics of study, the nitty gritty, the hard miles which need to be travelled to get to a position where an exam pass can be gained.

The Study Tools and Techniques are, if you like, the real guts of the machine. They are the cogs, wheels, gears and so on which need to be there if the machine is going to produce an end product capable of standing up to a detailed inspection. So they need to be set up and operated correctly if disasters are going to be avoided.

Pragmatism Rules

In chapter 13, we saw that, despite what other books on study might tell you, there really is no one single methodology that can be used to assure success. Rather, a common-sense, pragmatic approach to studies needs to be adopted, incorporating the principles of active learning and multiple encoding.

In the same chapter, we also introduced the idea of viewing your studies as the process of building a house. There are many helpful parallels to be drawn between the two processes. Both require the best possible environment, the right foundations, a decent plan and above all, a strong core upon which to build the finished article.

FAST

Chapter 14 introduced the Five-step Active Study Technique (FAST), which allows you to build that strong core. Make sure you fully understand what each of the five steps entails, and follow the principles contained. Remember, skim reading a study manual and then writing some poorly structured notes is simply *not* good enough if you want to be sure you're getting the most out of your study time. Follow the principles of FAST and you can be sure you're on the right road.

The Magic Ingredient

Chapter 15 set out the thinking on Question Practice. I hope you took on board how and why the introduction of question practice at the earliest opportunity is *so* crucial to your endeavours. Look at it this way. You're going to be assessed almost certainly purely on your ability to answer questions in an examination situation. Not on anything else.

If so, doesn't it make all the sense in the world to get as much question practice in as you can? Ignore this home truth and the only person you're going to kid is yourself.

The More Mistakes the Better

Please, please, please, do not be too hard on yourself. You *will* make mistakes during your studies. This is normal. And not only is it normal, it is healthy. Because only from making mistakes can you identify what you know and what you don't know and then learn from these mistakes.

> ***"Mistakes are the portals of discovery."***
> **James Joyce**

This means that, put simply, the more mistakes you make, the more you are learning. Look at it this way the next time things aren't going well and you feel like giving up.

Moving On...

No doubt working your way through your study manual (or manuals) using the tools and techniques contained in Part Five will take you some length of time. Throughout this period you should of course be continuing to use and monitor your study timetables to make sure you're still on track to meet the deadline of finishing your studies by the start of your revision period. And taking corrective action where necessary to meet that deadline.

Sooner or later however, you're going to reach that moment when study ends and revision starts. You need to know what to do. Part Six of this book covers the whole area of Revision. So read on...

Part Six

REVISION

Revision Basics

Reaching the End of Your Studies

You've reached the end of your allotted study period. The date you set during your initial timetabling for the start of your revision period has arrived.

Now starts the hard work!

The Bad News

It's a daunting prospect. No more can you hide behind your studies, ignoring the day of reckoning coming all too soon, the day when you have to sit in that exam hall and give it your all. Reaching the start of your revision period brings that big day very much back into sharp focus.

You might have produced the world's best ever study notes during your study process, but on their own these notes aren't going to be enough to help you pass your exam. Something more is needed. And that something more is revision.

> ***"I'm a great believer in luck, and I find the harder I work the more I have of it."***
> **Thomas Jefferson**

Using the correct revision technique is absolutely crucial if you want to pass your exams. The revision period, perhaps more than any other time during your studies, is a time where you simply must do everything you possibly can to ensure you're doing things the right way. So many students get it wrong, with dire consequences for their examinations. Let's make sure you too don't fall into the many traps that there are.

The Good News

The good news is that you've already started your revision. Yes, you've read it correctly. I repeat – you've already started your revision, even if perhaps you weren't aware of it. How can that be?

Well, throughout your studies you've planned and carried out a process of continual review of your study notes. This continual review is in fact the first stage of your revision, because during the review process you're committing facts, figures, concepts, ideas and procedures to your memory, for later use.

This is why the review process is so important – it gives you a head start when it comes to your revision. Had you failed to carry out any review whatsoever, simply reading your study text, writing some notes and then forgetting them until the start of the revision process, you'd have to waste far too much time getting back up to speed on the material itself. And this is time you simply don't have. Every second of your revision period needs to be put to good use.

In addition to the ongoing review process, having followed the advice I've given, you'll have also been building in question practice from an early stage in your studies. This too is a form of revision, and in the process you'll also have gained some experience of answering questions, which will stand you in good stead when you start your revision question practice.

So take heart – there may indeed be some hard work ahead, but you've already made a start. Allow yourself to feel good about that, give yourself a pat on the back for being prepared, and give your self-confidence a boost. You're still on the right track and going full steam ahead.

Objective of the Revision Process

The Main Objective

What's the main aim of revising, that is, what are we trying to achieve?

In a nutshell, it's this.

By the end of your revision period, you should be as prepared as you can be to face the exam.

Simply stated, but perhaps not so simple to put into practice!

Your Best is Good Enough

Notice that I state you should be as prepared "as you can be". Nobody can ever be 100 percent ready for an exam. It's not possible to understand everything there is in the syllabus. This is normal, and it's important you remember this fact during the course of your revision. You should be doing everything you can to be fully prepared, yes, but don't beat yourself up because there are still areas you're not completely happy with, or that you haven't had the time to cover in the detail you would have liked.

> ***"I am careful not to confuse excellence with perfection. Excellence, I can reach for; perfection is God's business."***
> **Michael J. Fox**

The important thing is to approach your revision in the right way. Then, the feelings of "I haven't done enough" will be reduced to a manageable level. Get the preparation right and you'll minimise the inevitable exam stress.

So, what is the right way? Well, we'll look at the keys to successful revision shortly, and what you should be doing to maximise your chances of success. But before we do that, let's have a look at what you should *not* be doing.

Common Mistakes

There are some all-too-common mistakes that students make when revising that you need to avoid.

Mistake 1 – No Planning

Often students will start their revision without any plans whatsoever, detailed or otherwise. They work in a completely unstructured and ad-hoc way, with no attempt to ensure an even coverage of the syllabus. They simply pick up the study notes nearest to hand and start reading.

"It is not enough to be busy…the question is: what are we busy about."
Henry Thoreau

But just as planning was important before and during your studies, it's fundamentally important when entering your revision phase. How can you be sure you've covered everything you need to if you don't check? And if you don't have any targets to aim at, how can you give yourself rewards when you've reached them? All of the benefits we saw in Part Three on Planning apply here to revision too.

Mistake 2 – Using a Passive Approach

Throughout this book we've seen the importance of approaching your studies in an *active* way. And yet may students adopt a completely passive method of revision. In their minds, revision consists of sitting down and reading their study notes, perhaps in the hope that some of the material will somehow "stick".

Using passive methods in this way will mean you are doomed to failure.

Mistake 3 – Treating Revision like a Memory Test

Perhaps a hangover from school tests, where it was simple *recall* that was being tested, many students treat their professional level exams as if they were simply a massive test of memory and recall. Remember this list of names, and you'll pass, that kind of mindset. Rote learning and nothing more.

Almost invariably, memorising facts is only a small part of the skills needed to pass a higher level exam. We've seen already that the main thrust of these types of exams is about *application*. So simply memorising everything you have read is not going to get you a pass mark.

Mistake 4 – Trying to Learn New Things

The time allocated for revision is for exactly that – revision, and nothing else. It is far too late to be thinking about trying to learn new areas that for whatever reason haven't been covered previously.

And yet so often, students make exactly this mistake, trying to learn new material instead of consolidating the knowledge they already have. In reality, this is a poor use of time. Five minutes spent revising will always give you better returns come the exam than five minutes spent studying new material.

Learn to accept this fact. What's done is done. If you haven't managed to cover everything during your studies, forgive yourself. It's quite normal anyway. Get on instead and strengthen further your understanding of what you've already learned. Revision, not study.

Mistake 5 – Misallocation of Time

There are many facets to this mistake, some examples of which are set out below.

- Not spreading the workload over the entire revision period, but instead trying to do everything at the last possible minute. Sometimes called "cramming". This isn't sensible or even practical with the amount of material and level of understanding required for a higher level exam.
- Spending too much time re-reading study notes, and not enough (or any) time actually practising questions. Question practice, as we shall see, is the key to success.
- Working late into the night ("burning the midnight oil") the night before the exam. How many times have you personally heard others boast of doing this? And yet, it simply isn't necessary, nor is it desirable.
- Not building in any time away from the revision process. As with during your studies, it's important to always build in leisure and relaxation time, even in those days and weeks immediately preceding the exam.
- Where the student is sitting more than one exam in different subjects, not allocating time evenly or sensibly between these subjects, often leading to the "preferred" subject being studied at the expense of the "difficult" subject or subjects. Such an approach is OK if you're happy to only pass one out of the set of exams you are taking!

Mistake 6 – Rewriting Study Notes Too Many Times

Some students spend most of their revision time writing and re-writing their revision notes many times, often with the aim of making them neater, or condensing them down to a more manageable size.

Whilst this is a noble enterprise, it is not the time to be undertaking it. One rewrite might be acceptable, but no more. And anyway, if you've followed the instructions contained in the study tools and techniques chapter, your study notes should not really need to be rewritten!

Mistake 7 – Poor Question Practice

It's already been stated more than once that question practice is a crucial part of the revision process. Often students get this wrong too. Here are some of the mistakes they make.

Little or No Timed Question Practice

Not spending enough or any time attempting *timed* questions. By "timed" I mean attempting the question under exam conditions, giving yourself only the time you would have in the exam to produce an answer.

Many students enter the exam hall having *never* attempted a question under timed conditions. How can they ever hope to pass when they have no comprehension of what's required to produce an adequate answer in the time provided? This is a mistake of no less than absolutely *catastrophic* proportions.

Insufficient Experience of Producing Full Essay Answers

Where the exam consists of questions requiring essay answers, not spending enough time on practising writing *full* essay answers to timed questions, but instead producing outline answer plans only.

Whilst the use of outline answer plans to questions has a valid place in your revision techniques (their use allowing you to attempt a greater number of questions and ensuring therefore a greater coverage of the syllabus), it's still important to make sure you can produce a full essay under timed conditions. This is a skill that takes time to develop, both in terms of getting the content right and making sure you can write at a speed which leaves your answer still legible!

No Mock Exams Attempted

Never attempting a full mock exam under exam conditions.

Most professional level exams last for a minimum of three hours. Again, if you have no experience of what it feels like to sit there for this length of time producing answers to the prescribed standard, you're likely to come unstuck in the exam hall, where the experience may be simply overwhelming. It's going to be a tough experience and you need to be ready for it.

Avoiding Exam Standard Questions

Only attempting practice-level questions and never looking at exam standard questions or real past papers.

Self-delusion it may be, but I have met students who, during their revision, only ever attempted questions at the "practice exercise" level (the sort of questions that might be included at the end of a study chapter, for example).

There is simply no substitute for attempting *real* questions from *real* past papers. This is the only way you can be sure the level of difficulty of the questions you're trying is right.

Mistake 8 – Using Question Spotting Techniques

Question spotting is essentially guessing what topic areas the examiner is likely to set questions on, and then concentrating revision into these areas only. The idea is that not only does this stop you wasting valuable time in revising areas that aren't going to be examined, but also that in so doing, you can produce better answers in those areas that are.

As such, it is a high-risk strategy, because unless lady luck happens to be on your side (and the probability is that she won't be), the questions you expected to come up in the exam won't, and visa versa. This will severely limit your chances of answering sufficient questions well enough to secure a pass mark.

Such a technique therefore has no place in the well-prepared student's revision phase.

Mistake 9 – Allowing Panic to Set In

It's all too easy for the revising student who is close to the exam to find themselves unable to maintain a positive mind-set when faced with the enormity of the task ahead. The panic starts to set in, and very soon their negative state of mind starts to adversely affect their self-confidence, and ultimately their performance.

> ***"Our doubts are traitors***
> ***And make us lose the good we oft might win***
> ***By fearing to attempt."***
> **Shakespeare (Macbeth)**

If not nipped in the bud, this pernicious problem really can turn a pass mark into a fail. I lost count of the number of times during my student days when I personally witnessed students entering the exam hall with so resigned an air that it was no surprise to learn subsequently that they had indeed failed. Expect to fail and you undoubtedly will!

It is important therefore to try and maintain as positive an outlook as possible throughout the revision phase. Following the advice you're about to read in the next few chapters, and avoiding all of the potential mistakes listed above, will help ensure this happens.

The Three Keys to Revision Success

Having now seen all the potential mistakes there are to make, how do you ensure you don't make then?

There are three keys to successful revision, and they are

1. Revision Planning
2. Active Review
3. Timed Question Practice.

Each of these is important in its own right, but by far the most important is timed question practice. Reduce the time spent on any other part of your studies if you must, but not this one.

Chapters 18, 19, and 20 will look at the details behind each of these three keys in turn, whilst Chapter 21 will give guidance on answering specific question types. However, before we move on to look at these areas, we need to consider another issue that you may need to address. And that is whether to carry out your revision alone or in a group environment.

Solo Revision versus Group Revision

The Choice is Yours and Yours Alone

Ultimately, it's going to be up to you, and only you, to put in a performance worthy of that first time pass. Only you can sit in that seat on the big day, unless of course you're planning on getting your identical twin to take the exam on your behalf! (And yes, before you ask, it has been known!)

What this means in practice is that you can't absolve yourself of the responsibility you have to make sure you undertake all the preparation necessary to get you through the exam. It's up to you.

This needs to be taken into account when you're considering whether to adopt a solo revision approach, where you revise alone, or a group revision approach, where you join up with a number of other people also taking the same exam as you. As far as the decision whether to revise alone or as part of a group goes, you need to be brutally honest with yourself. If you really feel that you will able to contribute to the group's progress equally along with the other participants, by all means set up your self-help revision group and make a start. But if you think that in all honesty you're more likely to be a bit of a wallflower, give it a miss.

Group Revision – The Advantages

For the record, some of the advantages of revising as part of a group are as follows.

- The group can provide invaluable moral support when things don't seem to be going well for you.
- Being part of a group can help eliminate the sense of loneliness and isolation that might come from spending a lot of time on your own deep in revision mode.
- You can learn from other students' ideas, and from their mistakes.
- Firing questions at each other to test memory and understanding is a far more active approach than asking yourself questions, and as a result, more of a valuable revision/learning experience.

Group Revision – The Disadvantages

However, there are disadvantages to group revision too, and these need to be borne in mind.

- Your revision time is very valuable and you can't afford to waste it. If the group's agenda and activities are not closely controlled, there is a strong possibility that valuable time that could have been spent on something more beneficial, such as timed question practice, will be frittered away.

> ***"He travels the fastest who travels alone."***
> **Rudyard Kipling**

- A large part of your revision needs to be timed question practice and you can't do this in a group. Being part of a group means you might spend too long on your initial review of your study notes and not enough time on the crucial timed question practice.
- Where the group's personalities aren't evenly matched, one person may lead the rest of the group in the wrong direction or place the wrong emphasis on less important syllabus areas.
- If you're a little sensitive to criticism, even constructive criticism offered by other group members may severely dent your self-confidence at a stage where you really need to be boosting it as much as you can.

Only you can decide which method is best for you – solo revision or group. Just be aware of the positives and negatives each gives when you make that decision.

Revision Courses – A Good Thing?

Yes, is the answer to that question. Generally, attending a professionally run revision course will give you an advantage over those who purely revise alone. I would always recommend booking yourself onto a course if you possibly can.

Some of the benefits are the same as we've just seen when discussing group revision. The ability to learn from others' ideas and mistakes. Removing the isolation of studying alone. And so on. But attending a revision course can give even greater benefits.

- The course should be led by an experienced, knowledgeable tutor. This means you will cover the most important syllabus areas, whilst avoiding peripheral areas. It also means that someone is on hand to answer problems quickly and correctly (contrast this with a self-help revision group which can sometimes be a case of the blind leading the blind!).
- Timed question practice is often factored into revision courses, so not only will you be actively reviewing the syllabus but you'll be getting that valuable question practice too.
- Where timed questions are set in class, the tutor will normally run through the answer step-by-step. This allows you to identify where you went wrong, and allows access to the tutor's expertise should you require further explanation or guidance. When you're on your own at home, this is far more difficult.
- Revision courses often give you the opportunity to sit a full mock exam, and then have your answers professionally marked. This can be an invaluable experience, allowing you to both experience examination stress in advance of the real thing, and to get a measure of your performance.

Having said all of that, it may simply not be possible for you to attend a revision course. In this case, stay disciplined and stick to the approach to revision set out in this book. You'll still be maximising your chances of success if you do this.

Key One – Revision Planning

Planning – as Important as Ever

Planning is as important now as it ever was, in fact, even more so. Whereas at the start of your studies you had the luxury of time, now you have no more room to manoeuvre at all. As your exam day approaches fast, there's very little time left to correct mistakes.

As a result, it is imperative that every one of the days you've allocated to your revision phase is planned in detail. And when I say in detail, I mean *in detail*. Literally down to the nearest hour, morning, afternoon and night.

Two Stage Process

Your revision phase should consist of two stages, taking place in this order.

- Active review of study notes
- Timed question practice

Each of you will have a different period of time allocated to your revision, depending on individual circumstances, so it's not possible to give you a prescriptive number of hours or days for each of the two stages. However, what I can say in guidance is that as much time as possible should be allocated to, and spent on, the timed question practice stage.

In fact, out of the total time you have available for revision, spending as much as 75 percent on timed question practice would not be unreasonable.

Building to a Crescendo

How might you imagine you should allocate your efforts over the revision period you have selected?

An Even Spread

Perhaps it should be an even effort over time, something like this (see figure 18.1 overleaf).

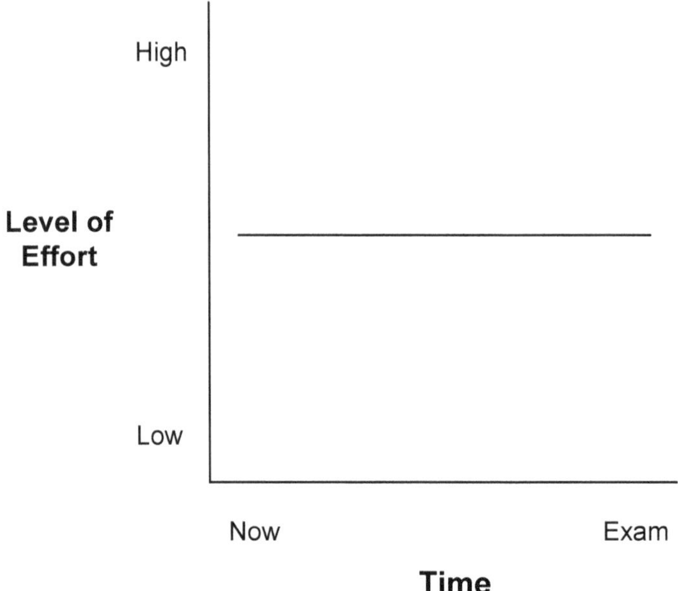

At first sight, this might seem sensible. The same amount of effort every day, avoiding peaks and troughs, maintaining a constant workload.

However, such an approach has its downside. Bearing in mind you'd be doing the same amount of work each day, it's unlikely you could maintain your maximum effort day after day throughout the whole revision period. Hence the horizontal line on the graph is only half way up the y-axis and not at the top, as it's simply not possible to maintain your maximum level of intensity for long periods.

As a result, following an even allocation of effort over time in this way, you'd only be firing on half of your cylinders come the day of the exam. And this is not a desirable situation to find yourself in. You need to be ready to work at maximum output in the exam hall, and if you're not used to working at these levels prior to your exam you're unlikely to be able to do so in the exam itself.

Reaching a Peak Just Before the Exam

The Right Way

Clearly, therefore, you need to be gradually building your levels of effort to a peak just before the exam. Notice the wording I use here as well – I talk about a *gradual* increase in effort over time so that a peak is reached *just before* the exam.

In other words, the ideal approach to revision could be represented graphically by something like figure 18.2 below.

Figure 18.2

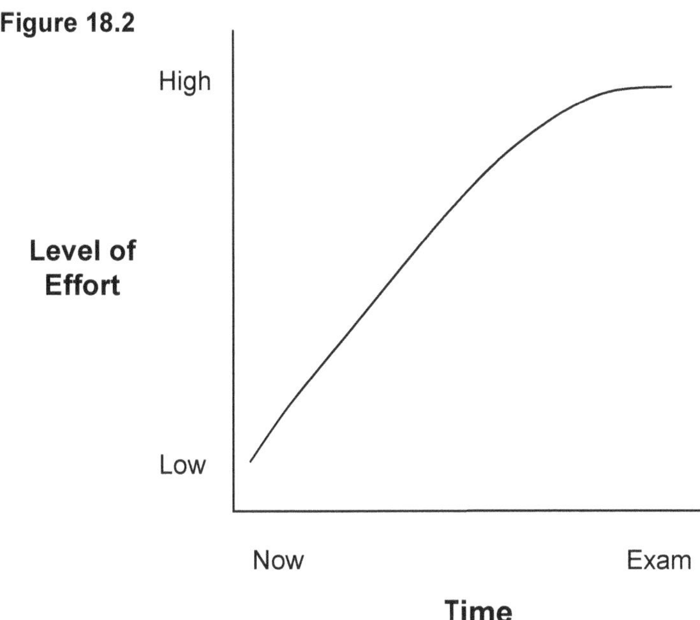

Notice how effort levels increase gradually over the entire revision period, so that for a relatively short length of time before the exam, maximum levels are reached. Such an approach avoids two potential pitfalls that can trap the unwary

The Wrong Way – Cramming

In figure 18.3 overleaf we can see that the student has left it too late to do the necessary work. This has led to a situation where cramming is the only possibility – trying to fit everything in to a very short period immediately prior to the exam. Sure, there's a crescendo. But it's a pretty steep curve to get up. For the reasons we've already discussed, this is not to be recommended.

Figure 18.3

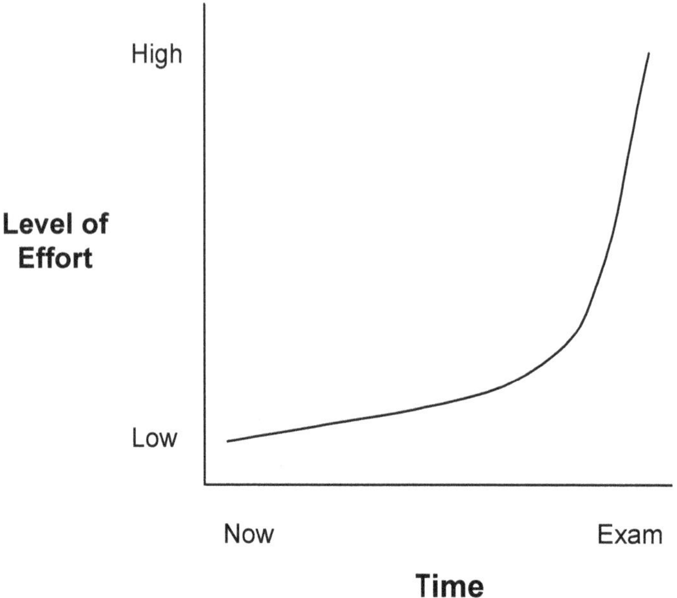

The Wrong Way – Peaking Too Early

The other common mistake is peaking too early.

Figure 18.4

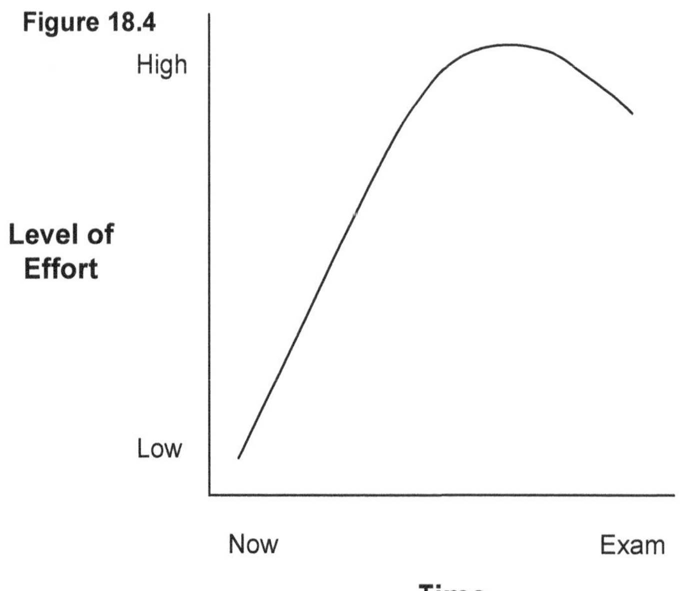

In this scenario, the student works very hard but builds to a peak of effort too quickly. Both boredom and tiredness then set in, leading to a fall in effort levels prior to the exam date. The student literally becomes stale, and does not perform to the best of their ability in the exam.

Admittedly, it's a fine line to tread. On the one hand you need to ensure you don't peak too early, whilst on the other hand you need to cover all the material in good time so that not everything is left until the last minute.

But you do need to give it your best shot and orchestrate that rise in volume, so that by the time your crescendo has reached its peak, you're operating at full volume and close to the exam date.

And the best way to make sure you get this balancing act right is to plan in detail up front.

The Revision Timetable.

Yep, you've guessed it – we need another timetable! This time, one covering the revision period.

The mechanics involved in producing the timetable are largely the same as for producing your original study timetable. All of the concepts we looked at there are still relevant.

These include

The 45 Minute Rule

The idea that you should spend a maximum of 45 to 50 minutes on study before a break.

Little and Often

Where faced with the choice between studying for a given period in one single lump or splitting that period into a number of smaller parts, the latter is always preferable.

Subject Variety

Build in variety so that boredom is reduced.

Level of Difficulty Variety

Build this in to ensure that you don't get stuck in a problem area.

Study Method Variety

Make sure that wherever possible a variety of techniques and tasks are involved to maintain interest.

Repetition and Review

Use repetition and review to help strengthen recall and memory formation.

When producing your revision timetable, try to incorporate these principles into your timetable. However, because of the time pressure you'll be under, you'll need to adapt the normal timetabling process to suit your revision situation. Let's look therefore at the steps involved in producing your revision timetable.

Stage 1 – Defining the Time Available for Revision

The Process

- Obtain or draw up a day planner for the period between now and the exam date(s). Make sure each day has enough space allocated to it so that you can enter details down to the nearest hour. (The daily planner introduced in Chapter 7 that you used for your weekly timetable production will be ideal.)
- Add the exam date(s) to the relevant days on the planner.
- Add any other significant known dates which you are aware of. This might include, for example, revision course dates, or other calls on your time which mean you won't be able to build in study (you have kept these to an absolute minimum though, haven't you? There'll be plenty of time for holidays after the exams!).
- Block out the time you'll spend at work if you haven't already done so. Only block out actual working hours though – every other hour during working days should be viewed as a potential revision hour.
- This might be your revision phase, but you still need to make sure you build in some leisure time. In fact, when you're working so hard, it's even more important that you set aside time for exercise and relaxation. As we've already seen, you can't work at maximum intensity indefinitely. So timetable in those gym visits, or an evening out with friends every so often.
- This may sound obvious, but build in sufficient time for sleep! Working late into the night will not improve your chances of success. In fact, cutting down on your sleep may well lower them, for reasons we have already seen in earlier chapters. Sleep is important if you want to function well – so make sure you get enough.
- Whilst you don't need to actually timetable this in as such, try to incorporate humour into your revision day, perhaps in one of the ways we saw in Chapter 3. Now more than ever you need to retain a sense of perspective about what you are

> ***"Always laugh when you can. It is cheap medicine."***
> **Lord Byron**

doing – taking things far too seriously and not finding time for laughter is in reality not going to boost your chances of success.

Identifying Free Time

Having followed the process above, you should now be able to identify how much spare time you have left to allocate to revision. As with planning your original study timetables, there can be no hard and fast rules here. I can't give you a minimum number of hours you should be aiming to spend on your revision, as everybody's situation will be different. Only you can best judge what's possible and achievable within the deadlines you have.

Important Points

There are some points worth making here.

- The 45 minute rule doesn't mean you can only do a maximum of 45 minutes study per day! Just make sure you build in short breaks between your 45 minute sessions, and a longer break every so often when you are stringing a number of 45 minute sessions together.
- The Little and Often rule still stands, but apply it sensibly and don't use it as an excuse not to work hard! For example, if you have three hours available on one particular day for revision, break it down into four separate 45 minute session spread throughout the day, say two in the morning and two in the afternoon. Little and Often does NOT mean you have to allocate the sessions across four days, one 45 minute session per day.
- Remember that you should be aiming to build to a crescendo in terms of level of effort. Build this gradual rise in revision hours in when deciding how much revision time you have available over the entire revision period. *Do not assume you will be able to work flat out for the entire period.* Be sensible – be realistic. Setting yourself unrealistic targets will only dent your self-confidence when you can't reach the goals you have set.

Stage 2 – Producing the Revision Timetable

You have now defined the number of revision hours available for every day of the revision period. Hopefully you've taken into account all of the points above, in particular the need to gradually build your efforts to a crescendo from now until your exam date.

Having done this, you now need to define how each hour of your revision time is going to be spent. At this stage, you can't be certain how your revision will go, which areas you will find easy, which you will find hard, which you will need to revisit a number of times before you fully understand them. As with your long term and weekly study timetables therefore, inevitably you will need to update your revision timetable as you progress.

However, what you can do now is at least attempt to sketch in how, and on what, you'll be spending your time.

Step 1 – Allocate Between Review and Question Practice

We've already seen that revision consists of two stages, firstly an active review of your study notes and secondly, timed question practice. We've also seen that a larger proportion of time (as much as 75 percent) should be spent on the latter. From this, you should be able to identify which revision hours are spent on which of these two processes.

For example, let's say that you've identified that you can spend a total of 80 hours on revision over the next 3 weeks, 15 the first week, 25 the second and 40 the third (notice the gradual rise in workload over the period). This would mean that 25% x 80 hours = 20 hours should be allocated to active review, and the remaining 60 hours to timed question practice. Thus the first week (15 hours) and 5 hours from the second week would be spent in active reading.

Step 2 – Allocate Between Subjects

Where you are studying for more than one subject, you now need to allocate the time you have appropriately between the various subjects. By now, having spent some time studying them, you will have a good feel for their relative levels of difficulty. You may want to allocate proportionately more time to the more difficult subjects and visa versa for the easier.

For example, taking the 80 hour example above, and assuming you're studying for two subjects, you might decide to allocate between the two subjects in this way on the basis that you find Subject A more difficult than Subject B.

	Subject A	***Subject B***	***Total***
Week 1	9 hours	6 hours	15 hours
Week 2	15 hours	10 hours	25 hours
Week 3	24 hours	16 hours	40 hours
Total	48 hours	32 hours	80 hours

By all means do this, but do make sure you don't skew the revision hours so far in the direction of one subject that it is at the expense of the other. It is important to maintain a relatively even coverage over *all* the subjects you are taking if you want to pass in every one.

Conversely, don't spend proportionately more time on those subjects you find easier at the expense of the more difficult subjects. You'd be amazed how often students do this – it seems to be human nature to avoid the more troublesome or complex, even if it involves self-deception!

If you're one of these people, remember that ultimately you're only kidding yourself. If you really want to pass these exams, you're going to have to face up to the hard work ahead of you. Just tell yourself it'll all be over in a matter of weeks, grit your teeth and get stuck in.

Step 3 – Allocate Subjects to Revision Sessions

Having arrived at a number of revision hours in total for each subject on a weekly basis, it's time to allocate subjects to the individual revision sessions you have pencilled in to each of your revision days.

Sticking with our example above, during week 1 there are 9 hours allocated to A and 6 hours to B. If we were to simply start revising for Subject A, finish after we'd done the 9 hours required and then move onto Subject B for the remaining 6, this would not be the best use of our time. Remember the importance of varying both subject and difficulty?

Instead, wherever possible vary the subject and difficulty from day to day and even within any one day. In this way you'll avoid getting stale. The only note of caution I would add is to make sure you don't switch between subjects *excessively*. For example, when you're in the question practice phase, attempting one question from Subject A then the next question from Subject B, then the next from A and so on, is probably taking the idea of subject variety a little too far. Some sort of continuity does need to be maintained.

So instead, perhaps you could study Subject A in the morning of one day, and then switch to Subject B in the afternoon.

Step 4 – Allocate the Syllabus to Revision Sessions

If you have followed the instructions so far, you should have in front of you a timetable detailing the targeted number of revision hours per day and which subjects these hours are to be spent on.

What you have not done yet is allocate syllabus areas across the revision sessions you have timetabled, so this needs to be done now. Otherwise you're not going to know what area it is you're supposed to be revising for when you start your revision session.

In many respects this is the same as the process you went through when producing your initial study timetables i.e. use the exam syllabus to identify syllabus areas and spread evenly across the revision sessions available. The difference here is that you can give more prominence (more time in other words) to those areas you found more difficult during your studies. Again, do make sure you maintain a relatively wide and even coverage though.

Note – It may be that the questions you are intending to use during your timed question practice do not identify which syllabus area they are seeking to test. If so, you will have to skip this step, in which case each of your timed question practice revision periods will simply have an overall subject assigned. It will then be up to you to select the questions you want to attempt on the day.

An Example Revision Timetable

The revision timetable that you end up with having followed the instructions above will of course be unique to you and your own particular circumstances. Nevertheless, to give you an indication of what you should be aiming at, set out in figure 18.5(a) and (b) is an example of a revision timetable, based on the subjects and associated syllabi which were used in Chapter 7 on timetable production and the information contained in Steps 1 to 4 above.

Note that only Week 3 of the revision period is shown here – in practice you would have a weekly timetable for each of the weeks that make up your total revision period.

Figure 18.5 (a)

Revision Period - Week 3

Time	Monday		Tuesday		Wednesday		Thursday	
00:00								
01:00								
02:00								
03:00								
04:00								
05:00								
06:00								
07:00							G Gym 07:00-08:30	
08:00								
09:00	W Work 09:00-17:00		W Work 09:00-17:00		CAQA QP D2	3	FA QP B1 and B2	3
10:00	W		W					
11:00	W		W					
12:00	W		W		FA QP A3g	1	Lunch	
13:00	W		W		Lunch		CAQA QP E1	3
14:00	W		W		FA QP B1	2		
15:00	W		W					
16:00	W		W		CAQA QP D3	1		
17:00	W		W				CAQA QP E2	1
18:00								
19:00	FA QP A3d/e/f	2	CAQA QP D1 & D4	3				
20:00								
21:00								
22:00								
23:00								
00:00								
Total		2		3		7		7

Figure 18.5 (b)

Revision Period - Week 3

Time	Friday		Saturday		Sunday		Notes	
00:00								
01:00							Total budgeted study hours	40
02:00							Split into	
03:00							CAQA	24
04:00							FA	16
05:00								
06:00								
07:00			G Gym 07:00-08:30					
08:00								
09:00	CAQA QP E3	2	FA QP C1	3				
10:00					CAQA QP F3	2		
11:00	FA QP B3	2						
12:00			Lunch					
13:00	Lunch		CAQA QP F1	2	Lunch			
14:00	CAQA QP E1/2/3	3						
15:00					CAQA QP F3 and 4	2		
16:00								
17:00			CAQA QP F2	2	FA QP C1	3		
18:00								
19:00								
20:00			Night out - Dog and Gun					
21:00								
22:00								
23:00								
00:00								
Total		7		7		7		40

Reviewing and Maintaining the Revision Timetable

Following the steps above will give you a revision timetable that you can use on a daily basis to identify

- The time and length of each planned revision session.
- The subject and syllabus areas for each session.
- The type of revision session i.e. active review or question practice.

Compare Actuals to Plans

Use your timetable to guide your revision, and log your actual performance for each session and day on your timetable against your plans. Make sure you review your progress regularly, preferably daily. Doing this will allow you to clearly identify whether you're still on track or whether some correction of your course is required.

Reward Yourself

Where you find you have reached the targets you originally set yourself, allow yourself the luxury of feeling good about the progress you're making. Even better, allow yourself some kind of reward, whatever suits your personality best. Rewarding yourself in this way makes the whole process seem somehow slightly more bearable!

Reach Your Targets Then Walk Away

Don't be tempted either to do "just a little bit more" when you reach your targets. This is a noble gesture, but the wrong one to make. You need to pace yourself over the long haul, so save that energy and enthusiasm for the next planned revision session. Reach your targets, pat yourself on the back, put your books away, and rest.

Key Two –
Active Review

Reading Alone is Not Enough

Probably the biggest single misconception about revision is that it consists purely of sitting down and reading study notes.

Don't Just Read Study Notes

This couldn't be further from the truth. Merely sitting there, passively reading study notes, hoping that if you read them enough times you're going to understand and remember enough to pass your exam, is simply not going to work. You need to do more.

Don't Just Read the Textbook Either

And this doesn't mean you should be going back to read from the source textbooks either. Although many students still use their textbooks for revision right up to the day of the exam itself, this is a flawed approach. Having the textbook in your hands might well give you a feeling of security that you have accurate information "from the horses mouth", but you don't have enough time at this stage to trawl through the text trying to find nuggets of important information. Instead, you should be using your time wisely and working from your study notes.

What Should I Do Then?

So if you shouldn't be just reading your textbook, or your study notes, what *should* you be doing? Working actively, of course! We've seen the importance of being active already – it's crucial if you want to ensure that you make the best use of your brain's enormous powers.

> ***"Like swift water an active mind never stagnates."***
> **Author Unknown**

What's Involved

You've already produced your revision timetable, so you know *when* your revision study periods allocated to active review are, *how long* these periods are, and *what subject(s) and topic area(s)* you'll be covering during each revision period. (Remember, as a rough guide, around 25 percent of your time should be spent on this first stage of active review.)

So all you need to know now is *what* you should be doing during these revision periods. Here's the what.

Step 1 – Revisit Your Big Picture and Study Notes

Assuming you used the methods outlined in the Study Tools and Techniques chapter to produce your study notes, you should already have both a "big picture" of the chosen subject area (in diagrammatic form) and some written study notes. Read these through now to remind yourself of the contents.

Step 2 – Sketch Out the Main Points

Bearing in mind the ongoing review process that you should have been undertaking during your studies, reading through your notes now should merely act as a reminder of the issues contained rather than as a method of memorising the data.

Having reminded yourself of what's involved, the aim now is to produce some highly summarised revision notes. Put your study notes to one side, out of sight, and try to sketch out the main points from your notes. This only needs to be done roughly, as you'll be producing some final revision notes shortly.

Step 3 – Check Your Knowledge

The aim of producing these rough notes is to ensure you do indeed have all the key points stored in your memory and can reproduce them when required. Compare your rough notes back to your study notes and big picture diagram(s) to check whether you have indeed committed everything of importance to memory. Identify where any gaps between your knowledge and the notes exist. Be honest with yourself. Where gaps do exist, revisit these areas until you are happy with them. Ideally, repeat steps 2 and 3 to ensure that you have filled these gaps in your memory.

> ***"To be conscious that you are ignorant is a great step to knowledge."***
> **Benjamin Disraeli**

Step 4 – Produce Revision Notes

The Aim

Once you're happy that you have committed the salient information to memory, you need to produce some revision notes. The idea here is to summarise even further your study notes, condensing them down until a subject area can be represented on a single sheet of paper, or at least as few sheets as possible. Some students prefer the use of "cue cards", which are postcard sized, but use the same basic principles of holding highly summarised data. They find these cards portable and therefore easier to pull out and review whenever the opportunity arises.

The Process

To condense your notes down to one sheet of paper (or revision card, or whatever format you decide works best for you), identify the main themes around which the subject area is based. Distil these down into key words only – there should be no full sentences appearing on your final revision notes. It's likely too that to represent an entire subject area on one page, you'll need to use some sort of diagrammatic approach (i.e. like the patterned notes method detailed earlier in the book), as this allows you to represent the relationships between the main themes and key points.

Figure 19.1 overleaf gives an example of revision notes.

Figure 19.1

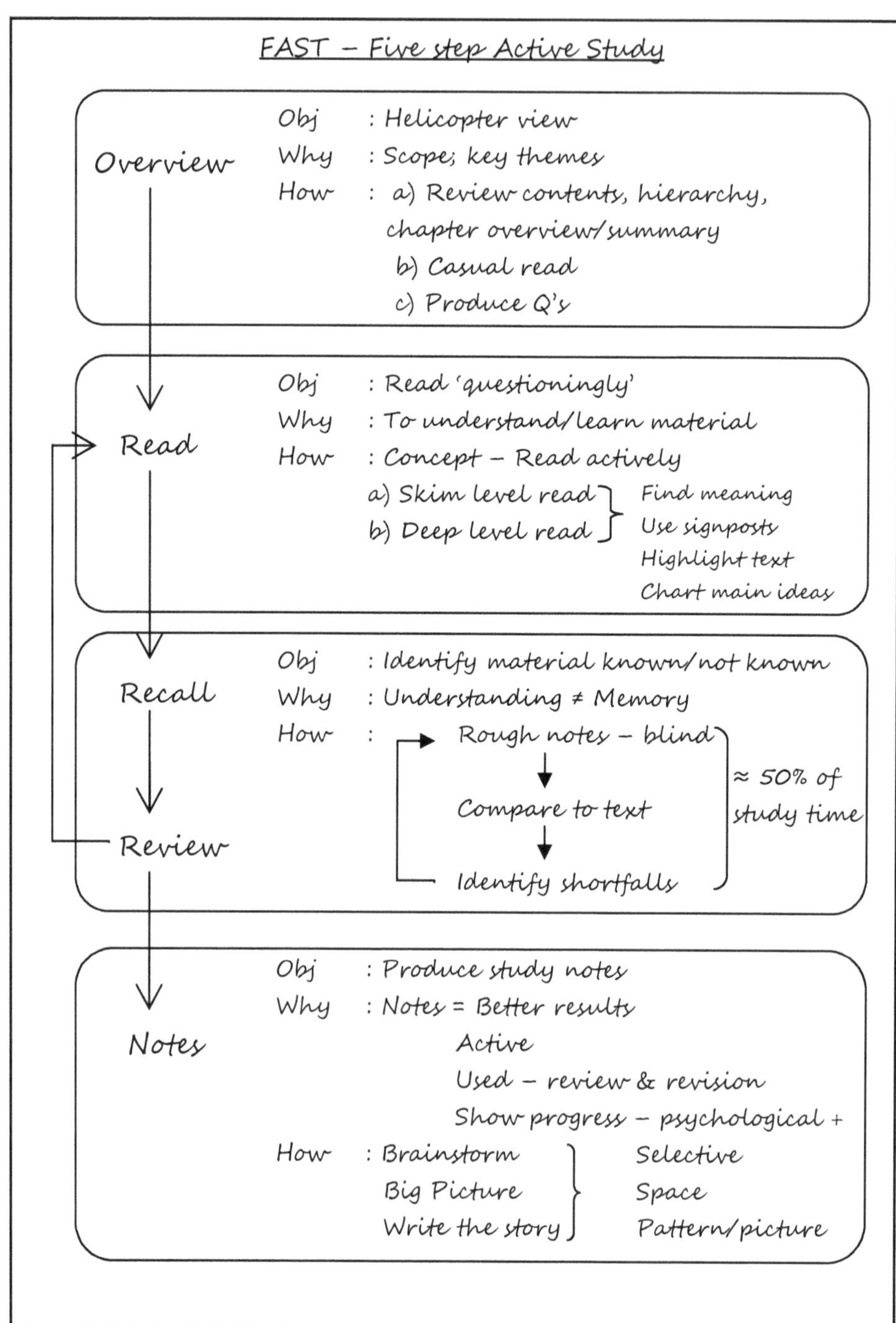
FAST – Five step Active Study
Overview
Obj : Helicopter view
Why : Scope; key themes
How : a) Review contents, hierarchy, chapter overview/summary
b) Casual read
c) Produce Q's
Read
Obj : Read 'questioningly'
Why : To understand/learn material
How : Concept – Read actively
a) Skim level read
b) Deep level read
Find meaning
Use signposts
Highlight text
Chart main ideas
Recall
Obj : Identify material known/not known
Why : Understanding ≠ Memory
How :
Rough notes – blind
Compare to text
Identify shortfalls
≈ 50% of study time
Review
Notes
Obj : Produce study notes
Why : Notes = Better results
Active
Used – review & revision
Show progress – psychological +
How : Brainstorm
Big Picture
Write the story
Selective
Space
Pattern/picture

Step 5 – Check Your Revision Notes

Having produced your revision notes, ensure that they encapsulate everything you need to know about the subject area. This doesn't mean they should contain every single piece of information you need to know. If they did, they would be study notes and not revision notes. Rather, the notes should act as a catalyst, firing off neural pathways in your brain that bring to mind all of the subject matter you've studied.

Step 6 – Review Examiner's Comments and Past Papers

In addition to producing condensed revision notes, at this active review stage it's also worth getting hold of both past papers and examiner's comments for the exams you're about to take, if you haven't already done so. Some examining bodies won't release these, but the majority will.

Past Papers – Set the Scene

Now is a good time to remind yourself exactly what you're aiming at, to see both the structure of the exam and some examples of content. Have a look through the past exam papers, make sure you identify how the exam is structured (what format the exam takes, the number and type of questions, the time available etc.), and have quick read through some of the questions to get a feel for the way they are set.

Examiner's Comments – Invaluable Advice

The Examiner's Comments are often an invaluable guide to avoiding costly mistakes in the exam hall. Not only do they usually contain general advice and comment, including the oft repeated

> ***"Candidates are again reminded of the need to read the question carefully, and to answer the question which has actually been set – and not the one they wish had been set!"***

but often guidance or comment on particular areas of the syllabus, for example

> ***"Candidates for future examinations should ensure that they can draw simple Entity Life Histories or State Transition diagrams."***

This is the kind of guidance you would be wise not to ignore! There is a strong possibility that if the Examiner is unhappy with the way a particular question has been answered, he will seek to test that subject area again in the very next sitting. Using this information in this way isn't question spotting, it's common sense.

Gaining An Advantage

So, taking note of what the examiner wants and doesn't want to see in the exam scripts he marks really *can* pay dividends. That's why looking at these comments now is worth doing. They'll hopefully still be fresh in your mind when you sit both your timed question practice and the exam itself, and you'll avoid making some of the common mistakes that others who haven't taken the time to read the examiner's comments will. Remember – any advantage you can gain over your fellow student is worth taking.

> ***"It's them as take advantage that get advantage i' this world."***
> **George Eliot, Adam Bede**

What *Not* to Do for Active Review

There are some mistakes which need to be avoided.

One Rewrite Only

You should be aiming to rewrite your study notes in the form of condensed revision notes *once only*. If you need to go through a serious of rewrites, each one reducing your original study notes down a little further, you are wasting valuable time on an activity which is going to yield you little extra value come the day of the exam.

Read your original study notes, check you can recall them, and then rewrite them in the form of condensed revision notes. And then move on.

For the Visually Orientated

Compromising Photographic Memories

There are some people whose memory works in a predominantly visual way. Whey they recall something they have studied, they literally "see" the study text (or more likely their study notes since these were produced actively) in their mind's eye. A lucky one or two of these people literally have a "photographic memory".

If you are one of these people, rewriting your study notes is *not* a good idea, for fairly obvious reasons. Your new revision notes would not look the same as the original study notes, and the existing memory might be compromised. In this case, it's probably best to stick with your original study notes and follow the advice below.

An Alternative to Revision Notes – Index Cards

Instead, keep your study notes as they are to allow your visual memories to stay undisturbed, and produce a set of "index cards". These are similar to cue cards, but as the name implies, simply act as an index for the key points and main themes.

To produce these index cards, as before, identify the main points contained in the study notes, and then list them in a logical order on the index card. Cross reference each entry on the card back to your original study notes, showing the position of the item in your notes (this will require you, if you haven't already done so, to sequentially number the pages in your study notes). Figure 19.2 gives an example of an index card.

Figure 19.2

Learning Theories & Memory

Guidelines for TT production

Notes Page Ref

1) ≤ 45mins per study period
+ short break (5mins) — 10

2) Little & often — 11

Effort — NOT

Time

3) Include subject variety — 11
Subject, subject area, study method,

4) Repetition + Review = Recall
(Understanding ≠ Recall) — 12-13
Builds brain pathways

Using index cards in this way brings big advantages.

- Your existing visual memory remains intact.
- To revise, you use the index cards in conjunction with your cross referenced original notes, and not just the original notes alone. Thus you don't waste time trawling through the notes every time you want to

revise something, but instead go straight to those areas of importance via the index.

- Your existing visual memories are further strengthened as you revisit the same places in your study notes every time you revise.

Wrapping up the Active Review Stage

The Active Review stage is an essential part of the revision process, but it is important not to get too hung up on it and get stuck. There is often a temptation to drag one's feet here and not move onto the next crucial stage, the timed question practice.

Reasons for this tardiness include

- Not being 100 percent happy with the way the active review process has gone (certain areas of the syllabus may have been difficult to understand and commit to memory).
- Not feeling that the active review process is 100 percent complete (certain areas of the syllabus have not been covered or have not been covered in sufficient depth).
- A feeling of blind panic at the thought of actually attempting some timed questions (there's no more escaping or hiding from the truth when understanding and skills are tested in this way).

In reality,

- You're never going to be completely happy with your progress. No one is perfect. There is no model student in existence (not one I've ever met anyway!).
- There will *never* be enough time to completely cover every area of a subject.
- It's normal to feel panic at this time. The whole point is that in dealing with it now, whilst you still have time to practice before the exam, you can learn to overcome it *before* the exam.

So, when you get to the end of the time allotted to the active review stage, wrap things up and move on. Don't be tempted to adopt the "just a little bit more, only another couple of days and then I'll move on" attitude. The timed question phase awaits, and this is without doubt the most crucial phase of your entire study process. You need to spend all the time you can on it.

Key Three – Timed Question Practice

No Substitutes Available

Timed question practice is all about attempting exam standard questions under exam conditions. For many it is a daunting task.

There is no substitute for timed question practice. It's a simple as that. You can't replace it with something less stressful which will still do the same job.

So, accept that this is an inevitable part of the study process, and make the most of it. To convince you that the benefits gained from timed question practice make the blood, sweat and tears worth it, let's look at *why* question practice is so important – what are these benefits that you're going to enjoy?

Why Timed Question Practice?

Timed question practice will benefit you in a number of ways.

- It allows you to develop the skill of providing a reasonable answer to a question in the time frame set.
- It increases your fluency in the subject, as you get used to using the ideas, terminology and so on within your answers.
- It allows you to practice applying your knowledge in range of different contexts and scenarios. As we know, *application* of knowledge is what the examiner will want to see demonstrated at professional level, not just the ability to memorise facts using rote learning.
- It allows you to integrate what you have learned from a range of syllabus areas into a single specific task. Questions at this level are likely to cover a number of syllabus areas – you need to demonstrate that you understand the relationships between these.

> ***"Chance favours only the prepared mind."***
> **Louis Pasteur**

- It allows you to experience exam stress and anxiety in advance of the real exam, and the familiarity you gain by doing so allows you to learn to manage and reduce these negative feelings before the big day.
- It reinforces your self-confidence by making you realise you *are* capable of providing exam standard answers. And the stronger your self-confidence, the better your exam performance.

Overall, timed question practice is always going to be far more beneficial than just sitting down and reading study notes. Reading notes alone does not test

- Your recall.
- Your ability to apply the knowledge you have.

- Your ability to plan, organise and write your answer in the time given.
- Your presentational skills and grammar.

> *"The work will teach you how to do it."*
> **Estonian Proverb**

Timed question practice will test *all* of these. Again, it's all about being *active* and not *passive*. And you can't get more active than sitting there and producing an answer to an exam question under timed conditions!

The Meaning of "Timed"

You may be wondering exactly what I mean when I use the term "timed" to describe your question practice. Let's just make sure therefore that you understand what the use of the word implies.

Set Duration

Every exam will have a set duration. You should already be aware of how long your exam lasts, but if not, check with your examining body who will be able to provide you with this information. Often, professional exams last for 3 hours per paper, although there are no hard and fast rules here.

Set Number of Marks

Every exam will also have a set total number of marks available to the student. Normally, exams are marked out of 100. That is, a total of 100 marks are available – assuming a perfect answer to all questions, the student would receive 100 marks (or 100 out of 100, being 100 percent).

Set Paper Format

Each exam will have its own format. For example, some may consist of 5 essay questions of 20 marks each. Others may be a 60-mark case study and two 20-mark essays. Others again may be different, consisting of smaller individual questions going to make up in total 100 marks. Again, there is no hard and fast rule here – you need to make sure you're aware of exactly how the exam you're going to sit is formatted. Past papers can help here, but do make sure you read all the latest guidance and advice produced by the examining body – exam formats do change from time to time.

The Minutes Per Mark Calculation

Now, assuming you know (i) how long the paper lasts, (ii) how many marks the paper is marked out of, and (iii) the exam format (and also by implication the mark allocation per question), you can work out how long you have to answer each question.

An Example

Say our exam lasts for 3 hours and requires five essay questions of 20 marks each to be answered.

The total number of minutes available to you in the exam will be 3 x 60 = 180 minutes in total.

Theoretically, this means that you have -

180 minutes ÷ 100 marks = 1.8 minutes per mark available, or

20 x 1.8 minutes = 36 minutes per essay question.

However, this ignores the fact you will need a certain amount of time to read the paper through when you open it and a little time at the end to check you have complied with all the exam requirements, such as entering your candidate number onto all answer booklets and sheets.

For a 3 hour exam, allow 20 minutes for these tasks. This means we have 160 minutes (180-20) available for answering questions. This equates to 1.6 minutes per mark (160÷100), or 32 minutes (1.6 x 20) per 20 mark essay question.

Any by the way, do *not* be tempted to ignore the deduction for those admin and checking duties (the 20 minutes shown in the example above) to give yourself extra time to answer each question. This is a false economy. The reason you need to build this time in is precisely because what you'll be doing during it is so important – things that can make all the difference between pass and fail. We'll look at this in more detail in Chapter 25 – The Exam.

Where "Pre-Exam Reading Time" is Given

Some examining bodies allow a certain amount of time as "pre-exam reading time". What this means in practice is that you will be given a specified amount of additional time, normally between 10 and 20 minutes, at the beginning of your exam. This time is to allow you to read and understand the exam requirements, read the questions themselves and to start planning your answers (although it's unlikely you'll get very far with the planning in the small amount of additional time given). Usually during this period you will only be able to annotate the exam question paper and not to actually start writing in your answer booklet – you will only be able to do this from the time your invigilator tells you that you can do so.

If this is the case for you, still allow 10 minutes checking time at the end of the exam but do not build in any adjustment for reading time at the start as you've got this as an added bonus for free (wow – aren't you the lucky one!). In the example above, assuming a 3 hour exam with five 20-mark questions, the marks per minute figure would be 1.7 ((180-10)/100), so for each essay you should allocate 34 minutes (1.7 x 20).

Using the Minutes Per Mark Calculation

Calculate Your Minutes Per Mark

Work out how many minutes per mark you have available to you in your particular exam. Remember to build in some reading and administration time to your calculation as we've seen above (unless you're going to be given some pre-exam reading time, in which case you should adjust only for some checking time at the end of the exam) – it's not practical to expect that you'll be able to open the exam paper and start writing the answer to your first question immediately!

Use It For Every Question

Once you have the minutes per mark number calculated, use it when you're attempting *every* question during your timed question practice revision period. Normally both past exam papers and exam standard practice questions will show the number of marks allocated to a particular question – simply multiply the number of marks indicated by your calculated minutes per mark figure to find out how much time you should assign to producing an answer. For example, if the question is for 15 marks and you've calculated you have 1.6 minutes per mark, you have 15 x 1.6 = 24 minutes to answer the question.

Multi-Part Questions

Often, where a question has more than one part, each part will have a mark allocation too, for example, using our 15-mark example question, there might be three parts, each of 5 marks each. If so, each part should take approximately 8 minutes to complete (24÷3).

But What if No Allocation Between Parts is Shown?

Where no allocation between parts of a question is shown, you will need to apply your common sense and judgement to decide what the likely allocation is. This is often obvious from the wording of the question, for example

Under existing UK law, all limited companies are required to maintain certain registers, books and records. These are known collectively as statutory books.

Required

(a) List the names of any four such statutory books
(b) State the contents of each book you have listed in (a) above and explain the purpose for which each is maintained.
(16 marks)

In this question, it would be a perfectly reasonable assumption to presume that

- Part (a) has four marks allocated to it, one mark for each of the four statutory books listed.
- As part (b) has the remaining 12 marks allocation (16 marks total less the 4 for part (a)), this must mean there are 3 marks available for each of the listed statutory books (4 books x 3 marks=12), probably 1 mark for stating the contents of the book and 2 marks for explaining its purpose.

Cut and Run

When attempting questions during revision, you need to develop the discipline of stopping when you have got to the end of your allotted time, and moving on.

This is the case even if you haven't finished the question. (You have read this correctly!)

That means not overrunning on time *by even one minute*. If you have 24 minutes available to answer your 15-mark question, *only take 24 minutes and not a minute longer*. Then cut and run – stop your answer and move onto something else. Do not be tempted to spend "just another 5 minutes" on trying to complete your answer. This is a false economy, for reasons we shall come back to in Part Seven – Exam Technique.

"I wasted time, and now doth time waste me."
William Shakespeare

It might seem a little over the top to be quite so ruthless with your time allocation, especially as you're still only in your revision stage and not actually in the exam. But believe me, it's better to start getting into the routine now rather than to try to get it right for the first time in the exam hall when the pressure's really on. It seems to be a natural human need to complete a task set, but this is an instinct you need to eradicate by the time you sit the exam. Starting this process now will give you the practice you need. Trust me on this – you'll be pleased you did!

Implementing Timed Question Practice

You've calculated your minutes per mark. Your revision timetable shows you when your timed question practice revision periods are, how long they last, and which subjects they are for.

So, armed with this information, exactly what is it you should do now? You should be following the four steps shown below in figure 20.1.

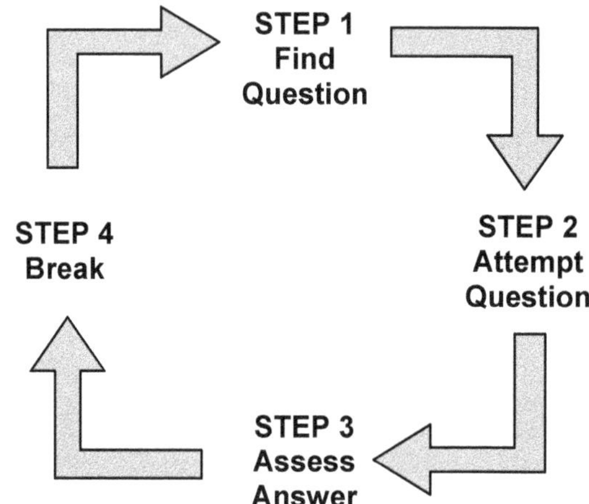

Step 1 – Identify the Question

Select a question from your question bank (this might be from either an actual past exam paper or from a question manual produced by a third party, such as the training company who supplied you with your distance learning materials).

You may find that, depending on the source of the questions, you are told which areas of the syllabus the question seeks to test. If you are provided with this information, make sure that you use it to further target your studies by ensuring that you attempt questions covering a wide range of syllabus topics.

Step 2 – Attempt the Question Under Exam Conditions

Using the minutes per mark figure you arrived at above, calculate how long you have to complete your answer (i.e. your minutes per mark figure multiplied by the mark allocation for the question gives the total time available). Where the question is multi-part, work out how long you have for each part of the question.

Using this information and the time now (the start time), calculate and jot down finish times for each part of the question and the question as a whole. Then put all available study and revision notes out of sight and attempt the question (we shall cover the techniques to use when attempting the various question styles that there are in the next chapter). When answering the question, make sure you stay within the allotted times you noted down at the start of the question. Do not overrun on time in order to complete any part of the question, or the question as a whole.

Step 3 – Mark Your Answer

Having finished writing when your calculated time was up, now it's time to assess how well you've done.

- Turn to the model answer produced by the examiner or the question provider, and compare your answer to the model one.
- Identify any differences between your answer and the model one, and where gaps in your knowledge exist.
- Revisit any problem areas you identify as a result of this comparison process in your revision notes, and make sure you are happy that you understand where you went wrong.

It's important to remember that a model answer is just that, i.e. a *model*. It is an ideal answer, which includes *everything* you might correctly put into your own answer. The examiner would definitely not expect you to produce so comprehensive an answer under timed exam conditions, so don't beat yourself up when there are things in the model answer you've missed.

Step 4 – Take a Short Break

Now is the time to sit back and switch off for a short time. Get up, walk around and stretch your legs, maybe get yourself a drink. You only need to take five minutes, no more, before you sit back down and start the process again, selecting another question, producing an answer under timed conditions, comparing your answer to the model answer, and so on.

Additional Guidance for Timed Question Practice

We've seen the basic question/answer/assess/review process to be used for your timed question practice, but how about some more guidance to ensure you get the most out of it?

Using Outline Answer Plans

For computational questions, there's no choice but to work your way through the entire question as it is set. For example, if you're an accountancy student and the question asks you to prepare a profit and loss account with the information provided for 20 marks, that's what you're going to attempt for the next 32 minutes (20 x 1.6 minutes). There's no way of short-cutting the process.

However, where your exam includes essay questions, during your revision you have the option of either producing a *full written essay* answer in the allotted time, or alternatively producing only an *outline answer plan* in, say, 10 minutes. An outline answer plan sets out the structure of the essay you would write, along with the key points you would make in it. As such, producing it allows you to attempt a question without having to waste time writing a full answer, with all the words, sentences and paragraphs that this entails. An outline plan can still be compared to the model answer to see where gaps in knowledge or understanding exist.

In fact, as we will see shortly when we look at how to approach the various different question types you might encounter, producing an answer plan is an integral part of the essay writing process anyway. It is always the first step taken *before* you start writing the essay itself. Getting into the habit of producing these outline plans is therefore a good discipline to instil in yourself now.

And not only does getting practice in producing outline answer plans help you come the day of the exam, it also allows you to attempt a far greater number of questions during your revision, leading to a wider syllabus coverage, which can only be a good thing.

A word of caution however. Using outline answers to allow you to attempt *more* questions in *more* syllabus areas *is* a great idea. However, actually sitting an exam having *never* attempted to write a full essay answer under timed conditions is *not* such a good idea! Writing full essay answers is a demanding activity – you will be writing at pretty much full speed for the entire time available. You need to produce a complete answer with a beginning, a middle and an end, and at the same time you need to maintain legibility and comprehensibility (in other words, your answer has to be readable and it has to make sense). These are not skills you can simply acquire in the exam hall – you need to practice them up front.

What I'd suggest is this

Step 1

Produce a full written answer to the first essay question you attempt. This will give you an idea of what it feels like to produce an answer under timed conditions. Don't panic if you don't do very well the first time – it's only to be expected. That's why you need to build practice into your revision plans.

Step 2

Attempt the next few questions using only outline plan answers. Doing this ensures that you build your confidence levels by getting a few questions under your belt.

Step 3

Then try producing another full written answer to the next essay question you attempt. Build on the experience you gained in Step 1, and try to put those lessons you learned into practice.

Step 4

Continue Steps 2 and 3 until you are happy and able to produce a complete answer in the time set. Once you feel you have got to this level, attempt the majority of essay question using outline answer plans, but include a full written answer every so often to maintain the skills you've acquired.

Full Mock Exams

At some point during your question practice phase, you need to build in the time to attempt a full mock exam *under timed conditions*. You should do this at least once.

Why? Because sitting in an exam hall for (say) three hours and producing a decent answer script is extremely demanding, both mentally and physically. You need to know what it feels like, so that you don't find the real thing too much, and perform below your abilities. Unlike your revision, there can be no five minute breaks between questions in the exam hall!

By full mock exam I mean either a past exam paper, or a mock exam prepared by the provider of your study material. If these aren't available, you should select a set of questions whose time allocations equal the length of your exam (normally this means selecting questions whose combined marks equal 100).

Whatever you select as your mock exam, make sure you sit it as if it were the real thing. No getting up and making a cup of tea. No sitting back and day-dreaming. No looking out of the window. Pretend it's exam day, start the clock, open the paper, and do the best you can. Finish writing your answers after the allotted time.

You will find this an invaluable experience, although a uniquely demanding one. However you do, remember – there is no substitute for experience. By sitting this mock exam, you are adding to your experience, and increasing your chances of success. Tell yourself this if you are tempted to avoid this task.

Don't Use Hieroglyphics

Readable Answers Please

Do make sure that the answers you produce under timed conditions are *legible*. If they are not, whatever wonderful insights your answer may hold will remain unread and unmarked. However wonderful they are.

Of course, the examiner does not expect you to produce answers in inch-perfect copperplate script – this would hardly be possible in the time pressured environment of the exam hall. But you *are* expected to produce answers which can be read with the minimum of difficulty.

Exam Markers are Not Charities

Why is this so important? Well, think about it for a moment. The poor unfortunates who have to mark exam scripts have to mark many hundreds of them in a very short space of time. With a script that is largely illegible, the marker will do their level best to decipher the answers given, however, there is only so much leeway, and so much marking time, that they can give. Ultimately, if they cannot read the answer, they cannot award the marks, and they will have no choice but to move onto the next question or the next paper.

Get Your Writing Checked Out

So make sure this fate doesn't befall your answers. Check to make sure you can read your script. And go one step further – give one of your answers to a friend and ask them if they can read it. You may be surprised to find what you thought was perfectly clear is actually far from it.

Less is More

If so, you need to work hard to write in a legible way. It's too late to change your writing style now, but the likelihood is that it's the time pressure that is making your writing unreadable. This is a common mistake – trying to write as much as you can using as many words as possible. Perhaps students think they get marks by the hundred words written, I'm not sure!

In reality, short, punchy, to-the-point answers are what's required in the exam. So work hard on writing your essays in this way, and avoid the urge to write a paragraph when a sentence will do. By cutting down on the amount you write, you should find that its legibility automatically improves.

Maintain that Variety

Whilst you're carrying out your timed question practice, *do* remember to build in as much variety as possible. At this stage of the game, you need to be on absolutely top form, and doing everything you can to stave off boredom and avoid becoming stale is a sensible approach.

For example, if you're studying for two exams in different subjects, do timed question practice for subject one in the morning and timed question practice for subject two in the afternoon. And within each subject, don't spend the whole revision period doing questions only from one area of the syllabus – keep the variety going.

When Things Don't Go Well

The Wrong Answer

There will be times when the answer you produce to a timed question falls dismally short of what's required.

That's life. You should expect to get a fair number of the questions you attempt wrong – it's inevitable.

The important thing is to *learn* from the mistakes you make. And that's what you're doing by attempting these questions now and not in the exam itself – learning. Please do not underestimate just how much value you add to your ultimate chances by making a mistake, looking at the answer, and working out where you went wrong. This is an invaluable process.

> ***"Mistakes, obviously, show us what needs improving. Without mistakes, how would we know what we had to work on?"***
> **Peter McWilliams**

So next time you get a question wrong, pat yourself on the back! You've learned something. And, more importantly, you're going to be better prepared than many of your fellow examinees, who won't have attempted as many questions as you, if any. This is good news!

Not Enough of an Answer

Instead of getting the conceptual or factual information wrong in your answer, you may find you simply didn't have enough time to produce an answer of sufficient length.

Again, do not get disheartened when this happens – it *is* inevitable. Getting used to producing a decent answer in a time pressured situation takes some degree of practice – which is precisely what you're getting as you struggle through your timed questions. Gradually, if you persevere, you will find that working to the tight deadlines involved really does become easier, and eventually second nature to you. Honestly!

> ***"You may be disappointed if you fail, but you are doomed if you don't try."***
> **Beverly Sills**

And that's what you're aiming at – making ruthless time allocation a habit, so that come the day of the exam, you give every question a fair crack, maximising your chances of success. This ruthless time allocation is so important that we shall return to it again in Part Seven of the book on Exam Technique.

"It's All Going Pear-Shaped"

The days and weeks immediately preceding your exam are without doubt among the toughest you will have to face. Mentally and physically, they demand a tremendous amount from you.

In the face of such pressure, it's not surprising if occasionally it feels like it's all getting too much and that you just can't see your way through to a happy ending. You're only human, after all.

If you find yourself feeling like this, falling into a black pit of despair or unable to shake a feeling of almost blind panic, stop doing what you're doing immediately. Shut up your books, put away your pens and paper, and go and do something completely different. Preferably get away from wherever you're studying and find another environment. Take a "Time-Out".

This may feel like you're wasting valuable time but you won't be. If you were to stay there, doggedly trying to work through it, you'd be in danger of doing yourself more harm than good, perhaps sending yourself into such a tailspin you'll have trouble pulling out of it. And the last thing you need at this stage is to place a huge dent in, or even destroy, the confidence you have built over the past weeks and months.

As to what you should be doing during this time out, and how long it should last, that depends on you and what you enjoy. Maybe an hour's walk outside in the sunshine, maybe a visit to the gym to burn off that frustration, whatever you can do to take your focus off of the exams and your performance. And when the despair and panic have subsided, return to your studies. You will be refreshed and in a more receptive state of mind than you would have been had you tried to stick with it.

> ***"Self-confidence is the first requisite to great undertakings."***
> **Samuel Johnson**

Remember also the power of positive affirmations and visualisations. Use these techniques (and others) shown in the Success Factor section to further improve your state of mind and confidence levels.

How to Approach Questions

How Do I Answer the Question?

We've seen that timed question practice is fundamental to your exam success, and the procedure you should use to implement it. However, what we've not yet looked at is exactly *what* approach you should be using when you actually attempt a question. In other words, *how* do you answer a question? That's what we're going to look at now.

Furthermore, the exams you take may seek to test your knowledge, and the application of that knowledge, in a number of ways. Whilst essays may be the question type of choice for some examining bodies, many will use a range of different testing techniques in their exam papers.

These include

- Essay style questions.
- Report style questions.
- Questions requiring short prose answers.
- Case study questions involving a given scenario and using a range of answer formats.
- Multiple choice questions (sometimes known as Objective Testing).
- Mathematical/calculation/numerical questions.
- Open book questions/exams (where certain material can be taken into and used in the exam itself).
- Seen exams (where some material and/or the questions can be seen a predetermined time before exam, i.e. pre-seen as opposed to unseen).

Each particular question type will require an answer in a given style, and as such, each requires its own particular approach. You need to know what these are.

General Approach to Answering Questions

Whatever the question type, there are some ground rules you should always apply when attempting a question. These are

RTFQ (Read the Full Question)

Whether the question is one sentence or one page, you need to make sure you have read the question and its requirements *properly*. Read it through once to get a general feel for what the question is about, then re-read it more slowly, underlining what you believe to be the key words and phrases. Make sure you read what is printed on the page and *not* what you would like to see printed.

There is no doubt that at some stage you will fall into the trap of not reading the question properly and so will produce an answer which is likely to pick up few marks. When you make this mistake, you might want to berate yourself with a variation of RTFQ, where the F stands not for "Full" but instead for a well known Anglo-Saxon expletive also beginning with F! Repeat this variation of the RTFQ acronym to yourself (in your mind only of course, rather than out loud, if you happen to be in a public place) and hopefully this will fix in your mind just how important reading the question properly really is! *Answer the question set, not the one you want to see.*

"Furious activity is no substitute for understanding."
H.H.Williams

Understand the Requirements

Reread the requirements again (i.e. what it is the examiner wants you to do). Underline the key words contained in these instructions. The appendix at the end of the book sets out some of the most commonly used terms in exam questions and their meaning. Make sure you understand the differences between these, as getting the wrong meaning will mean you will not be answering the question correctly.

For example, answering the question

"Describe the views on industrial relations taken by (a) management and (b) employees."

requires a markedly different answer to the question

"Compare the views on industrial relations taken by (a) management and (b) employees."

even though they might look similar at first glance. The former question requires the presentation of the details and characteristics of the views of each group, the latter an explanation of the similarities and differences between the views of the two groups. This difference stems from the use of the use of the key words "describe" and "compare" – miss this point and you could end up answering the question the wrong way. Doing so would seriously impact your chances of getting a pass mark for this question.

Reflect on the Question

Take a few moments to consider the question and its requirements. Don't feel panicked into starting to answer it yet. Be thinking about what areas of the syllabus the question is based around. Consider what specific issues, concepts, theories or knowledge concerning those areas of the syllabus the examiner might be seeking to test. Ask yourself what is implicit in the question as well as explicitly stated. If necessary, jot down notes to help your thought processes.

Making sure you follow these ground rules before you actually start answering a question should ensure you avoid the most common mistake made by students. It's a fatal error to make – not answering the question set.

> ***"Think first, then do."***
> **Albert Schweitzer**

Not Answering the Question Set

If you were to read a selection of Examiners' Comments produced by a range of examining bodies for a variety of different subjects and for any exam sitting you care to select, one common theme would undoubtedly stand out. And that is, students persist in producing answers which don't match the questions' requirements. They don't answer the question that has been set.

This mistake generally takes two forms. Either

- Instead of answering the question they have been asked, the student answers the question they would have liked to have been asked, perhaps the one they revised for; or
- The student writes all they know about the subject in general, not addressing the specifics of the question, perhaps in the hope that by throwing everything they know into the answer they can somehow fool or impress the examiner into giving them a pass mark.

In either case, students are unlikely to score highly if they don't produce a focussed answer which addresses the requirements of the question itself. In fact, they may gain no marks at all. And time spent on an answer which gains no marks is time wasted – which you can ill afford to do.

So make sure you don't fall into this trap. Read the question slowly and carefully. Take notice of *every* word. Understand the question's requirements. Ensure you think about what it is the examiner is seeking to test. And don't make assumptions based on your own particular preferences. Answer what is there in front of you in black and white.

Answering Specific Question Types

Having looked at the general approach you should be adopting whenever attempting a question, let's now focus in turn on each one of the specific question types you might encounter during your exam. We'll start with perhaps the most common question type of all, the essay.

Essay Style Questions

These questions require an answer in the form of an essay. In general, essays tend to be

- "Argumentative" – that is, they contrast and compare different theories and arrive at an opinion or judgement in the form of a conclusion, or
- "Factual", where relevant factual information is presented in a logical and structured way in order to meet the question's requirements, or
- A combination of the two, where the first part is factual and the second part requires an evaluation to be made and opinions to be expressed.

Whatever the style and length of the essay (the length will be determined by the number of marks allocated to the question), the approach is basically the same.

Step 1 – Read/Understand/Reflect

Carry out the three steps listed above under the general approach to answering questions i.e.

- Read the full question.
- Understand the requirements.
- Reflect on the question.

Step 2 – Produce an Outline Answer Plan

Why Bother?

Students often skip this stage, reading the question and then getting stuck into writing their answer immediately. This is a mistake. Time spent planning your essay is most definitely *not* time wasted. Instead, it allows you to collect and marshal your thoughts and ideas together so that your finished essay is well-structured, coherent and presents a strong argument backed up by fact.

> ***"Whatever we conceive well we express clearly."***
> **Nicolas Boileau-Déspreaux**

Another reason for producing an answer plan is that it acts as a reference point whilst you're writing the essay. Without a map to work to, you can end up taking the essay in the wrong direction as you get diverted from your original path, and miss points that you were going to make along the way. Either that or without a map, or plan, you have to keep stopping to decide where to go and what to say next, leading to a lack of fluency in your writing. Having that plan to refer to significantly reduces the chances of these things happening.

And where you don't get to finish your essay due to time pressure, you'll likely still get credit for the points you would have made because they are in your original answer plan which your examiner can see.

What to Do

As guidance, producing your plan should take no more than 10 minutes for a 32 minute essay. Adjust this time accordingly dependent on the mark allocation for the essay itself.

You'll have already started jotting down some notes whilst reflecting on the question. Now you need to construct a plan which is capable of being used to produce your essay.

All essays have essentially three parts, an introduction, a main body and a conclusion. So set out space for these three areas on a sheet of paper. The main body will require the most space, as that's where the bulk of your work will be.

Then make brief notes (key words and bullet points only, not full sentences) using the guidance on content shown below.

OUTLINE ANSWER PLAN CONTENTS

Introduction

- Comments on the essay topic, noting what aspects of the syllabus will be dealt with.

Main Body

- List of the main points to get across.
- Ensure that some kind of logical progression of points exists. Where necessary, indicate relationships with arrows.
- Note of any examples, illustrations and factual evidence/information which needs to be included.

Conclusion

- Sum up your main ideas.
- Offer your conclusions (it may be more difficult to define a conclusion where the essay is a factual one).
- Point out any further implications of your conclusions.

When producing an answer plan, I often found one of Rudyard Kipling's verses very relevant when deciding what to include –

> ***"I keep six honest serving men***
> ***(They taught me all I knew);***
> ***Their names are What and Why and When***
> ***And How and Where and Who."***
> **Rudyard Kipling**

Asking yourself what, why, when, how, where and who in the context of your question can be a very useful way of driving the production of your answer plan.

Set out below is an example of a question that might be set in a paper examining “management and strategy” type issues and an answer plan constructed to address this question is set out in figure 21.1.

‘Long-term strategic planning is an obsolete practice’.

Discuss the benefits of long term strategic planning for an organization and examine the case for its abolition.

Figure 21.1

Answer Plan

Introduction

LTP - Define – formulation, evaluation, selection of strategies → plan to attain objectives

2 parts

Formal process – identify objectives, evolve alternative strategies

Translate to detailed operational plans

Benefits of long term planning

Some decisions irreversible – sensible to fit into plan

Forces objective setting

Allow risk identification

Environmental appraisal

Identifies resource issues/shortages

Helps integrate long/med/short plans

Gives metrics

Defines responsibility authority

Can help foster innovation, participation – better working environment

Performance targeted – performance up

Can act as early-warning system

The case against long term planning

Obj setting

Forecasting difficult- complex - inaccuracies

Pressure on mgt short term

Rigidity - straitjacket

Stifles initiative

Cost

Small businesses – no LTP – so why now?

Mgt distrust – techniques

Divergent personal interests – lead to conflicts?

Only useful if all mgt involved – CEO buy-in??

LTP - conclude a worthwhile process

Why ? –

Large orgs – complex, diversified, decentralized – no effective mgt without LTP

No LTP – uncoordinated, fragmented, divergent mgt

Uncertainty a given – LTP helps manage

Creates suitable environ for creativity

On balance – strong arguments in f/o LTP

Step 3 – Write Your Answer

Having produced your plan, now start writing your answer, basing it on the points you've jotted down. Bear the following guidance in mind when putting pen to paper. An essay incorporating all of these points should be of sufficient quality to get you a pass mark.

Don't restate the question

Don't restate part or all of the question as the first part of your answer. You will not gain any marks for it and it simply wastes valuable writing time.

Assume the reader is an intelligent layman

Your essay should assume that the examiner is an "intelligent person in the street". Of course, we know that's not the case, but pretend anyway! Don't assume any prior knowledge of the subject – this means defining any terms that you use, and not using abbreviations or acronyms where they are not in general public use (at least not without defining them in full first).

Appear confident

Write as if you are confident about what you are saying, even if you are not! And, at all costs, avoid putting in apologies to the examiner for any weaknesses you think there might be in your work. (You'll be amazed at the number of times I've marked scripts which contain phrases such as *"Dear Examiner, I wasn't in class when this area was studied hence the gap in my answer"!* Don't draw attention to your shortcomings.)

> ***"The man who has confidence in himself gains the confidence of others."***
> **Hasidic Saying**

State the obvious

Remember that the reader (i.e. the person marking your exam script) can't see into your mind, and may not be able to see the connections between the points you make in the way you can. Always clearly state what I call the "blindingly obvious" – you'll still get marks for it!

Maintain objectivity

Your essay should be as objective as possible, presenting *all* the arguments and points of view around the case before you give your opinion. Don't just present one side of the argument.

Present evidence

Back up your case with evidence. Do *not* make unsubstantiated or unrealistic assertions or assumptions which cannot be justified. For example, when asked to comment on a company's financial position and forecast future earnings, stating in your answer that you have made an assumption that interest rates will be 20 percent when the prevailing market interest rate is 4 percent, is likely to be viewed as unrealistic by the examiner.

Regular review of question and plan

Whilst writing, frequently refer back to both answer plan and question to ensure you are not departing from the question's requirements. Remember, you will not get marks for points made when they have no relevance to the question set, however groundbreaking your comment might be.

Maintain presentation

Although this is difficult when working under such time pressure, you need to work hard to incorporate good presentation to your essay. Break up the text with headings, sub-headings, bullet points and, where relevant, diagrams. And keep that writing legible!

Maintain rules of English

Following on from the above point, your use of grammar, punctuation and general spelling needs to be good too. Theoretically, in most exams you should not be marked down for bad spelling, but try telling that to your marker. First impressions do count! It's unfair, but that's the reality.

Maintain readability

Use short sentences (ideally one sentence should contain one point only and as a rule should be less than 20 words long), avoid the use of either slang or ponderous language, and keep to one main theme only per paragraph. And avoid excessively long paragraphs, which tend to hide the points you make, instead of making them clear and therefore easier to award marks to.

(Remember, each paragraph should contain one main idea only, the first sentence setting out the idea, the middle sentences developing that idea, and the last sentence returning to the main idea to show how it has been developed.)

Logical progression

Ensure that there is a logical flow of information through the essay, and that the links between points are made clear.

Show how your answer addresses the question

Make sure that your conclusion shows the reader how your essay has answered the question set.

Quality not quantity

At the risk of repeating myself, do not write everything you know about the subject. Don't waffle. And don't pad. Your answer must be focussed and answer the question set. The maxim "Size isn't Everything" is very relevant here – it's not the size of your essay, it's what you do with it that counts! Quality, not quantity, is what's required.

> ***"It is quality rather than quantity that matters."***
> **Seneca**

Report Style Questions

The approach to answering questions which require your answer to be in the form of a report is very similar to that used for writing essays. However, the end result, the report, is more formal in structure and language than an essay.

Reports generally have the following structure containing some or all of these elements.

- Title
- Date
- To and From details
- Contents
- Terms of Reference
- Summary
- Introduction
- Problem Description
- Analysis and Possible Solutions
- Conclusions
- Recommendations
- Appendices

Although all of these potential headings may at first sight appearing confusing, in reality the basic outline of the report will be the same as for the essay i.e.

- Introduction
- Main Body
- Conclusions/Recommendation

Some marks are generally given for using the correct format for your answer. In fact, one of the common gripes seen in Examiner's Comments relate to students using essays to answer questions specifically asking for an answer in the form of a report. Again – *make sure you answer the question set, and don't throw away the easy marks by not using the correct answer format.*

To recap, the following steps should be followed.

- Read the full question
- Understand the requirements
- Reflect on the question
- Produce an outline answer plan
- Write your answer

All of the detailed guidance already given for essays is relevant for reports too. For example, the presentation of evidence to back up statements you make, and the avoidance of uncorroborated opinion. However, some additional advice specific to reports is also worth noting.

Purpose of the Report

Make sure you know who the audience for your report is, and write your report accordingly. What are their characteristics and needs? For example, are they technical people or not? If not, you will need to use non-technical language. What level are they at – are they directors of the board or supervisory staff? Again, adapt your report accordingly. The language used for a report to the board is likely to be far more formal than one to lower management levels.

Also, make sure you understand exactly what the end result of the report will be. Is it meant to inform only, or is it meant to recommend? Clues to this will be given in the question and its requirements. Once more, the aim of the report will have a bearing on what you put in it.

Structure of the Report

Examples of the types of headings generally used in reports were set out above. Do be aware however that it is not always necessary or possible to include *all* of these headings in your report, and there is no one single correct format you should use. You will need to adapt the structure of your report according to the question and its requirements that you have in front of you.

But whatever you do, make sure the structure you are using is *clear*. Use clear headings and sub-headings, and consider numbering your sections to make things even clearer. A common system is to number main sections using integers (1, 2, 3 etc.) and then sub-sections as 1.1, 1.2 and so on. Further sub levels of the report can be numbered in the same way e.g. 1.1.1, 1.1.2 and so on.

Content and Style of the Report

It's very important to use appropriate language in your report. To an extent this depends on who the report is aimed at. Nevertheless, some general rules can be applied.

- Be concise. Never use two words when one will adequately convey the same meaning.
- The language should be precise. For example, avoid the use of "may" and "might" if possible.
- Where abbreviations are used, always write the first instance of the term in full with the abbreviation immediately afterwards in brackets. Thereafter you may include the abbreviation only when referring to it in your report.

- Explain technical words or terms in general laymen's terms where appropriate.
- Write the report in the third person and do not switch between third and first e.g. "it was thought that…" and not "I thought that…". This helps to introduce the air of formality that the report requires.
- Avoid introducing your own feelings into your report by making sure you avoid emotive words and phrases e.g. "There appears to be some resistance amongst operational staff to the introduction of new management directives" and not "Operational staff are being downright bloody-minded and refusing to take any notice of new management directives".
- Do not include humour, as what may be funny to one person may not be to another.
- Try to avoid introducing any *bias* into your report. Are you viewing information and evidence from a particular standpoint, without acknowledging other points of view? Remember, you should be objective and present all sides of the argument.

Questions Requiring Short Prose Answers

This type of question can come in many forms, so it is not possible within the confines of this book to give you examples of all of them. Here's just one.

Explain the meaning of each of the following terms and comment on their relevance in relation to the operation of a budgeting system. Give specific examples to help illustrate your answers.

a) Programmed and non-programmed decisions	***(6 marks)***
b) Feedforward control and feedback control	***(6 marks)***
c) Open systems and closed systems	***(5 marks)***

Clearly, with these types of questions there is no point producing an answer plan, as each section of the question is too short to warrant producing one. However, good presentation is still important. What you should do is

- Read the full question
- Understand the requirements
- Reflect on the question

before you start writing your answer. Use the mark allocation to estimate how much you should be writing. Although no outline plan is required, still try to structure your answer in a logical way, and maintain good presentation, spelling, grammar, punctuation etc.

Break your answer up with separate paragraphs, as opposed to one long diatribe contained in a single paragraph. This makes it easier for the examiner to spot the different points you've made and award marks for them. And don't waste time writing paragraphs of text only vaguely linked to the subject area being tested. Remember – answer the question set.

Case Study Questions

The use of case study questions has increased over the past few years as more examining bodies catch on to the fact that they are arguably a better way of testing candidates effectively than the more traditional question styles.

As the name implies, case study questions give the candidates a "real-world" scenario or situation around which the question is based. They seek to test the candidates' ability to relate theoretical knowledge to the practical situations they are given. In other words, you need to be able to apply what you have learned during your studies to the problems set out in the question.

Often, case study questions will contain significant amounts of data, which all go to help set the scene. Not only this, but the question will often be open-ended. By that, I mean that the information you are provided with will be incomplete. You will have to make assumptions and adapt what you already know to help fill in the gaps.

Because of these factors, you cannot answer a case study question by simply regurgitating facts. Rote learning is not enough to help you here. This is why the use of case studies is now so popular, as it requires you to not only select and understand facts, but also to examine, analyse, interpret and then apply them in order to develop solutions to the problems set out in the question.

Here's the way I'd recommend approaching these questions.

Work out Your Time Allocation

Make sure you work out your time allocation up front. Often, case studies can account for a significant percentage of marks on a paper, often 50 percent or more. (For a 3 hour paper with a 50 mark case study therefore, you'll be answering the case study for 1½ hours – a long time!) Allocate a generous amount of time to read the question – at least 10 to 15 minutes for a 50-mark question (adjust this time as appropriate, depending on the mark allocation and the amount of data presented as part of the question). Also allocate a similarly generous amount of time to creating an outline answer plan. This might be as much as 20 to 25 minutes for a 50-mark question.

Thus, for a 50-mark question in a 3 hour exam, you should be spending the first 30 to 40 minutes reading and planning. At this stage you haven't even started writing your answer! This fact will be difficult for some students to come to terms with – they feel that if they don't start getting something down on paper immediately, they are wasting valuable time. Try to avoid falling into this trap. You are *not* wasting your time if you are actively reading and planning your answer, even if it takes 40 minutes to do this. Time spent in preparation *now* will mean a better answer later.

Read the Full Question

You will recall that this involves reading through the question relatively quickly the first time in order to get a feel for it, then going back and reading it again, slowly and carefully this time. Underline, highlight and draw boxes around key words, phrases and information provided.

Understand the Requirements

Reread the requirements of the question and make sure you understand what it is exactly the examiner is asking you to do. This is very important because if you go off at a tangent in a question of this size, and do not score highly as a result, you're likely to fail the exam.

Reflect on the Question

As with any other question, be considering which areas of the syllabus the question appears to be based on, and consider what specific issues, concepts, and theories might be relevant to the situation given. Remember to think about what might be implicit in the question and not just what's explicitly stated. Jot down any rough notes that help you. Due particularly to the sheer amount of information provided, doing this will ensure you don't forget anything when you come to produce your outline answer plan.

> ***"When the task is done beforehand, then it is easy."***
> **Yuantong**

Produce an Outline Answer Plan

Set out the various sections that your answer will use (often the answer is required in report form) and start making notes on what you want to include.

Do bear in mind that you have been set a real-world situation as a question and so you need to provide a *real-world answer*. In other words, your answer should

- Focus on and provide comments in relation to the real world example given, and not merely on the background theories which might be relevant.

- Incorporate some or all of the information provided as part of the case study (it will be up to you to decide on what is relevant – as with the real world, some of the data you are provided with may remain unused).
- Be specific as opposed to overly-generalist in style.
- Be based on assumptions which are realistic and justifiable (for example, "I expect the dollar/sterling exchange rate to move from 1.50 to 2.50 during the next 12 months" might not be a particularly believable assumption to be making unless you can back your assertion with strong argument and preferably factual evidence.)
- Include practical recommendations.

Write Your Answer

Once you have the basis of your answer down on paper, start writing your answer. The advice already given for writing essay answers is equally relevant and important here, so go back and re-read this section if you can't remember what's involved.

Multiple Choice Questions

Sometimes known as objective testing, multiple choice questions are generally short, structured questions which contain a number of possible answers as options, one of which will be the right (or best) one.

For example,

During a period of war with a neighbouring country, a government imposes a system of rationing on all consumer goods. This is most likely to result in

A ***Deflation***
B ***Hyperinflation***
C ***Stagflation***
D ***Suppressed inflation***

Multiple choice exams are in many ways a very different beast to written exams. For a start, you often won't really be writing anything! Instead, you'll be marking your answers off on an answer sheet provided by the examiner, which is then normally marked by computer. Either this or you'll be taking the exam entirely on computer, reading questions on the screen and inputting your answers via the keyboard or mouse. As a result, layout, presentation, grammar, spelling and so on aren't tested (which might be good for you if you find these things difficult!).

Added to this, the examiner has already provided you with the right answer. All you've got to do is select it from the alternatives provided. Because of this, and because there's no writing involved, students often fall into the trap of thinking that multiple choice exams are somehow "easier" than written exams.

Please, please, do not fall into this trap. Do *not* underestimate multiple choice exams. When set correctly (which depends to an extent on the skills of the question writers and examiner), they can be as challenging as any written exam. If you plough through the questions in front of you at speed, picking the first answer which seems to be right, you could well be in for a nasty surprise when you get your results!

So what approach should you be using? Let's look.

Work Out Your Time Allocation

With so many individual questions in a relatively short amount of time (for example, 50 questions to be answered in 1 hour) working out your time allocation might seem to be a waste of time.

However, whilst I'm not advocating an approach where you take exactly 1.2 minutes for each of the 50 questions in the above example (60 minutes divided by 50 questions), knowing approximately whether you are on target time-wise is an important factor in ensuring you attempt all of the questions set.

For example, if you're on question 20 out of 50 and you're 20 minutes into the exam, you know you're OK for time (as you had 20 x 1.2 = 24 minutes available to answer the first twenty questions). If however you've taken 35 minutes to get that far, you know you have got to speed up if you're going to answer all the questions.

Keep an eye on the time expended versus your time budget as you move through the questions.

Get Started

You will likely have a lot of questions to answer, so get started straight away with the first question on the paper. There's no point in reading the entire question paper first.

Read the question

Read the question and each answer option carefully. Underline or highlight key words, phrases or data. Missing a single word can change the entire sense of the question, or make a one of the incorrect answer options (sometimes known as distracters) seem right. The questions are written this way on purpose, so make sure you don't fall into the trap.

Answer the question (or move on)

If you *know* which one of the answer options is right, select it. But check the other options again anyway just to make sure. Sometimes it's easy to rush these questions.

If you *think* you know which one of the options is right, carefully look at the distracters first. This will hopefully allow you to identify what's wrong with these other answer options and eliminate them. If you're left with your original choice of option, use this as your answer.

If you *can't decide* whether your choice is right, or you *don't know* the answer, skip the question and move onto the next one. You can come back to this question (time permitting) later on.

Do the Easy Before the Hard

Using the above methodology will mean you answer all the questions you find easy first. This should give you a sense of confidence having hopefully got some marks under your belt.

Once you've got to the end of the questions, go back to the beginning of the paper and start again, this time looking at the harder questions you skipped over on your first pass.

With these harder questions, try a process of elimination with the answer options. Try to find one which is definitely incorrect. Then look for another which seems suspect and give it careful thought. Can you possibly eliminate this one too? Do so if you can. Carry on the process of elimination if you can, until you can go no further. If you've reduced the possible options down to one, you've got your answer. If not, you're going to have to take a guess between the options that are left. At least you've reduced the odds of getting it wrong!

So guess, and then move on.

Other Guidance

A few other matters are worth noting.

Negative marking

Although arguably educationally unsound, some examining boards persist in using negative marking, perhaps to reduce the chance of a student achieving a pass grade through mere guesswork. (After all, for a multiple choice exam where each question has four possible answers, using basic probability theory would suggest that a student can gain 25 percent by mere guesswork alone.)

Negative marking simply means that for each wrong answer you give, the examiner will deduct a mark or marks from your overall score. If negative marking is part of your exam, you clearly need to change your strategy as a result! Answer only those questions you are certain of, or can be reasonably certain of (those you *know* or *think you know*). Do *not* guess if you don't know the answer.

Computer based exams

With paper-based multiple choice exams, you have complete freedom as to which questions you answer and in which order. Some computer based exams offer this same ability to move forwards and backwards through the questions as you see fit, but *others do not.*

If the multiple choice exam you're taking is computer-based, make sure you know which style it is. If you have to answer the questions sequentially (one after the other), you'll have to adapt your approach accordingly, as you can't go back and do the harder questions later.

Multiple choice exams are hard work

If I haven't already managed to disabuse you of the mistaken notion that multiple choice exams are easy, let me try again now!

Sitting multiple choice papers is incredibly hard work. Every word of every question has to be read carefully. A large number of questions have to be answered in a short space of time. A wide range of syllabus areas can be covered. A large number of decisions have to be made by the student.

So I suggest that you get as much practice as you can with this type of question. Get to understand what it feels like to work in this way. And don't practice written questions at the expense of multiple choice questions where your exam(s) involves both types.

Mathematical/Computational Questions

For some exams, the majority of questions may be largely numerically based, involving the use of mathematical theory, formulae and computation for some or all of a question. This is particularly true for science-based subjects and a number of areas related to finance, such as accountancy.

There are clearly a number of differences between a computational question involving mainly numbers and an essay/report style question using written English. These differences need to be taken account of when attempting to produce an answer.

How Computational Questions Are Different

The answer to a computational question is either right or wrong

Unlike an essay where one single incorrect sentence does not affect the ultimate conclusion, getting one part of a calculation wrong can mean the final answer is wrong too.

Perfection is possible

Because the answer to a numerical question can be assessed and marked completely objectively (i.e. "does the answer provided match the one in the marking scheme?"), it *is* possible to get maximum marks for this type of question.

Getting maximum marks for a question type involving a more subjective and qualitative approach, such as essays and reports, would be far more difficult, if not impossible.

Getting started can be a bigger hurdle

With an essay, it's possible to make a start even if you're not quite sure what you're going to say or which direction your answer is going to take (not that you're going to make this mistake, are you?). With a computational question, it is a lot more difficult to get started if you're not sure how to answer the question.

You either know it or you don't

Either you know how to perform the calculation by applying the relevant technique from your syllabus, or you don't – you can't use your common sense alone to get you through. This is unlike an essay, where sometimes it might be possible to use a common sense approach to write an acceptable answer, even if you can't remember the background theory.

No One Universal Method

These differences need to be taken into account when attempting computational questions. However, unlike a number of the narrative-type questions, such as essays, reports and case studies, where the same basic approach can be used, there can be no universal method of approaching numerical/computational questions. This is because this label covers such a wide range of very different subjects and tasks.

For example, calculating the expected internal rate of return (IRR) associated with a particular project is very different from calculating the taxable profit for a given company/period. Each requires its own particular methodology to be applied in order to arrive at the correct answer. It is outside the scope of this book to cover each and every one of these techniques applicable to your own particular set of exams – your study material and/or trainer should provide you with guidance on these.

General Guidance

However, what we can say is that there is some general guidance which *can* be applied, whatever the specific question.

Computational versus Narrative

Where you have choice of computational or narrative-style question (some exams will offer such a choice), choose the computational question over the narrative question where you *know* how to deal with it and what computational techniques to use. This is because it should be easier to obtain a greater number of marks for the numerical question. (And remember to "RTFQ" before you make this choice – are you *sure* you can definitely answer the numerical question?)

Show your workings

This is important lesson number one when it comes to answering numerical questions. **Always show your workings**.

Ignore this lesson at your peril. In an exam situation, when under the immense time pressure an exam brings, you will undoubtedly make mistakes during some of your calculations. This may be as simple an error as keying in a number to your calculator incorrectly. If you don't show your workings, the examiner will have no way of knowing whether you were following the right process or not. As a result, you will gain zero marks. (Contrast this with a mediocre essay, where you'll still get some marks even though you got some things wrong.)

You therefore need to make sure that the examiner can follow your thought processes from beginning to end. Show *all* workings in detail, with every step set out so your calculations can be followed (remember, treat your examiner as if he or she is an intelligent layman. Assuming no prior knowledge in this way means that you should not skip any steps in your explanation).

Depending on the exam, it might be more appropriate to include these calculations in an appendix to your answer, but if you do this make sure you clearly cross-reference your workings with your answer so that the examiner does not have to search for your work.

Making sure you show your workings can make all the difference between a pass and a fail. Show your workings and even when the ultimate answer is wrong, you should still gain credit where due for your work. After all, the examiner wants to see you demonstrate your ability to apply your knowledge – you're not going to be failed merely because your fingers slipped on the calculator keys. But fail to show any workings and you could end up with no marks, even though you *did* know how to answer the question.

Do you really want to take the risk? No? So make sure you practice producing answers which include detailed workings as a part of your timed question practice. Then, come the exam, this will be second nature to you, and you won't throw good marks away unnecessarily.

Do the easy before the hard

Where the calculation parts of the question are not inter-linked (one part does not build on the answer from an earlier part), consider answering the easy sections first to build up your confidence, then go back and attempt the more difficult ones. Normally, there is no penalty for answering questions non-sequentially.

Good presentation

Make sure you lay your answer out clearly. Align columns of numbers correctly. Label any diagrams, graphs and tables that you include. Identify what units you are working in where relevant, for example, if you produce a balance sheet in your Financial Accounting exam, are the units £, $ or €, and are they shown in single units, thousands ('000) or millions (m)? Make it clear.

(Don't assume that by merely not stating the units you're working in there can't be a dramatic and adverse result. When the $125m Mars Climate Orbiter was destroyed as it began its initial orbit around the planet, the two government agencies involved in the project quickly realised that the cause was down to one agency using imperial measurements (feet, inches, pounds etc.) to transmit flight date whilst the other was using metric measurements!)

Reasonableness checking

When working with numbers, some students seem to have a tendency to switch off any common-sense circuitry in their brains that they might otherwise have! As a result, they make an error in calculation which ends up with a wildly improbable answer being produced, and yet don't think to question it.

Always try to filter the answers you produce through your reasonableness checking equipment. Does the answer make sense? Does it fit within the context of the question you are answering? If not, rework your answers through.

Stick to your time allocation

Whether you have finished answering the question or not, when you come to the end of your allocated time, *move on to the next question.* This is particularly important in the context of some numerical questions, where trying to find the "right" answer can be a temptation difficult not to succumb to, for example, trying to balance that balance sheet we mentioned earlier. If it doesn't balance and your time is up, don't worry. Forget it and move on.

Open Book Questions/Exams

Like case study questions, open book questions and exams have come increasingly into vogue in recent years. As the name suggests, unlike traditional exams, you can take certain study material (or "open books") into the exam, which can be used for reference when answering some or all of the exam questions.

The idea behind these questions and exams is that they allow candidates to be examined in a more "life-like" manner. After all, if a candidate can use reference material during the course of their chosen career out there in the real world, then why shouldn't they do so during their professional exam? Added to this, with the emphasis on rote learning of facts and figures removed, the exam can concentrate on testing higher level skills such as analysis and application, which can only be a good thing.

As a concept, it seems too good to be true, doesn't it? You get asked a question, you look up the answer in your study book. Simple. Surely you can't fail?

Well, unfortunately, it *is* too good to be true, and if you're not careful, you might very well fail. Here's why.

Why Open Books Exams Aren't Necessarily Good News

Insufficient time

You only get marks for the answers you produce in the exam, not the time you spend reading. The bottom line is that there simply won't be enough time in the exam itself to spend searching through a reference book to find the answer if you either don't already know it, or don't have a pretty good idea of where to look.

Predefined materials only

Only certain approved material will be allowed in the exam hall. So it's not just a case of taking all your notes in there to help you out. Normally your own notes would not be allowed.

Everyone has them

As everyone has the same "open books", you're not going to gain any undue advantage from having them yourself. Everyone in the exam will be in the same boat. So, ultimately, nothing has changed.

Full knowledge required

To be able to use the approved material in the exam, you need to know it inside out, back to front, and generally be able to know where to find what you are looking for at a moment's notice.

Irrelevant material

Often, the approved material may contain sections that are not relevant to, or at the very least tangential to, your studies. You need to know which sections are which for your exam.

"Harder" questions

Because the examiner isn't testing your recall, he can focus on asking the questions that really test your ability to solve a problem via the application of the material provided. This can make the questions harder to answer than traditional exam questions.

So, although the idea behind open book exams is sound, the reality is that they bring burdens of their own. To deal with these successfully, you need to adopt the right approach.

Approaching Open Book Exams

Familiarise yourself with the approved material

Not only get hold of the approved material before the exam, but make sure you are *fully* familiar with its contents. This doesn't mean reading it through once to get a general idea of what's involved – you need to know the material *in detail*. Even better, you should know it inside out.

Make sure you know who's providing the material

This may sound obvious, but do make sure you know whether the material will be provided for you in the exam hall or whether it's your responsibility to provide it. Turning up to your exam without the necessary materials when you're supposed to be providing them will put you at a rather significant disadvantage when compared to your fellow examinees!

Practice using the material during revision

Make sure you get used to using the approved material when you're attempting your timed question practice during your revision phase. This requires a different approach to answering questions. Instead of answering questions purely from what's in your head, you are expected to incorporate into your answer any relevant information from the approved material. Practice doing this.

> ***"Practice is the best of all instructors."***
> **Publilius Syrus**

Practice finding material quickly

Get used to finding things *fast* from the approved material. This should follow naturally from the points above, but there's no harm in testing yourself by picking a relevant subject area from your syllabus and then making sure you know where to look in the material to find it.

Don't just copy

When answering open book questions, don't just copy chunks of the approved material as part of your answer. For one thing, it wastes your time, and for another, you won't gain any marks for it. Where something is relevant, frame it in your own words, putting your own spin on the idea or concept.

Clear cross references

Where a particular piece of information is directly relevant, and it's not possible or necessary to put it into your own words in your answer (for example, objective data presented in tabular form, such as economic statistics provided by a governmental body), ensure that you include clear cross references in your answer to show where the information was taken from.

Use the right approach

Open book questions require you not just to describe what's in the approved material, but to use the parts of it you think are relevant to *apply* to a scenario you are given. In other words, you need to make decisions, produce discussions and argument, provide comment and arrive at a solution, conclusion or recommendation as a result of your analysis and thought processes.

This process needs to be communicated clearly to the examiner. Whatever you do, don't simply answer the question using the "write all I know about the subject" approach. You won't gain many marks. You need to move beyond the purely factual and demonstrate instead your higher level skills.

Seen Questions and Exams

A variation on the open book exam is where either the questions that will appear on the exam paper, or some information relating to these questions, are handed out in advance of the exam. In terms of professional level exams, the latter approach is far more prevalent.

For example, an exam on "Interpreting Financial Statements" might involve the provision of financial statements for, say, three publicly listed companies one month in advance of the exam date. Students would then be expected to fully familiarise themselves with the contents of these financial statements before the exam, knowing that out of the three, one of the companies will be selected in the exam as the main case study question.

Although similar to an open book exam, this takes the idea one stage further. Not only are students expected to be familiar with the material, it is expected that they will carry out a significant degree of preparatory work before the exam itself. Using the example above, students would need to carry out a detailed analysis of the financial statements for each of the three companies prior to their exam, calculating key financial and accounting ratios, interpreting financial information and producing comment on the companies' general performance.

Much of the advice on answering questions that we have already seen in the Revision section is still relevant to these types of question and exams; however, some additional advice is necessary given the differences that exist.

Specific Guidance for Seen Exams

Treat the preparation as part of your exam

In essence, although you're not yet sitting in the exam hall, as soon as you have information or questions provided to you by the examining body, you *are* taking part of your exam *now*. Treat this stage with the respect it deserves therefore. Make sure you allocate as much time as you can to this. There won't be time in the exam, as the examiner will assume you have done all of the preparatory work in advance.

Put yourself into the mind of the examiner

Where information is provided upon which the questions will be based (but not the questions themselves), try to imagine what sort of questions the examiner might throw at you. If it were you setting the questions, what would you seek to test? What syllabus areas seem ripe for questions? What areas of interest are there that would really test students? Using this questioning approach can help you pre-empt questions in the exam.

Don't assume the examiner won't introduce new material

Just because you're given key information relating to the question, don't assume that the examiner won't introduce new elements in the exam as well. For example, going back to our earlier example where financial statements for three companies were disseminated prior to the exam, the examiner might introduce additional written material relating to the company selected in the exam itself, such as a hypothetical Stock Exchange Press Release issued by the company.

So don't think that you can limit your revision to certain syllabus areas only. There's no guarantee they won't come up in the exam, even if you do think you know the questions.

Where the questions themselves are "seen"

Occasionally, you might be given the questions themselves before the exam date, although this is unusual. If this does happen

- Where you have a choice of which questions to answer, try *all* of the questions out first. What looks easy at first sight might prove to be otherwise.

- Get practising *immediately*. The more you practice, the more polished your answer. Remember to practice under *timed* conditions.
- As you practice, try to increase the *quality* of your answer and not just its length.
- Try to work out what's really important in the question – what are the fundamental underlying issues involved? This is particularly important in the context of "seen" questions because there's the possibility of including so much relevant material.
- Remember to stick to the question set.
- In the exam, still check that the questions are exactly the same as the ones you have been working on, just in case.

Revision Revisited

Big and Important

It may not have escaped your attention that this section, on the subject of Revision, is one of the largest in the book. It is not mere chance that this is the case.

Revision accounts for this many pages because it is without a doubt the most important part of your whole studies. A poor study record can still be pulled round with a good revision phase; conversely, a poor revision stage can ruin what has been promising study progress to date.

Make or Break

Revision is the make-or-break time when all of the strands created during the study phase are woven together into a seamless single structure or fabric capable of bearing your weight during the examination itself. Get it wrong and you could be heading for a fall. Get it right and you know you've built a solid framework around you capable of supporting you through any difficulties you might encounter.

So do make sure you treat the revision phase with the respect it deserves – follow the guidance contained in the last five chapters and you'll be doing just that.

In Case You Need Reminding

- Realise that your best *is* good enough – keep a positive mindset and tell yourself that you're following the right approach for success.
- Remind yourself that what's done is done and now is the time to focus on revision, not on what you missed during the study phase. Look forward, not back.
- Plan your revision phase like a military campaign. The better planned it is, the more value you'll get from it. And aim to peak just before the exam.
- Remember that to be effective, revision has to be active, not passive. Merely reading your notes is not revision.
- Spend as long as you possibly can on timed question practice. There really is no substitute for it.
- Make sure you use the right approach to questions in general, and the right approach for each specific question type.

The End is in Sight

Congratulations!

You've got the end of your revision period. The end is finally in sight.

You've done all the hard work. All that remains now is for you to demonstrate the results of all that effort in the exam hall.

Allow yourself to feel good that you've got this far. And boost your self-confidence by reminding yourself how well prepared you are. Just like home decorating, the key to success and a superior finish is all in the preparation. Get that right and the end result is almost assured. Your preparation has been first class.

Think for a moment about an iceberg. Only the very tip shows, whilst perhaps 90 percent of the overall mass remains hidden deep beneath the ocean's surface. If you were to judge an iceberg's destructive power based on what you could actually see of it, you'd be making a big mistake. The real power lies in the bit you can't see, the hidden bit.

Similarly, imagine all of your work is represented by that iceberg, and that the visible tip represents what the examiner sees when you hand in your answer script. The real power lies in what is hidden beneath the surface, your study and revision programs. These are the substance, the bulk, upon which the tip of the iceberg, your examination performance, has been built.

You have built your potential and power through hard work. Although it is hidden, it is there all the same. All you have to do now is demonstrate that hard work. The next part of this book will show you how.

Part Seven

EXAM TECHNIQUE

Exam Fundamentals

The Big Day Approaches...

The big day approaches. Your very own day of reckoning is almost here. No more avoiding the issue, pretending to yourself that somehow it's not going to happen. It is!

No doubt you are feeling nervous, wondering what's in store for you, perhaps panicking because you feel you haven't done enough to pass. There will be a lot going on inside your head right now, thoughts about what you've learned, the questions you've attempted, concern as to what's going to appear in the exam paper, worries about whether you will get to the exam hall on time. If you're not careful, all of these things and more can get on top of you in the immediate run up to the exam and cause you to lose your footing at the worst possible time.

In this part we're going to make sure that the path you've been following continues clearly right up to and beyond your exam day. First, we're going to look at some exam basics, things which you should keep in mind throughout the examination process. Then we'll look at the process itself, pretty much in the sequential order that it will happen, from before the exam, to during the exam, and even a chapter on after the exam too, strange though that may seem right now!

The Examiner

Friend or Foe?

We've already used the term "the examiner" many times in this book. But who is this amorphous person we keep talking about? Are they really to be treated as our sworn enemy? Do they really have it in for us, or does our perspective need to change? We need to find out, even if only in the spirit of "know thy enemy". Far better we go into the exam knowing what and who we are up against, rather than going in blind.

So, is the examiner an ogre? Is their sole *raison d'être* in life to trip up unsuspecting students and to find as many faults as possible so they can fail them?

Make the Examiner Your Best Friend

The answer is a resounding, NO, they are not. They are normal people (honest!) who will give you every opportunity to prove yourself and pass the exam they are setting. But, that said, you need to make sure that you take that opportunity given, and do what the examiner wants you to do in order to give yourself every chance of passing. That means *making it easy for the examiner to give you marks,* by both

- Following his or her instructions given in the examination rubric and questions *to the letter*, and also
- Producing answers to the questions which are logical, well structured, coherent, clearly presented, that demonstrate an understanding of the syllabus and that answer the question set.

Do these things and the examiner will want to be your best friend! So make it easy for the examiner and give them what they want.

But What Exactly Do Examiners Want?

Maybe you're still not clear exactly what it is the examiner wants you to do in the exam. So let's make it crystal clear for you.

They want you to

Follow the Exam Instructions

Examination instructions, also known as the *rubric*, are normally printed on the front of the exam paper. For computer-based exams, which are generally multiple choice based, the instructions are normally shown on the initial screen you view. The rubric will tell you things such as

- How many questions there are on the paper.
- How many questions you have to answer.
- Whether there are any compulsory questions.
- How long you have to complete the paper.
- Where the paper is split into sections, how many questions from each section you should be answering.

You need to make sure you follow these instructions *to the letter*. And that means reading them slowly, carefully and with your utmost attention, *before* you begin the exam. You'd be amazed at how many students fail their exam because they don't do this. Answering two questions from Section A and one from Section B when the examiner wanted you to answer one from Section A and two from Section B isn't going to do you any favours!

Answer the Question Set

We've already seen this, but there's no harm in reiterating just how important it is that you answer the question that the examiner has set, and not one which you would have liked the examiner to set, based on your own pet preferences and favourite syllabus areas! There is a big difference between the two. The former will get you marks awarded; the latter will likely get you none.

So, you need to read every question carefully and *think* before you start writing. Don't feel pressured into starting your answer just because every one else around you in the exam room has started theirs. Remind yourself that they are the fools and not you. Read, think, plan and then write.

Demonstrate Your Knowledge of the Syllabus and Your Ability to Apply It

Answering the question set will ensure that you do this. Remember, it's not just about regurgitating facts, it's about applying concepts to the specific situation the examiner has presented you with. Make sure that you select the appropriate material from your syllabus and weave it into your answer. *And leave out what you don't need.*

Don't be tempted to try and pad your answer with irrelevant detail. You really won't fool the examiner, and may only succeed in making it more difficult for your paper to be answered, as the examiner tries to sift through the mass of material you have presented to find those points which actually deserve a mark.

Produce a Well-Structured, Logical and Coherent Answer

To do this, you're generally going to need to plan first. It's not possible to produce a written answer to a question of any significant length without doing so. Use your exam time wisely and build in time to produce these outline plans. Remember, it is *not* time wasted.

As to your answer, make sure that it makes sense. It should include objective analysis and avoid presenting unsubstantiated facts or argument.

Produce an Answer which is Clearly Presented

Can the person marking your script read your answer? Is it clearly laid out on the page, using plenty of white space to separate the answer into sections? Are your paragraphs and sentences short? Are you using the correct spelling, grammar and punctuation?

Don't count on the examiner's charity – they may not be an ogre, but they are only human! Ask yourself how many times would you try to read an illegible script when you had to mark twenty in an evening? Make sure your script is as easy as possible to mark by using the correct presentation.

Produce a Balanced Answer Script

In other words, the examiner wants you to give equal weight to each mark. This means attempting *all* the questions that are set, and allocating your time and efforts evenly across them according to the mark structure.

Failing to answer all the questions set, or producing one really good answer whilst the rest of the answers are at best mediocre is most definitely *not* what the examiner wants. Do ensure that you manage your exam time properly and be strict with your time allocation. It will pay you dividends.

Perfection is Not Required...

It's worth just reminding you at this stage that you do not need to have reached perfection in order to pass your chosen exam. Not only is that not the aim of the exam, it would actually be impossible to achieve in practice.

As long as you can demonstrate that you have a reasonable awareness of a broad range of syllabus topics and areas, you should have no trouble getting that first time pass. Remember – the majority of exams have a 50 percent pass mark. This means you only have to get half of everything right to pass – and that doesn't sound too difficult, does it?

> ***"Aim for success, not perfection."***
> **Dr David M. Burns**

Give yourself credit for all the hard work you've put in so far. You have done all you can to prepare yourself for the task ahead. In many ways the worst is over. One final effort and you can retire to that sun lounger and relax with that cocktail you have been craving for the past few months. Again, tell yourself, "I do not have to be perfect".

Perfection is not required.

...But Anxiety Is

Anxiety *is* required if you want to perform to the best of your abilities in the exam.

This may seem like a contradiction. On the one hand I'm telling you not to get stressed by aiming for perfection. On the other I've just said that anxiety is required. What could I possibly mean? Don't the two statements contradict one another?

The answer is no, they don't. You do not need to become overly-anxious by assuming that, because you're not perfect, you'll never be able to pass your exam. But on the other hand, it's a scientifically proven fact that small to moderate amounts of anxiety can actually improve your performance.

The Science

In fact, a large body of scientific research and evidence has demonstrated the following relationship between levels of anxiety and mental performance.

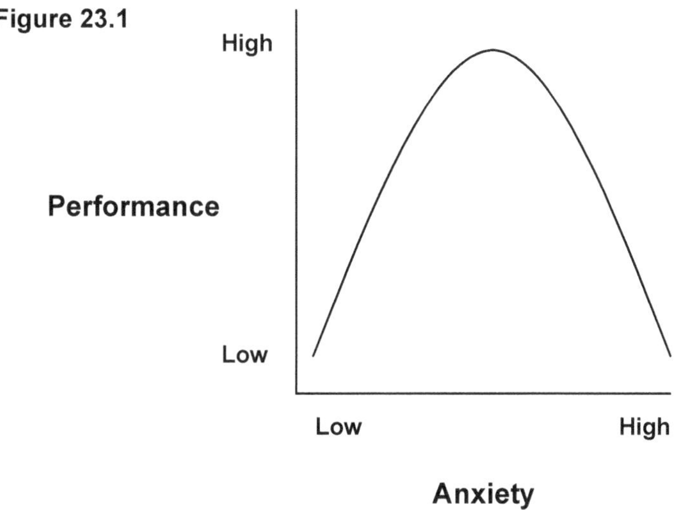

In other words, the highest levels of performance are shown when anxiety is at a moderate level, and not when these levels are either low (relaxed) or high (stressed).

Implications for Your Exam

This has profound implications for your preparation. You need to accept that it is normal for you to feel nervous about your forthcoming exam. *And that it is OK to feel like this*. As long as you don't let your level of anxiety reach blind panic levels, you don't need to worry.

Or put another way, don't worry about getting worried! It's normal, it's healthy, and it'll be good for your exam performance.

A Feeling of Quiet Confidence

We've already said that a moderate degree of anxiety is both an understandable and a necessary part of the examination process. After all, no matter how much you tell yourself not to worry about the exam day, you're not going to be able to completely free yourself of the feelings of worry (not to say fear!) that are part and parcel of the experience.

But you *do* need to make sure that you can manage that worry/fear level down to acceptable levels if it's in danger of getting too high. By the time you walk into that exam room your aim should be to be feeling quietly confident of your chances and above all, in control. It's when the feeling of control vanishes that fear has chance to take hold. Don't let it.

"Skill and confidence are an unconquered army."
Proverb

To achieve that feeling of quiet confidence

- Remind yourself about all the hard work and preparation you've already put in towards the exam and how well you've controlled your studies and revision.
- Use your visualisation techniques to see yourself performing well in the exam.
- Use your verbalisation techniques to tell yourself that you're doing all you can to ensure you perform well in the exam.
- Replace every negative thought that comes to mind. For example, replace the statement *"I never got a chance to do a practice question on that really difficult area of the syllabus, I'm bound to fail"* with a positive one such as *"I've made sure that I've fully covered a broad range of syllabus topics, and missing one peripheral area isn't going to harm my chances – nobody's perfect"*.
- Remember that what other students are doing or saying is irrelevant – let them get on with their preparation and concentrate on your own – you are the only person that matters.
- Tell yourself that all of the techniques you have learned during your studies will put you at an advantage in the exam – you'll let the others make the silly mistakes, such as not allocating their time correctly, whilst you'll be applying these techniques to ensure your success.

Becoming a Mark Mercenary – Time Allocation Revisited

By now you'll no doubt understand the basics behind time allocation – using the minutes per mark calculation to work out how long to spend on any one particular question (remember, minutes per mark multiplied by total marks available for the question = length of time to spend on the question).

And on a number of occasions already, I've made the point that you should be sticking to the time you've allocated to a question and not overrunning, even if the temptation is there to do so.

This concept is so crucial to your chances of success that I want to spend a little more time convincing you of the absolute necessity of following it to the letter, without exceptions. So let's do that now.

Easy Versus Hard Marks

Take Two Essay Questions...

Imagine a situation. You have two questions to answer. Both are for 20 marks. Both are essay questions. By definition, as both have equal marks, you should spend the same length of time on both.

But let's assume you feel more comfortable with question one than you do question two. You think you could produce a really good answer to question one, whereas your answer to question two is likely to be mediocre at best.

Concentrating on the "Better" Essay

In this situation, there will be a strong temptation to spend longer on question one than on question two. Why not "borrow" some of the time for question two to spend more time on producing a really good answer to question one? Or so the logic goes.

At first sight, this logic seems attractive. Which is why many people fall into this trap. But it *is* a trap, make no mistake about it. You should always spend an equal amount of time on each mark available on the paper. No exceptions. Period.

But why?

The Relationship between Marks and Difficulty

It comes down to easy versus hard marks. If you were given the choice of spending one minute chasing an easy mark or one minute chasing a hard mark, which would you choose? Chasing the easy mark of course. Well, that's exactly the decision you are making when you consider whether to overrun on one question at the expense of another (or others).

Marks 1 to 5

If an essay is marked out of 20, the first 5 marks are probably going to be pretty easy to get. They'll be for obvious points that anyone who has done a reasonable amount of work is likely to score. There may even be marks available purely for using the right format asked for by the question, such as report format. Easy marks!

Marks 6 to 10

The next 5 marks (marks 6–10) will be a little more difficult. You'll need a little more in-depth knowledge to manage these. But a reasonable candidate should still be capable of getting them.

Marks 11 to 15

The next 5 marks (marks 11–15) are going to be harder still to get. You've already picked up the easier marks, so there's less material available that you can now bring in which will gain credit. The points you need to make to get marks 11–15 may also be more complex in nature, being less about basic factual awareness and more about detailed analysis and application. This makes them more difficult to get.

Marks 16 to 20

The last 5 marks (marks 16–20) are the hardest of all. To score more than 75 percent (15 out of 20), you are going to have to be an exceptional candidate. And given the reluctance of many examiners to give a perfect score for an essay (based on the idea that an essay can always be improved upon in some way), the last few marks will in practice be almost impossible to achieve.

In fact, the relationship between marks and their relative difficulty can be summed up nicely by the following graph. Notice how much more difficult relatively it becomes to earn the higher marks when compare to the first 50 percent of the marks – this is shown by the increasingly steep slope on the curve as we go from left to right.

Figure 23.2

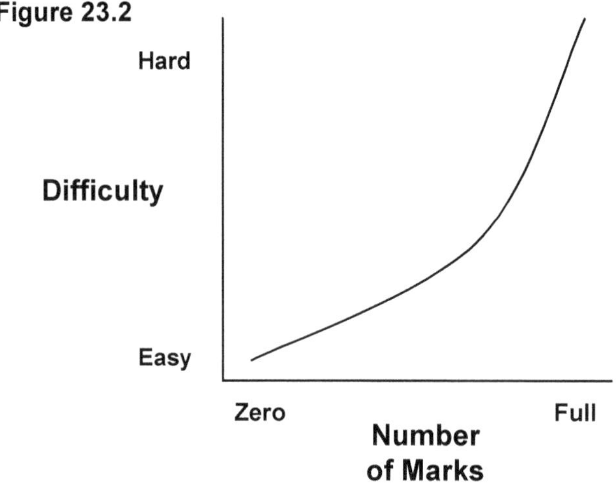

Back To Those Two Essay Questions

So, going back to our scenario of the two essay questions above, you've got to the end of time you've allocated to question one and you've managed to produce a reasonably good answer. Let's say you've reckon you've managed to score 14 out of 20. At this point, do you choose

Option 1

Steal 10 minutes from the time allotted to question two and try to pick up the (very hard) marks 15 to 20 for question one, or

Option 2

Start on question two and spend the first 10 minutes picking up the first (very easy) 5 marks?

What do you think? It's a no-brainer when you look at it like that, isn't it! Who on earth in their right mind would choose option one and chase the hard marks instead of selecting option two and picking up the easy ones? No one. The easy marks are just that, easy. So pick them up. Make sure you *are* in your right mind! The probability that you'll earn the easy marks for question two is far higher than it is you'll manage to scrape those last few marks out of the first question.

Work out your minutes per mark. Calculate the time available for the question you're about to attempt. And stick to it, come what may. When the time is up, move onto the next question. Never, ever, turn down easy marks at the expense of chasing hard ones. Unless you really do want to fail.

The Mark Mercenary

I used the term "Mark Mercenary" at the beginning of this section on the importance of time allocation. And I did so with good reason.

Because the term "mercenary" accurately describes the manner in which you should approach your forthcoming exam. You need to be ruthless. You need to be calculating. Decisions you make should be cold and clinical. Emotion should have no sway over this process.

Playing to Win

You need to grab every mark you can. Take the easy ones on offer, don't turn them down. Never go after difficult marks at the expense of easy ones. Realise that in many ways the whole exam process is a game, a game played between you and the examiner. You need to make sure you play by the rules, follow the instructions, but ultimately, you need to make sure that you win. Allocate your time ruthlessly and you make sure you have the best chance of doing so.

> ***"If winning isn't everything, why do they keep score?"***
> **Vince Lombardi**

After all, your success or otherwise may come down to a single mark. 49 is a fail. 50 is a pass. One mark really can make all the difference.

Even Allocation Across the Entire Paper

The example of the two essay questions seen in the Easy Versus Hard Marks section above clearly demonstrates that ruthless time allocation is the key to examination success.

And yet, some students will still come up with a "Yes, but…" when they are confronted with the evidence. So just in case you're one of them, we'd better take a quick look at another fallacy.

The "Yes, but…" in question goes something like

"Yes, but surely if you managed to score pretty well in at least a couple of questions by taking extra time on them, this would more than compensate for the lower scores on the others, and you'd still pass as a result".

Disproving the "Yes, but..." Theory

Imagine an exam paper with a pass mark of 50 percent and containing 5 essay questions, 20 marks per question. Assume that the student has spent the majority of time producing polished answers for the first two questions, and had little time left to attempt the remaining three questions that were answered.

The scores awarded might therefore be

Question 1	16
Question 2	15
Question 3	8
Question 4	6
Question 5	4

This gives a total of 49, a marginal fail. But marginal though it may be, it is still a fail. And this is even though two questions have been awarded very good marks of 16 and 14 – they count for very little in the grand scheme of things.

The reality is that, in this example, too much time was spent chasing difficult marks at the expense of the easy ones. Had a little more time been allocated to any of questions 3 to 5, just one more of those easy marks might have been awarded, and the end result would have been very different. Instead, an even spread of effort might have resulted in no one single outstanding mark, but a better overall average. For example,

Question 1	12
Question 2	11
Question 3	10
Question 4	9
Question 5	8

In this scenario, no one question has scored particularly well. In fact, only two are marginally above half marks. Nevertheless, this is enough to score 50 marks and earn a pass. Remember, perfection is not required. An even spread of effort over the entire paper is. So make sure you maintain that time allocation for *every* question you attempt.

A Word About Computer-Based Exams

We've touched upon the subject of computer-based exams already. In the context of professional level exams, assessment by computer is generally restricted to multiple choice papers, with those exam papers normally testing the lower levels of a multiple level qualification.

Although this may change at some stage in the future, at the time of writing assessment of the upper and final level papers for most professional qualifications is still very much carried out in the traditional way, using a pen and paper based approach. The written exam is still the gold standard by which most professional bodies measure their student members.

This is largely because it is the only sensible way to properly assess whether the student has reached the standard necessary to become professionally qualified. To reach this standard, they need to demonstrate that they are able to understand and apply a wide range of complex and interrelated concepts, information, rules and practices relevant to their profession – and written exams allow exactly these things to be tested.

Given the preference for written exams, the next three chapters are understandably based on the premise you will be taking a written exam rather than a computer-based one. However, pretty much all of the advice given is relevant whatever type of exam you're taking, so when reading on just use your own common sense to decide what's relevant to you – you'll still gain maximum value from following the suggestions provided.

Build Up to the Big Day

In this chapter we've covered some of the background to your exam. We've learned what it is your examiner wants from you. We've also been reminded that we don't need to be 100 percent perfect in order to pass the exam, and that anxiety can be better for you than perhaps you imagined. And most importantly, we've learned why strict time allocation is just so important – remind yourself of the concept of easy versus hard marks whenever you feel tempted to give just a few more minutes to the question you're on at the expense of the next one.

Now we need to look at the countdown to your big day. In the next chapter, we'll start the clock from one week prior to your exam, and see what you should be doing. As you will see, organisation and preparation are very important in ensuring you arrive at your exam desk in the best possible condition, ready to perform.

Then, in chapter 25, we'll cover that most feared of events, the exam itself.

Before the Exam

One Week Before

Overview

With a week to go to your exam, you'll still be head down working hard at your revision. You should be well into your timed question practice by now, which as we've seen is a crucial phase in your overall revision strategy. The more time you can spend on this the better.

Nevertheless, your exam is fast approaching and you need to take a little time out from your revision now to make sure you're actually ready for the big day. It's no good looking up from your revision on the morning of the exam and realising you don't even know where the exam hall is!

> ***"Common sense is not so common."***
> **Voltaire**

Much of the advice offered within this chapter could be categorised under the banner of "logistics", but in fact, most of what you will see is just good old plain common sense. That said, I make no apologies for including it. At this stage, common sense has a tendency to fly out of the window as anxiety or even utter panic starts to set in.

So forgive me if it sounds like I'm stating the blindingly obvious – I am! Trust me – it's in your best interests. If in reading this section just one single student is saved from turning up to the exam one day too late I will feel I have done my job well.

What You Should Be Doing

Find your examination booking confirmation or attendance docket

You should have been sent a confirmation of your examination booking when you initially applied to sit the exam. This may have confirmed the exam details, or alternatively you may have been sent these subsequently as part of an exam attendance docket. If you do not have these details, contact your exam provider immediately so that any problems can be rectified before the big day.

Check your exam timings

Some exam boards set a provisional exam timetable, and then publish a final one at a later date. Make sure you have the final timetable in your hands. Then make sure you know the correct day, date and time of your exam. Check this against your revision timetable/calendar to make sure you've got it right. Mistakes do happen – students regularly get the date of their exams wrong, or turn up in the afternoon for a morning exam. Ensure you're not one of them.

Check the exam centre and plan your journey

Which location is the exam being held at? Have you been there before? Do you know how to get there? How long does the journey take? You need to make sure you know the answers to all of these questions.

If you haven't been to the location before, I'd strongly recommend a dummy run in advance.

- ♦ Plan your route, and attempt the journey at the same time of day as you'll be making it on the exam day itself.
- ♦ Find out how long it takes, and then add a generous contingency for unexpected delays on the day to calculate what time you need to leave.
- ♦ Make sure you can find the exact location that your exam will be held in (if it's in a large building, make sure you can locate the exact room you need to find).
- ♦ If you're driving, make sure you can easily find a parking space in a nearby location. If you can't, consider taking public transport.
- ♦ If your exam hall is a long distance away, think about staying overnight close to the hall in a hotel or bed and breakfast. This does involve extra cost, but is worth every penny. You'll avoid all the stress and worry that a long journey and unexpected delays can bring. Arriving late for an exam having sat stranded on a broken-down train for an hour is not conducive to a producing a good answer paper! (And that's assuming your examining body will even let you into the exam late – some won't.)
- ♦ Make contingency plans to deal with unexpected problems. If your train breaks down, do you have an alternative route? Will you have money to use a taxi cab? Do you have a mobile cellphone to call one? Try to cover every eventuality.

Check that you understand your exam procedures and rules

Your examining body should already have provided you with these details, but make sure you have them, read them, understand them and comply with them. Failure to comply with exam rules can mean your removal from the exam or at the very least a severe reprimand. It may also ultimately mean your removal from the student membership of your professional body. Don't take the risk.

- ♦ What are you allowed to take into the exam hall? For example, can you take a calculator and if so, is there a particular make and model which you must use?
- ♦ What equipment will you need in the exam hall (for example, an HB pencil to mark off your multiple choice answers on the computer-marked answer sheet)?

- What are the rules concerning late arrival and early departures?
- Will you need to bring proof of identity, maybe in the form of a student card or passport?
- Do you know whether you are allowed to take in other items, such as food and drink?

Check that you understand your exam's format and structure

You should have already made yourself aware of this during your studies and, more particularly, during your revision phase, but double check at this point you've definitely got it right. Better to find out now than in the exam.

You should know

- How many questions there are on the paper.
- What format the questions take e.g. case studies, essays, multiple choice questions etc.
- Whether the paper is split into sections, and if so, how many questions from each section do you need to answer.
- Whether questions are compulsory or optional.
- How long the exam lasts for and whether there is any pre-exam reading time allowed.
- Where the exam is an open book one, what the approved materials are and whether they will be provided in the exam.

Produce a list of "Things to Take"

Although your exam is still a week away, I would strongly recommend making a list of things you need to take with you on the exam day *now*. A simple thing it may be, but the less you have to worry about on the day before your exam the better. Far better to take a little time now and know you've dealt with it than leave it to the last minute and forget something vital, such as your proof of identity (in which case you would be not allowed to sit the exam).

So, what kind of things do you need to take to your exam? Your list might include

- Pens (yes, do make sure you have some spare ones!)
- Pencils (where your multiple choice exam is computer marked, you may be asked to bring a specific pencil type e.g. HB)
- Ruler
- Other drawing instruments e.g. compass
- Correction fluid
- Highlighter pens

- Calculator (you do have an approved model, don't you?!)
- Spare batteries for your calculator
- Mathematical tables
- Examination attendance docket
- Proof of identity (e.g. student card, passport)
- Details of your journey
- Sufficient cash to allow for emergencies (e.g. for a taxi)
- Drinks and snacks (where allowed)
- Any medication (e.g. painkillers if you are prone to tension headaches)
- Glasses
- Spare contact lenses
- Tissues/handkerchief
- Revision notes/cards
- Watch (or anything with a clock on it) to use for accurate time allocation
- Good luck charms (not that you're going to need them!)

One Day Before

Overview

24 hours to go. You wouldn't be human if by this stage of the game you weren't feeling at least a little anxious. Accept that this is normal, and remind yourself that a little anxiety can be a good thing when it comes to your performance on the big day.

"The best preparation for good work tomorrow is to do good work today."
Elbert Hubbard

However, anxiety can have a strange effect on some people. Panic starts to set in, and common sense seems to disappear. It's important to guard against over-reaction at this stage, for example, the temptation to work late into the night trying to cram every last detail into your mind.

To make sure you don't fall into any of the traps waiting for you, read the guidance set out below on what you should be focussing on the day before your exam.

What You Should Be Doing

Assemble your "Things to Take"

Get this one done first thing as soon as you get up in the morning. Whip out the list you've already prepared, and pull together all the items on it. Place them in a bag together and put the bag by your front door. Then you only have *one* thing to remember when you leave for the exam tomorrow.

Avoid last minute cramming

It seems to be an unwritten but accepted fact that the day before your exam you should be trying to stuff every last possible fact you can into your brain. The idea seems to be that if you throw enough information at it at least some of it will stick. As a result, many students spend their last revision day frantically reading through all of their study notes, and even in some cases returning to the original study texts. This is a mistake.

Tell yourself that your brain will not forget everything you have learned in just one day. If it's already stored in your brain, it will still be there tomorrow. And if it isn't, it's far too late to be trying to learn it now. Don't resort to last minute cramming.

Light to moderate revision and wind down early

Leading on from the point above, don't overwork yourself on the last day. You should aim for a relatively relaxed day so that you can build and sustain your energy levels for tomorrow's big effort.

This means preferably avoiding timed question practice, and sticking to some light reviewing of your revision notes. Now too is a good time to review the examiner's comments from the last exam sitting (if you have them). These can help remind you of the common mistakes that students make in the exam, so that you can avoid them on the day.

And finish working early – you should *not* be working late into the evening, or even worse, into the early hours of the morning. Put your books away, put your feet up, and relax for a few hours before you go to bed.

Be selfish and avoid stress

The most important thing in your life right now is *you*. And your exam. Taking an exam is by necessity a selfish act. So forget everything else. You need to be mercenary about this. After all, if you allow the stresses and strains of normal everyday life to creep in now, you're only going to be distracted from your primary goal, passing your exam.

> ***"The greatest productive force is human selfishness."***
> **Robert A. Heinlein**

In practice, this means avoiding anyone and anything which might lead to conflict or stress. If this means being anti-social, then so be it. Don't allow yourself to get dragged into an argument with your partner or your children. Ignore them, tell them that you'll deal with whatever it is they have a problem with after tomorrow, and remain focussed on what's important.

Partying can wait too

Some students take the advice to relax on their last revision day to the opposite extreme. Instead of relaxing at home and retiring to bed at a reasonable hour, they go out and seek the maximum excitement, letting their hair down and partying 'til they drop.

For fairly obvious reasons, this approach is to be avoided too. Excessive alcohol has a detrimental affect on the brain, and your brain needs to be in tip-top working order on the exam day. Not only this, you need to be saving your energy for the big day. Getting three hours sleep before your exam starts doesn't fall into this category!

"Water is the only drink for the wise man."
Henry Thoreau

By the same token, recreational drugs and any sleeping medication should be avoided. Also, spicy food might best be left until after your exam if you know you're affected by it.

Don't be a fashion victim

Before retiring to bed, get out the clothes you are going to wear for the exam tomorrow. This will be another thing less to worry about in the morning.

The key word here is *comfort* above all else. Any irritation you feel will be magnified under exam conditions – and the last thing you need in the exam is unwelcome distractions. If you're too cold, too hot, or some part of your clothing is too tight and is chafing, your mind will not be 100 percent on the job in hand. So don't treat the exam hall like a catwalk. Leave the fashion for after the exam when you go out to celebrate!

In practice, comfortable, loose, lightweight clothing should be worn. Much like the advice given to those participating in outdoor adventure sports, such as mountaineering, layers of clothing are best. You can then easily take a layer off or put another layer on if you feel too hot or too cold.

Get alarmed

If you have a morning exam, you'll need to make sure you're up bright and early with plenty of time to get ready, eat breakfast and journey to the exam hall with time to spare. Even if you think it's unlikely that you'll get any sleep at all the night before, arrange it so that you have something to wake you up at the appointed hour. And have at least one back-up too! There's no harm in having a contingency plan! Set your alarm clock, set the alarm on your mobile cellphone, arrange for an alarm call, get a friend to knock on your front door. Whatever it takes. Knowing that you'll be woken up at the right time whatever happens gives you one less thing to worry about.

Triple check the time of your exam

You should have already checked the time of your exam when you started your preparations a week ago, but there is no harm in double and triple checking now. Unless of course you'll be happy turning up for your afternoon exam only to find it you've missed it because it took place in the morning...

Get some sleep

Easier said than done, I hear you say. What with everything going round and round in your head, the material itself, worries about whether you'll get there on time, concerns about what will be in the paper itself, how can you ever switch off and actually get some rest?

- Try taking your mind off the impending exam before you go to bed by directing your attention onto something else you find entertaining. Maybe watch television or a DVD, listen to some music, or have a chat with a friend (but not about study or exams!).
- Don't try to go to bed earlier than you would on a normal day. This is a recipe for disaster. You'll likely lay awake and make things worse.
- Unless religious, medical or personal reasons preclude it, a *small* alcoholic drink can help you relax. But please, do make sure it really is small! No more than two standard measures would be my recommendation here.
- Think about using one of the relaxation techniques we saw in the Success Factor section. These can help calm your nerves and take your mind off of the things that are worrying you.
- *Don't* sit in bed and attempt last minute cramming. You'll just be wasting your time. If you do know it, you'll still remember it tomorrow. And if you don't, it's too late to learn it now.
- Consider using visualisation to see yourself in bed and asleep. Imagine what it feels like as you lay there in bed with sleep slowly creeping up on you. By visualising it in this way, you should find that what you have imagined starts to happen.
- If you really can't sleep, don't beat yourself up over it. It's not the end of the world. Simply lying in bed and taking it easy is still resting your mind. Listen to some gentle, soothing music and maybe use your visualisation skills to take you to your very own "Retreat".

Exam Day

Overview

The big day has dawned, hopefully bright and sunny, although it may not feel that way to you. All the work you have done up to now has led you to this point in time. Today is the day you're going to prove to the examiner that you're up to the challenge.

But strange though it may seem, it's not just about what you do in the exam hall that affects your chances of success. Go into the exam in the wrong state of mind and no matter how much work you've done, no matter how much preparation, you could still mess things up and fail the exam. So we need to make sure you get to that exam hall in perfect condition, unruffled, relaxed, confident and ready to perform.

Follow the advice given below to ensure you arrive at the exam raring to go.

What You Should Be Doing – When You Get Up

Feed your brain

Your brain needs energy in order to work at its best. And it gets this from the food you eat. So, breakfast is the order of the day. Make sure you have some, even if you normally skip it.

However, this doesn't mean a full English breakfast, with fried egg, bacon, sausage and all the trimmings. Too much heavy food will divert blood flow from the brain to help your digestive system, and may give you that feeling of lethargy that comes after a big meal. You need to be bright-eyed and alert come the exam.

> ***"A full belly makes a dull brain."***
> **Benjamin Franklin**

So instead, keep breakfast light, maybe a fruit juice and cereal, with perhaps a little toast. And avoid drinking too much tea or coffee, both of which have diuretic effect. The last thing you need is to have to keep leaving the exam hall to visit the toilet!

And even if you don't feel like food at all (which is a very normal reaction), do try to get something down. You'll be thankful you did part way through your exam, when otherwise hunger pains might distract you from the job in hand.

Time to go

You'll have already planned the timetable for your journey a week ago, so you know when you have to leave your house to start the journey to the exam hall. If you can, check beforehand for traffic and transport announcements (these can be found on television, radio and internet) to make sure there are no delays or known problems on your chosen route. If there are, instigate your contingency plans. Make sure you leave with plenty of time to spare. And, most importantly, don't forget to pick up your bag containing all the items you need for your exam.

If you have an afternoon exam

Afternoon exams can appear more attractive than morning exams because there seems to be less of a rush to get there. However, you also have a lot longer to get yourself into a real stew, so you need to guard against this. If your exam is in the afternoon, adopt the following approach.

- Don't lie in bed for too long. Too much sleep can be as detrimental as too little.
- Don't plan any heavy revision for the morning. Review your revision notes/cards if you really feel you need to keep yourself occupied, but no more than that. Do *not* attempt looking at any new topics.
- Try to fit in some relaxation or entertainment that doesn't require too much concentration to help take your mind off the exam.
- Remember to build in time for lunch. You may not feel much like eating, but it's important to get something inside you to act as fuel for all the work you're going to do in the exam. Like breakfast, keep it light, although a little lean protein such as chicken is fine for optimum performance.

> ***"Mental power cannot be got from ill-fed brains."***
> **Herbert Spencer**

- Don't be lulled into a false sense of security by the fact your exam isn't until the afternoon. Make sure you follow your planned journey and leave with plenty of time to spare.

Aim to arrive early

You'll have already built in a contingency to your travel plans to allow for unexpected delays, however, there is no harm in repeating the advice that you should aim to arrive at the exam hall with plenty of time to spare.

This means at least enough time to get your breath back from your journey, make a toilet stop, have a drink and a snack, and generally get yourself in the right frame of mind. I'd suggest that you allow at least 15 minutes before the start of the exam, although a more sensible margin might be half an hour. And when you do get to the exam hall, there are some do and don'ts you should follow.

What You Should Be Doing – When You Arrive at the Exam Hall

"Trust no one" – adopting an anti-social approach

There's always a crowd directly outside the exam room, busy testing each other, discussing what they know and what's going to come up in the paper. You need to make sure you avoid these people at all costs. This may sound very anti-social, and it is. But it's important you stay away from everyone. This means

- Do not talk to anyone unless you have to.
- Do not discuss anything to do with the exam at all.
- Don't even listen to other conversations.

If you don't avoid conversation in this way, you are in danger of having your perhaps already fragile self-confidence severely dented or even shattered.

- You might be psyched out by someone who seems to know more than you do. For example, someone says to you *"Oh yeah, that binomial distribution stuff is easy, it's the Poisson distribution you need to worry about"*, when you struggle just getting to grips with the binomial, and the only thing you can recall about the Poisson is that it's French for fish.
- You might get dragged down by someone else's negative viewpoint e.g. *"I heard that last time around only 20 percent of all the candidates taking the exam managed to pass"*.
- You might think someone else has more knowledge about the actual contents of the exam paper than you do. For example, you overhear *"My lecturer told us it's almost certain there's going to be a question on Black Scholes"* when you haven't even studied Black Scholes. (By the way, no-one other than those who set the exam really knows what's going to be in the paper. Things like this are educated guesses at best.)

So if you want to keep that positive mindset, stay away from everyone, friends included. If someone takes offence, tough. These are competitive exams remember – it's you versus the rest. So look after number one and save the social niceties until afterwards. Keep you focus 100 percent on your exam.

Find a quiet spot and relax

Leading on from the above, try to find somewhere quiet, away from your fellow examinees, where you can sit comfortably and wait calmly. Make sure you're within earshot of the exam hall though so that you can hear when the announcement is made that you may enter and go to your desk. If you really must do something, get your revision notes out and glance at them, but don't test yourself on them or attempt to learn anything new.

Remaining positive

Ideally you should be entering the exam hall with that feeling of quiet confidence we discussed earlier. To achieve this positive mindset

- Pat yourself on the back for having worked hard and prepared well for the exam.
- Use verbalisation and visualisation to tell yourself you're going to do well and also see yourself doing so.
- Push negative thoughts away and replace them with positive ones.
- Remind yourself that you have learned the techniques of success and that you're going to apply them in the exam.
- Above all, tell yourself that you are *in control* of the situation. There is nothing you are not ready for.

"The thing always happens that you really believe in; and the belief in a thing makes it happen."
Frank Lloyd Wright

Last minute pit stop

You're going to be sitting down in that exam room for a long time, as much as three hours or more. You don't want to waste a single minute on things you don't need to. Getting up to go to the toilet during the exam can be a time-consuming process as you have to first gain the invigilator's attention, then explain what you want to do, then wait whilst a spare invigilator is available to supervise you (just in case you've got an accomplice in the toilets ready to help you out!). Ideally you want to avoid this.

So do make sure you make a last minute toilet stop before you get up and walk into the hall.

Check for incriminating evidence

Before you enter the hall, double check that you have nothing about your person which could be construed by the invigilators as an intention to cheat. Examining bodies, especially professional ones, tend to take cheating rather seriously – often the person found guilty of cheating can be removed from the body's membership altogether. If this happens to you, your chances of a career in that particular industry or profession are over.

So check that your revision notes are stored away in your bag, that you have no scribbled notes in your pockets (even if it's only last week's grocery list) and so on. And please, do not be tempted to try and cheat. Not only can it ruin your future career chances if you're caught, it's actually counterproductive because trying to cheat takes your focus off of what's important. Instead of trying to produce answers to the questions set, you'll be spending half your time trying to surreptitiously read your hidden notes and watching where the invigilators are. You'll probably fail anyway.

Entering the Exam Hall Part 1

The announcement is made and the exam hall doors open. You are now ready to enter the arena. If you're not careful, this is where the panic can suddenly set in. Walk (don't run, there's no rush) into the room and find your allocated desk. Keep breathing slowly and deeply. Get all the equipment you need for the exam and put it on the desk. Put your bag where directed. Sit down and get comfortable. Check the table and chair don't wobble – if they do, sort this out with a piece of folded paper or card under the legs. The last thing you want in the exam is to be distracted by your desk or chair moving as you write.

At this point, you mind might go blank. Suddenly you can't seem to remember anything you've learned. If this happens, don't worry – this is perfectly normal. You'll find that once you start reading the questions, the contents will act as prompts for your memory, and all you have learned will come flooding back.

Now you're ready.

The Exam

Overview

This is it! Judgement day. That moment you've been both working towards and simultaneously trying to forget.

Sitting an exam is never going to be a pleasant experience, that we know. But there are ways and means of making it slightly less unpleasant, and ways of making sure you wring every ounce of benefit out of each single second of your time in the exam hall. This chapter contains guidance on how to achieve these things.

In fact, what's contained within this chapter is *so* important that if you only had time to read one chapter of this book before sitting your exam, this is the chapter I would recommend. So do make sure you take the time to read this chapter and understand what it's telling you before you sit your exam.

Entering the Exam Hall Part 2

You've followed the instructions contained in the last chapter under "Entering the Exam Hall Part 1" and you're at your desk. You've a few minutes to go before the start of the exam. Double check you have everything you need laid out in front of you. Pens, pencils, calculator, all of those items on your list. Are those spare pens to hand too?

Sit back on the chair, and try to relax. Loosen those shoulder and neck muscles. Breathe slowly and deeply. Run through one of your verbalisations in your head, for example *"I'm in control of the situation"* or *"I'm ready to perform well"*, whatever feels right for you. Try to ignore the candidates in the desks around you. What they are doing is unimportant to you. And remember that a certain level of anxiety is both normal and valuable – you need it to perform at your best. So don't get anxious about being anxious!

> ***"Act as if it were impossible to fail."***
> **Dorothea Brande**

Whilst remaining internally focussed, listen to what announcements are made by the invigilators, and do what they tell you to do. It's not a good idea to get on the wrong side of an invigilator before the exam has even started!

Waiting to Begin – Let the Countdown Commence

Check Your Paper

Either your exam paper will already be on your desk when you enter the hall, or it will be handed out immediately prior to the exam. Either way, take the time now to check that you have the right exam paper. It is not unknown where a number of different exam subjects are being sat in the same hall for the invigilators to make a mistake in handing the papers out.

Read the Rubric and Follow It

The exam instructions, or rubric as it's known, are normally printed on the front of the exam paper. Students often fail to read this section, assuming that nothing has changed since the last exam sitting. Don't assume anything – something may be different, and if so, you need to know so that you can follow the instructions given. Make sure you read the rubric carefully and thoroughly. And that you *do* follow the instructions given.

- If the examiner asks you to answer one question from Section A and four questions from Section B, do it.
- If he asks you to start a new page of your answer booklet for each new question, do it.
- If he tells you to use only blue or black pen, do as he says and don't decide to also use red ink because you happen to like it.
- If he asks you to indicate on the front of your answer booklet the numbers of the questions you have attempted, do it.
- If he tells you to write your candidate number at the top of your answer booklet and any additional loose sheets that you use, make sure you do.

You want to do everything you can to keep the examiner on your side. Make him your friend!

Deal with the Administration

Usually, you're allowed to deal with the necessary exam administration before the exam starts. This usually involves filling in your details on the front of the answer booklet you've been given – candidate number, subject, date and time, name and so on. Do this now before you forget it in the heat of the moment. An answer script with no name or number on it will not earn you a very good mark! And filling in the details at least gives you something to do and takes your mind off the task ahead.

Don't Start Until You're Told To

You're keen to get going, but resist the urge to open the paper and take a quick peek at the questions. Officially this could still be classed as cheating. Anyway, 30 seconds extra time scanning a question really isn't going to make that much difference. Be patient and await the OK to start.

One Last Cheer

Give yourself one last pat on the back. Tell yourself how you've put yourself in the best position possible to get that first time pass. There is no more you could have done. You're ready.

> ***"They can conquer who believe they can."***
> **Virgil**

Open the Paper and Start – the First Few Minutes

The invigilator utters those immortal words – *"You may begin"*. It's time to make a start. So what do you do now?

Consider a Brain-Dump

If your exam is the type requiring you to memorise a fair amount of data, you may have resorted to using mnemonics to store these facts for the exam. You may also have had to memorise all of the formulae you'll need to use in calculations. If so, you may want to consider quickly writing all of these things down now either on the exam paper itself or a scrap piece of paper. Psychologically this frees up your mind for other activities and can give you an immediate confidence boost.

Ignore Everyone Else

Take no notice of those people around you who start writing almost as soon as they have opened their question paper. Don't feel somehow inferior and start to panic because you're not yet in a position to pick up your pen. This is not a sign they know more than you – it is a sign they know a lot less, in particular about those exam techniques most likely to ensure a pass mark. These people will likely have to come back for a resit when your exams are long over and done with.

> ***"Fools rush in where fools have been before."***
> **Unknown**

Read the Paper First – Or Not?

Every other How-To-Pass-Exams book I have ever read tells you in no uncertain terms that having opened the exam paper, the first thing you should do is read every question through in detail, word-by-word, before you even consider starting to select and then answer a question.

This is a great idea in theory, but, frankly, not always so great in practice. The question paper might be many pages long – the information for a single case study question alone might take up four or five pages of solid text. (I myself have had personal experience of many three hour exams where the question paper was at least ten pages long.) By the time you've read all the way to the end of the paper, you'll probably have forgotten what was at the beginning, and all you'll have ended up doing is wasting a lot of valuable time.

Instead, I suggest being pragmatic and adopting a common-sense approach to the question of whether you should read the entire paper first.

- If the question paper is short, say 5 pages or less, or approximately 5 to 10 minutes reading time, go ahead and read the entire paper first, question by question, being careful to note all the key words and understand the requirements.
- If the question paper is any longer than this, scan or skim read the question paper only. You can generally get a good feel for each question by reading the requirements first and then quickly skimming the question narrative.
- In either case, do check the back of the question paper to make sure there is no question on it. Students have been known to miss entire questions through not doing this.

Once you have done this, you need to decide which question you will answer first. Advice on question selection is set out below.

Your Best Foot Forward – Question Selection

Unless your exam is computer-based, it's likely that the exam rules allow you to answer the questions in whatever order you choose. Make the most of this leeway you have been given.

Why Attempting Your Worst Question First is NOT a Good Idea

Some take the decision to answer what they think might be their worst question first, perhaps with the idea of "getting the bad news out of the way". But this is a bad idea. Firstly, it does nothing to your confidence, and can in fact dent it so severely there is no hope of recovery for the rest of the exam. Secondly, your examiner is only human, and with humans, *first impressions count*. This may not be entirely fair, but it is true nevertheless.

Why Attempting Your Best Question First IS a Good Idea

Instead, *always start with the question you feel you can produce your best answer for*. This will be good for you psychologically. Your nerves will go. If you have a tendency to freeze under pressure, this will get you started. Your mind will be in a more positive state. You'll know that you have put in a good "banker" to start your cause off well – in other words, you'll have banked some easy marks to stand you in good stead if things get rough further into the paper.

Not only this, but making a good first impression on the person marking your script really does count, even though theoretically and in all fairness it shouldn't really make any difference. Put the person marking your script in the right frame of mind with a good, easy to mark first answer and you might just get given a little bit more latitude, or "the benefit of the doubt", if you need it later on in your answers.

So, after you've read the paper, think carefully about the questions and choose which one you think you can answer best. It will also be well worth trying to grade the questions at this point in terms of how well you think you can answer them, perhaps giving a mark on a sliding scale from one to five, one being the best, five being the worst.

Work Out Your Time Allocation

Having selected your first question, now work out how much time you have to produce an answer. You'll already know the minutes per mark figure, so simply take the number of marks for the question you've selected and multiply by the minutes per mark to find the time available. (If you need reminding how to calculate your minutes per mark figure then refer to Chapter 20. Although you shouldn't need reminding at this late stage, should you?!) Look at your watch or the clock on the wall and work out the exact time you need to finish your answer by. Write this time down on the question paper as a reminder.

Don't Plan on Exam Suicide

Having dealt with question selection and time allocation, I cannot move on before I expose another commonly held but seriously flawed belief. Some students seem to believe that answering fewer questions than they have been set, with the idea of producing relatively better (but fewer) answers as a result, is a strategy more likely to get them a pass mark. For example, instead of answering five 20-mark essay questions, they only answer four.

I have to say that this is madness. If you try this, not only do you run the risk of severely irritating the examiner, whose instructions you have failed to follow, but also you haven't even attempted 20 percent of the marks available. Do remember the principle of easy versus hard marks. Taking time trying to score the harder marks at the end of four essays, instead of answering a fifth and picking up the easy marks available is utter lunacy. Don't fall into this trap. Attempt an answer for *all* of the questions set.

Dealing with Compulsory Questions

As the name implies, compulsory questions have to be attempted by all students sitting the paper. The question is, if your paper includes one or more compulsory questions, should this alter your approach to question selection?

Only slightly. Still select your best question first, whether it's optional or compulsory. It's still a good idea to try and create that good first impression. After this, weigh up the situation. If you still have to answer the compulsory question and it's a long one (for example, for 40 marks), you may want to attempt this next whilst you're still relatively fresh, as opposed to leaving it until the end of the exam when you're beginning to feel the pressure. If it's not so long, simply treat it the same as the optional questions. Pick the question you've graded the next best after your first question, and work on that.

What To Do If You Arrive Late

Even the best-laid plans can be thwarted. You may have planned your journey down to the last detail, and then a serious of horrendous coincidences conspired against you, leading you to be late for your exam. If you're unfortunate enough to be in this position, what should you do?

- Stop replaying your abysmal journey in your mind's eye. It has happened. It is history. There is no time for a post-mortem right now. You need to concentrate on the exam.
- Assuming you're not too late to be let into the exam hall (this depends on exam regulations), walk quickly and quietly to your desk, get what you need out of your bag, sit down and take some deep breaths. Try to relax yourself as best you can.
- Read the rubric carefully and complete your personal details (candidate number etc.) on front of the answer booklet as required.
- Work out how much time you have left and quickly calculate a new minutes per mark figure based on this. For example, you're 20 minutes late to a three-hour exam. That gives you 160 minutes. Take off 20 minutes for reading the paper, administration and checking your answers (remember, you must *not* ignore the importance of allocating time to these things), and that leaves 140 minutes. Divide 140 by the total marks available, say 100, to get your figure of 1.4 minutes per mark.
- Start the paper, and use the newly calculated minutes per mark figure to work out how long to take on each answer. In this way you will at least spread your efforts evenly across all the marks available. Remember, this even spread of effort is very important to maximise your chances of picking up the easy marks.

- If you run short of time on any particular question, consider writing very brief notes to the examiner to tell him what you would have included in your answer if you had the time. You might be given some credit for this. (But don't include an apology for being late or an explanation of why you were!)
- Don't panic – it's still possible to pass an exam having turned up late. Be ruthless with your time allocation, make sure your answers remain legible, and answer the questions set. You can still do it.

Where Pre-Exam Reading Time is Given

You might be wondering how the advice given above might differ if you're sitting an exam with pre-exam reading time allocated at the start of your exam.

Essentially, your approach should be exactly the same. You still need to check you have the right paper, read the rubric, deal with the admin and ensure you don't open the question paper until you're told to do so (at the start of the reading period).

When you do get to open the paper, you still need to consider a brain dump onto the question paper, ignore everyone else, read the questions as I've suggested above, and then select your best question.

The only difference is that until the reading period is over, you can't actually start to write anything in your answer booklet, whereas for an exam with no additional reading time, you can. And that's it, the only difference. Given however that it's probably going to take you all of the reading period to actually read the questions, decide which one to attempt first, and start to annotate your thoughts and plans onto the question paper, in practice this shouldn't be an issue. You should be ready to start writing in your answer booklet around the same time the invigilator tells you that you can do so.

Working Through the Paper

Apply Your First Time Pass Techniques

You've selected the question you think you can produce your best answer for. You know how long you've got to get that answer down on paper. You can begin.

We've already seen in Chapter 21 exactly how to approach questions, both in general and for specific question types. These techniques that you learnt during revision practice are what you need to apply now, for real. Let's just remind ourselves what these are.

- ***RTFQ***. Read the full question, carefully.
- ***Understand the requirements***. Read and reread the requirements, underlining key words as you go.
- ***Reflect on the question***. What syllabus areas might the examiner be testing? Think carefully about what the question is really examining.
- ***Answer the question set***, not the one you would prefer.

> ***"It's ain't what you do, it's the way that you do it... that's what gets results."***
> **The Fun Boy Three with Bananarama (song written by Sy Oliver and James Young)**

- ***Produce an outline answer plan*** for essays, reports and case studies.
- ***Don't waffle***, don't pad your answer.
- ***Remember to re-read the question's requirements regularly*** as you work through your answer in order to avoid going off at a tangent.
- ***Always pick up the easy marks*** – don't waste them. Picking up one mark for using the report format asked for by the question may be the difference between a mark of 49 and 50 – fail or pass.
- ***Always show your workings*** for calculation questions – this ensures you get credit for using the correct technique even if the calculation goes awry.
- ***Don't neglect good presentation*** – remember, make it easy for the examiner. If he can't read it, he can't mark it.
- ***Keep your common sense hat on***. Does your answer seem reasonable? Are your assumptions justified? Don't let panic rob you of your common sense.
- ***Mark off each section of the question on the exam paper as you answer it***. In this way you can avoid missing part of a multi-part question, which is easily done in the heat of the moment.

Be Ruthless on Time Allocation

This concept is so crucial, it deserves to be repeated. I simply cannot overstate the importance of this. Stick to your time allocations religiously. Never be tempted to overrun on one question at the expense of another. Remember the concept of easy versus hard marks. Never decide to go for hard marks at the expense of easy ones.

Be ruthless – you're a mark mercenary. Grab whatever's on offer. In so doing, you're building up a store of marks. Use this fact to help boost your self-confidence during the latter parts of your exam.

Moving On

You've produced your first best answer in the time available, and now you need to move on. Which question should you go with now?

I'd always suggest using a "best-to-worst" approach, where your first answer is your best one, your next answer is your next-best, and so on, until your last answer is for the question you felt least comfortable about. Leave the bad news until last. That way, you're less likely to psyche yourself out by the negative affect of producing a poor (or non-existent) answer. Use the "best to worst" gradings you made when selecting your first question to identify this order.

Keep Your Focus

Try to keep your attention at all times on what you are doing. You need to maintain that 100 percent focus on what's important – the exam paper in front of you, and the answers you produce for it. Everything and everyone else are unimportant at this moment. In fact, you should hardly be aware of what's going on around you, other than to keep one ear open for any official announcements from the invigilators. Anything else is a distraction to be ignored – whether it's other students holding their hands up for more answer paper, someone taking a toilet break, or the fact that it's started to rain outside.

Problem Questions

Realistically, you're not going to be able to answer every question on the paper well. No one can know everything about a subject, and every one has good and bad syllabus areas. So accept this as a fact and don't beat yourself up – after all, normally you've only got to get half of everything right to pass!

But if you do find yourself in the position of answering a "problem" question, what should you do?

> ***"Never give in, never give in, never, never, never, never..."***
> **Winston Churchill**

You can't answer part of a multi-part question

Questions often come in multi-part form. Frequently, it is not necessary to have answered an earlier part correctly in order to be able to answer a later part. So if you think you can't answer an earlier part, skip over it, leaving a space in your answer booklet in case it comes back to you, and move onto the next part. Brains are strange things – you may find that you suddenly remember what it is you need to be able to answer the question later in the exam! If so, you can go back and add the answer.

You get stuck

On some questions, it is not possible to skip over an area you're not sure about, as the answers required may build on each other sequentially. If you do get stuck on one of these, and are really unable to progress any further, don't try to force your brain to come up with the answer. Generally, the more stress you put yourself under, the less likely you'll be able to recall the information you need. Simply make a note of the time you've already used from the total time available for the question, leave a large space in your answer booklet, and move on to another question. You can come back to the question later when hopefully you'll have remembered what you needed to know.

You're not sure what the examiner is asking

Unfortunately, even with the most careful reading, and extensive thought, sometimes it's still difficult to understand exactly what the examiner wants you to do for a particular question. If this really is the case, and the question is either compulsory or the "best-of-the-worst" out of a selection of optional choices (i.e. you have no choice but to attempt an answer), what should you do?

In these cases, all you can really do is make a best-efforts guess. Make some assumptions, and stick by them. State your assumptions in your answer. You may find that your approach is perfectly valid – essay questions in particular are often very open-ended and can be answered in more than one way – there is no one right answer. Lastly, bear in mind that if you're having problems with a question, you can bet many of your fellow candidates are too. So don't convince yourself you're somehow more stupid than the rest.

What to Do if You Run Out of Time on a Question

This *will* happen. Some professional level exams are deliberately set in such a way that they are time pressured. The examiner, in addition to testing your knowledge and your ability to apply it, is also testing your time management skills and your ability to work under pressure.

Of course, you know by now that at the end of your allotted time, you're going to move onto the next question. But what should you do if you still have things to put in your answer and have run out of time? I'd suggest this. Firstly, leave some blank space just in case you somehow have some spare time left at the end of the exam to come back and finish the answer (although frankly, this is unlikely for most professional level exams).

Then, make a quick note addressed to the examiner, something like "I ran out of time but had I not done so I would have included..." and then *very briefly* summarise the points you would have included in your answer. You might be surprised to hear that you could gain some credit for doing this, as it tells the examiner you were aware of the issues involved. After all, the examiner has no other way of knowing this – he can't read your mind!

What to Do if You Get Ahead on Time

You'll be very fortunate if this happens, but just occasionally you might be presented with a question which you can answer in full *before* the allocated time is up. (Generally, this is more likely to be the case with numerical or calculation questions, which require a particular technique to be used to produce a single end result, rather than narrative questions, which are more open-ended.)

If this happens, allow yourself a smile, *but still stick to your time allocation on all subsequent questions.* Do not relax and assume you have that much longer to answer the next question. Instead, keep the time saved until you need it – either at the end of the exam to go back and thoroughly check your answers, or to deal with a problem question.

Coping with Tailspins

They Can be Fatal

A tailspin is where an aircraft gets into uncontrollable dive, spinning towards the earth, with the nose down and the tail up, spiralling out of control. It's often very difficult in these circumstances for the pilot to control the spin and pull the nose of the aircraft up from the dive, with potentially fatal consequences.

Tailspins in Exams

It's possible to get into the same sort of tailspin in the exam if you're not careful. Something starts the dive off, maybe a question you thought you could answer but then find when you're into it that you can't. The panic sets in, the adrenaline rushes around your body, your heart starts to palpitate, your stomach feels like its sunk to the floor and your confidence is shot to pieces. You feel that you have completely blown your chances. Everything starts to get on top of you. Before long, you've given up. I've seen many people actually get up and leave exams early after falling into this mindset, clearly resigning themselves to a fail.

> ***"Fear is the mind-killer. Fear is the little death that brings total obliteration."***
> **Frank Herbert (Dune)**

Controlling the Tailspin

If you're in difficulties and can feel the blind panic beginning to build, you need to nip it in the bud straight away, before the feeling really gets a chance to take hold and you ruin all the hard work you've put in. The ground is rushing up fast to meet your fall and you need to pull the nose up now before impact. Sit back on your chair, put your pen down, look away from whatever it is that has caused the problem, and breathe deeply. Try using the 60-second breather technique we saw in Chapter 3, or maybe visit your safe place via the Retreat Visualisation. Put the problems you are having to the back of your mind just for a minute or two.

But Isn't This a Waste of Valuable Time?

Taking valuable exam time to do nothing other than relax may seem counter-intuitive, but take my word for it, it can do you the world of good. It gives you the chance to gain a sense of perspective, and to stop the free-fall you're in. Returning to your exam you should now feel better prepared to continue. If the problem you had cannot be solved, you'll simply skip over it and move on, realising there are plenty of other marks to pick up elsewhere.

If it helps, I used this technique in my final Advanced Taxation exam when I was studying to be an accountant. Without it, I sincerely believe I would have failed the exam, instead of eventually going on to pass it comfortably. So, in an emergency, take a moment or two. It could mean the difference between pass and fail.

Beyond the Call of Duty – Producing Additional Answers

This is the flip-side of the *"I'll answer fewer questions than set but produce better answers"* strategy we've already seen. This time, the student hopes to gain additional marks by giving the examiner *more* than he has asked for. This might be by either, say, answering six questions from seven when the rubric asked for only five, or within a question, giving more answers than the requirements asked for e.g. giving five answers to the question "name three of the fundamental accounting concepts".

Be aware that you'll be wasting your time if you adopt this strategy. Using the examples above, the examiner will simply take your first five answers and cross out the sixth, or the first three concepts you've listed and ignore the rest. You will gain no credit for your additional answers. All you will have done is waste valuable time that could have been used more productively on another question. Remember – *answer the question set*. No more, no less.

Giving Alternative Answers

Unsure about how exactly to answer a question where more than one approach might be valid, some students present an alternative answer in addition to their first one, a kind of *"Dear Examiner, I wasn't sure which answer was right, so I gave you both anyway. Love Student"*! All this does is clearly signpost to the examiner that you are unsure about the subject. Don't do it!

What the Examiner Wants Revisited

We've already seen that the examiner wants you to –

- Follow the exam instructions.
- Answer the question set.
- Demonstrate your knowledge of the syllabus and your ability to apply it.
- Produce a well-structured, logical and coherent answer.
- Produce an answer which is clearly presented.
- Produce a balanced answer script.

But there are a few more practical tips here which are relevant.

Don't use red ink unless specifically asked to do so

Markers generally use red ink when marking scripts. If you also use red ink, this can lead to confusion during marking, and perhaps more importantly, can severely irritate the person carrying out the marking process. You don't want to do this – so steer clear of that red pen! Blue or black ink is generally best.

Keep the highlighter pens for the question paper

By all means use highlighters on the question paper to help identify key words, phrases, requirements and the like. But do not use them in your answers. If you need to emphasise something, underline it (with a ruler please, not freehand!).

Make any corrections clear

If you realise you've made a mistake and you have time to correct it, neatly cross out the section which is wrong and produce the correct answer. If the correction does not appear immediately after the original mistake, make sure you clearly cross-reference the two sections together so that the examiner can easily find your final answer.

Where you realise you have made a mistake and *do not* have time to correct the error, write a note to the examiner to this effect. Briefly summarise

- What it is you believe you've got wrong.
- What you would have done to correct it if you had the time available, and
- What effect this would have on your finished answer.

You may gain some credit for recognising what your answer *should* have included.

Errors on the Question Paper

As a rule, the processes of question setting and exam production are rigorously controlled to stop errors creeping into the final question paper. However, just occasionally mistakes do fall through the net.

If you think you have spotted an error or omission in the question paper, do ask one of the invigilators for assistance immediately. Don't sit there for ages before deciding you need to do this – you'll be wasting that valuable time again. Raise your hand to get the invigilator's attention, and then quietly explain what it is you believe to be wrong. It is then up to the invigilator to investigate the matter – usually there will be written procedures to deal with these types of occurrence. In the meantime, get on with another question. The invigilator will then inform you, and the other candidates if necessary, about the outcome of the investigations and any action that needs to be taken as a result (for example, correcting a typographic error in a question).

Unfavourable Conditions

Exams are sat in a range of locations, and sometimes circumstances outside the control of the invigilators or the examining body can have an adverse affect on those taking the exam. For example, I can recall sitting an exam in the middle of a very cold winter in a hall where the heating wasn't working properly. As a result, it was difficult to write well due to hands and fingers being half frozen! The invigilators actually noticed this themselves and announced that it would be bought to the examiner's attention and taken into account when answer scripts were marked.

If something about the conditions you are sitting your exam in causes you problems, whether it's intrusive background noise from outside or the effect of the cold, make sure you draw it to your invigilators' attention. They may be able to do something about it, but if not, it will be reported to the examiner. This may mean allowances are made during the marking process.

Once you've made your feelings known, try to put the matter from your mind as best you can and focus all your attention on the next question.

The End is Nigh – Nearing the End of the Exam

Last Minute Checks

Assuming you've stuck religiously to your time allocations, you should have some time left at the end of the exam to carry out some last minute checks. Many study books recommend that at this point you re-read all of your answers word-for-word and then make additions, corrections and adjustments as necessary.

However, I think that in many cases this advice is simply impractical. If your exam is a lengthy one, and consists mainly of narrative-style questions, you are simply not going to have the time to read every one of your answers in detail. Not only this, but editing your own work is notoriously difficult – you have a tendency to read what you *think* should be on the page, not what is actually there. For these reasons, I recommend what I consider to be a slightly more pragmatic approach.

For a 3 hour exam, you should have around 10 minutes left at the end of the exam after finishing your last answer. (Remember, when we calculated our minutes per mark figure we allocated 20 minutes out of the 3 hours to allow for reading the paper at the start of the exam and carrying out last minute checks at the end.) Use this time to

- Check that your candidate number is on everything it needs to be, both answer booklet and any loose additional sheets. You will not be allowed additional time after the end of the exam to do this.
- Make sure that, if asked to do so, you have indicated on the front of the answer booklet which questions you have answered.
- Ensure that you have clearly numbered every answer you have produced and that any separate additional work not presented sequentially as part of the question is clearly cross-referenced.
- Make it easy for the examiner by ensuring that it is really clear where each answer begins and ends, and for multi-part questions, where each part starts and finishes.
- Check that any workings included as an appendix are correctly cross-referenced.
- Cross out any rough workings you do not want to form part of your marked answer.
- Skim read each answer (unless you really have time to work through each one in detail, when you may do so). If you spot errors, make corrections, but do so *clearly and neatly*.

- If you decide to make additions to your answers (sometimes something will suddenly come to mind as you read the answer that hadn't occurred to you when you were originally writing it), do so, but again, make sure they are clearly and neatly cross-referenced. Don't just scribble squashed notes in the margin.
- If you've still got time spare after doing all of the above, go back to any questions you ran out of time on and complete them.

Leaving Early

Don't do it. That's the advice I'd give. I realise that the outside world will be a really tempting place right now, but do resist that temptation. (That is if your examiner will allow you to leave early – often exam regulations may prohibit students leaving the exam hall during the last half hour of an exam to avoid disturbing the other students who are still (sensibly) working.)

If you think you've done everything there is to do, and carried out all the last minute checks listed above, yet you still have time to spare, go back and start reading your script again. You may still find that you have additional flashes of inspiration that mean you can add further mark-scoring points. Do not stop until the exam is over.

"Put Down Your Pens"

The invigilators announce the end of your exam. Put your pen down immediately (generally invigilators don't take kindly to students writing after the end of the exam, even if it's only to add a candidate number to a loose page). *Now* you can sit back and relax. Stretch those legs, relax those shoulders. However you believe the exam has gone, feel good that you've done everything you could to secure that pass mark.

After the Exam

Isn't After the Exam Irrelevant?

It may seem strange for me to give you advice about what to do after the exam. After all, what difference can it make? Surely what you do after the exam isn't important?

Well, it depends. Particularly if you are sitting another exam the next day, or the next week, you need to keep your mindset positive. Getting yourself into a bad mood is not going to do your chances of passing the next exam any good at all.

And even if you aren't sitting another exam in the near future, do you really want to spend the next few days, weeks or months feeling depressed because you've got it into your head you've failed the exam? Probably not.

As a result, I would strongly recommend both reading *and following* the advice set out below.

Maintain Your Anti-Social Stance – Avoid Others

Immediately after the exam, by all means talk all you want to anyone who *didn't* take the same exam as you, but avoid at all costs those that did. Talking about the exam afterwards with others who took the same paper can often turn out to be a negative experience that it would have been better to avoid. This is because of what you might hear.

- Listening to how someone approached one of their answers and what they included in it might make you think you've made a mistake in yours or missed something out completely.
- When someone else tells you they found a question easy which you found hard, you're bound to feel that maybe you're just not good enough to get a pass mark.
- When someone else tells you they found a question hard which you found easy, you might begin to wonder whether you missed something important in the question's requirements.

What you have to remember is that others' judgement and memory, as well as your own come to that, are subjective, and as a result, are completely unreliable. You cannot trust what anyone else thinks or remembers about the exam, and neither can you trust yourself.

With that in mind, perhaps you can see the common sense in not discussing the exam with others, or even listening to others' conversations. It is a pointless and potentially depressing exercise. Get out of the exam hall, and get yourself off home by the most direct route.

Avoid a Post-Mortem

I use the term post-mortem for a reason. The exam you sat is now officially dead and buried. It is history. You no longer have any control over it. Nothing you can do now will change that. Carrying out a post mortem will just be a messy and unpleasant business which will not make one iota of difference to the result. This means that

- However much thought and energy you expend turning what you did in the exam over in your mind, you cannot change your performance now. So give yourself a break – why waste your energies on such a pointless task?
- *Under no circumstances* should you get your study materials out for the exam you have just taken in a vain attempt to see if you "got things right or not". Not even if all those around you on the train home have the study manuals in their hands and a dejected look on their face. If you must read something, buy a newspaper.
- If you have other exams coming up, you need to start concentrating on these. Get started straight away with some gentle revision, maybe reviewing your revision cards. Not only will this be an essential part of the build-up to the next exam, but also it will take your mind off of the last one.
- If you don't have any more exams, give yourself permission to go and enjoy yourself. Pick something you love and really let yourself get involved in it. Forget about the exam until you get your result.
- If you can't shake the feeling that you've done badly in the exam, remember that your analysis of how you did is subjective and liable to be inaccurate. And if you followed the techniques set out in this book, you may get a pleasant surprise when you receive your result.

A Contradiction in Terms – The Useful Post-Mortem

Having just said that post-mortems are generally a waste of time, I'm now going to give you the one exception to the rule. The only type of exam post-mortem which can add any value at all is the one where you consider not what you put in your answers, but *how you approached the exam* i.e. what your exam technique was like. This can be a useful exercise that you can learn from for the next exam.

For example, ask yourself, did you manage to stick to your time allocation? If not, why not? What would you do next time to avoid making the same mistake? Did you RTFQ or did you suddenly realise halfway through one of your answers that you'd missed a vital part of the question? Did you manage to produce decent outline answer plans for those narrative questions, or did the temptation to get writing straight away prove to be too much?

Answering these types of questions, honestly, outside the heat and stress of the exam situation, can allow you to learn from your mistakes for the next time. But again, don't be too critical about your performance. You did the best you could. Remember to pat yourself on the back for the things you did well, not just find fault where you went wrong.

When You Have Another Exam

You may have another exam to sit in the very near future. It may even be tomorrow. If that is the case, you need to swiftly put today's exam behind you and focus all of your concentration onto the next one.

As we've already seen, taking a look at your revision notes is a good way of switching your attention to the next task. Perhaps you can do this on the train on the way home. But don't go overboard and forget all you have learned about how to approach your exams. If your next exam is tomorrow, you should not be working too hard the day before the exam. Give yourself permission to take a little time out to relax, and don't work too late into the evening. Follow the advice already given in the chapter 24 on what to do the day before your exam.

When Your Exams Are Over

Throughout this book, there has been an emphasis on making sure you build in rewards to your studies. Hopefully, therefore, you've built in a really big reward to enjoy after your exams. Now is the time to allow yourself that reward! Give yourself permission to do whatever it is that you enjoy the most. Forget about the hardships you've endured over the past months, and go and get a life!

Exam Technique Revisited

Poor Technique Equals Poor Results

It is my belief that poor exam technique accounts for more failures than any other single cause. More than not having planned sufficiently. More than not having done enough study. More even than not having got the revision phase right. And by exam technique, I refer not only to what it is you do during the exam, but also to the time immediately preceding the exam.

Ultimately, exams are about getting enough marks to reach a pass mark set by the examining body. Everything you can do to scrape together a few more marks will make all the difference to your chances of success. Exam technique is what allows you to pick up those extra few marks.

This claim may sound melodramatic, but it is true. Here's why.

Can One Mark Really Make a Difference?

If you were to plot on a graph the number of candidates achieving each possible exam mark, and assuming a pass mark set at 50 out of 100, you would get something similar to the following graph

Figure 27.1

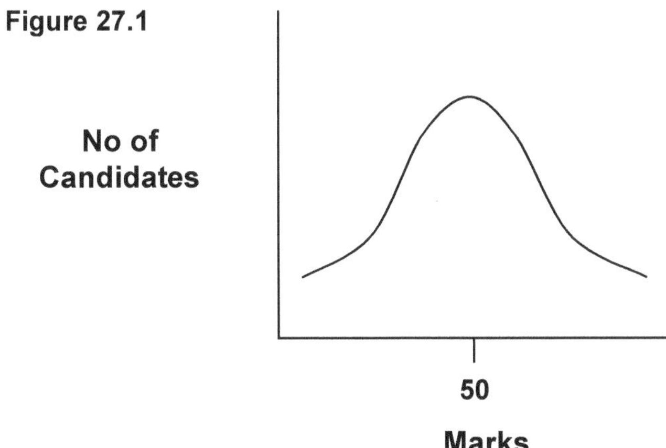

(For those of you of a mathematical bent, this is a classic normal distribution curve.)

As you can see, the highest proportion of those taking the exam will have their scores clustered in a range around the 50 pass mark, probably scoring between 40 and 60, with the highest number scoring 49, 50 or 51.

What this means is that probability suggests your exam score is most likely going to fall within this narrow range. And if that's the case, *one mark really can make all the difference between pass and fail.*

That said, don't you now think it's crucial you use the right exam technique? Here's a quick reminder of what you've learned in this part of the book.

Exam Technique

- Plan and prepare for your exam in advance of the big day. Make sure you can get there on time and with everything you need. This both reduces stress and greatly reduces the potential for disaster.
- Remain positive and single-minded immediately before the exam. Avoid anyone and anything which could dent your self-confidence.
- Once in the exam, select what you consider to be your best question first. But don't run over on time.
- Stick ruthlessly to your time allocations for questions. Remember, be a mark mercenary. Forget the hard marks and take all the easy ones on offer.
- Give the examiner what he wants. Follow instructions, write clearly, and answer the questions set (RTFQ!).
- If possible, leave your worst question until last. Then, if you do manage to get yourself in a stew, it isn't going to affect the rest of your performance.
- Take a 60-second breather where things really do get on top of you and you feel a panic attack coming on.
- After the exam, accept that you've done your best. Forget post-mortems as you can't change what has happened. Move on, either to the next exam, or back to real life!

That's it really. You're ready.

And Finally...

The only thing left for me to do now is wish you the very best of luck.

However, if you've faithfully followed the techniques set out in this book, you don't really need to have Lady Luck batting for you. Sure, it would be nice to go into the exam hall, open the paper, and find every question on it is on one of your favourite subject areas. No one is going to turn down an opportunity like that. But you no longer need that sort of once-in-a-lifetime good luck to secure your first time pass.

> ***"Always bear in mind that your own resolution to succeed is more important than any one thing."***
> **Abraham Lincoln**

For you have something far more valuable than luck on your side. You have knowledge. And knowledge, as they say, is power.

You know

- How to plan your studies.
- How to study and what study tools and techniques to use.
- How to revise and answer questions.
- How to approach your exam and what to do during it.

Above all, you know that every one of these things is affected by the way you think about yourself. You know that the psychology of success is what makes the difference between pass and fail.

So use this to your own advantage. Apply the ideas you learned in the Success Factor section and at all times *think positive*. Go into the exam hall really believing you are capable of achieving that first time pass, and you will.

> ***"Men are born to succeed, not to fail."***
> **Henry Thoreau**

Good luck!

Glossary of Terms Frequently Used in Examination Questions

Account for	Not the same as "give an account of", this requires an explanation of the reasons for something.
Advise	Present information, data, opinions or recommendations to allow someone to take action. See also "Recommend".
Analyse	Take something such as a process or concept and explain it step by step in depth, identifying, describing, and criticising its main features.
Appraise	Assess/evaluate the nature, quality, ability, extent or significance of something. See also "Assess" and "Evaluate".
Argue	Put forward an idea, discuss it and then defend it against possible counter arguments.
Assess	Examine something closely, consider its strengths and weaknesses, then discuss the case for and against in a balanced or cautious way, finally giving a clear opinion. See also "Appraise" and "Evaluate".
Calculate	Compute or reckon something using mathematical calculation.
Clarify	Explain more clearly and simplify the meaning of something.
Comment	State clearly your opinion on something and its relevance, supporting your views with evidence and mild criticism.
Compare	Set out similarities and differences between two or more things (concepts, items, processes etc.).
Consider	Express your thoughts and observations about something.
Contrast	Place two or more things in opposition to identify the differences between them.

Criticise	Present the faults and disadvantages in something, supporting your views with reasons and evidence.
Define	Explain what something means precisely using as formal language as possible.
Demonstrate	Show by reasoning the truth of something or how something works and prove it by giving examples.
Describe	Present the details and characteristics of something.
Develop	Expand on something and take it further, see also "Expand".
Diagram	Demonstrate your answer by drawing a chart or other visual element to illustrate your points.
Differentiate between	Explain the differences between two or more items you are asked about.
Discuss	Explain what you know about an issue or proposition with careful argument, demonstrating that you understand the opposing arguments for and against.
Distinguish	Specify the differences between items or propositions.
Elaborate	Add further details to clarify the meaning of something.
Enumerate	Provide a list in a particular order, giving the main features of something and omitting details.
Evaluate	See "Assess" and "Appraise".
Examine	Explore a topic and comment on significant elements, events, or acts, providing an opinion and explaining how or why you came to your conclusions.
Expand	Give more detail about something, see also "Develop".
Explain	Set out clearly and in detail the meaning of something, clarifying and interpreting in order to give a "why" response.

Explore	Examine or investigate something in a questioning and systematic manner, considering it from a number of viewpoints.
Give an account of	Describe something in detail, and explain it fully. Not the same as "Account for".
Identify	Pick out the main or essential feature(s) or part(s) of something, explaining clearly what is involved.
Illustrate	Use examples to explain something, this might be in words, drawings, diagrams or other evidence such as statistics.
Implications	Describe the likely results of an action, including those that are hidden.
Interpret	Explain clearly the meaning of something supplied to you, using your own judgement to read between the lines and draw your own conclusions.
Justify	State adequate grounds for, supplying reasons in support of an argument or event. Answer any objections likely to be made.
Limitations	Show where something will not work or will not work as well as something else.
List	Itemise; provide a series of answers.
Outline	Select and set out the most important points or main features of something, ignoring any minor details.
Order	Provide a list of several items in their correct placement using a chronological or value-based approach.
Prove	Show by testing the accuracy or false/truth nature of something by presenting evidence.
Recommend	Represent something favourably as an appropriate choice. See also "Advise".
Reconcile	Show how apparently conflicting statements or theories are compatible.

Relate	Demonstrate the connections between two or more things, showing how they may affect, cause, or resemble each other.
Review	Recall and repeat the important elements or facts about an item or subject, examining them critically.
Role	Explain the part that something plays, how it fits in, its causes and effects.
Significance	Explain the meaning of something and assess how important it is.
State	Express the main points of a subject or argument in a brief, clear form.
Summarise	State briefly the essential points in a logical order.
Support	Give reasons in favour of a proposition or argument, using relevant data or diagrams.
Tabulate	Set out the facts or figures in table form.
Trace	Explain step by step how something developed from a point of origin.
Translate	Express something in a different way, or restate from one language to another.
Validity	Whether the statement can be justified by the evidence and/or facts.
Verify	Show or confirm something to be true.

About the Author

Michael Bell is founder and principal consultant at FTP Development Limited, a specialist consultancy dedicated to helping both individual and corporate clients to realise their goals and achieve success in their chosen field.

He spent the first 12 years of his career in the financial services sector, working within banking and investment management firms in the City of London. He qualified as a Chartered Certified Accountant in 1994, gaining the ACCA's Silver Medal for his performance in his Final Exams. Subsequent to that, he moved into the professional education sector, working for a leading training company in both trainer and manager-director capacities. He then established FTP Development, where he applies the lessons he learned from his 15 plus years in the training arena to help clients reach their full potential.

Michael lives in the country with one wife, five chickens, three goats and his daughter, who thinks he should concentrate on writing about fairies and hamsters in future.

Further information about FTP Development and its services can be viewed at www.ftpdevelopment.com.

To contact the author, email michael@ftpdevelopment.com.

www.ingramcontent.com/pod-product-compliance
Ingram Content Group UK Ltd.
Pitfield, Milton Keynes, MK11 3LW, UK
UKHW051127260726
13967UKWH00010B/2909